A YEAR IN THE LIFE OF
VICTORIAN
BRITAIN

A YEAR IN THE LIFE OF VICTORIAN BRITAIN

FELICITY TROTMAN

AMBERLEY

First published 2015

Amberley Publishing
The Hill, Stroud
Gloucestershire, GL5 4EP

www.amberley-books.com

British Library Cataloguing in Publication Data.
A catalogue record for this book is available from the British Library.

ISBN 978 1 4456 4469 1 (hardback)
ISBN 978 1 4456 4475 2 (ebook)

Typesetting and Origination by Amberley Publishing.
Printed in the UK.

CONTENTS

AUTHOR'S NOTE

All text herein has been preserved in its original style and language, with minimal interference from the author.

JANUARY

1st – Celebrating the New Year

January 1st, 1856. – Last night, at Mrs. Blodgett's, we sat up till twelve o'clock to open the front door, and let the New Year in. After the coming guest was fairly in the house, the back door was to be opened, to let the Old Year out; but I was tired, and did not wait for the latter ceremony. When the New Year made its entrance, there was a general shaking of hands, and one of the shipmasters said that it was customary to kiss the ladies all round; but to my great satisfaction, we did not proceed to such extremity. There was singing in the streets, and many voices of people passing, and when twelve had struck, all the bells of the town, I believe, rang out together. I went up stairs, sad and lonely, and, stepping into J—'s little room, wished him a Happy New Year, as he slept, and many of them.

Nathaniel Hawthorne, *English Note-books*

Nathaniel Hawthorne (1804–64) had already established himself as a major literary figure in America when in 1853 his friend Franklin Pierce became President of the USA. Pierce made Hawthorne US consul in Liverpool – a position, according to Hawthorne's wife Sophia, 'second in dignity to the Embassy in London'. As consul, Hawthorne lived and worked in England from 1853 until 1857, when Pierce lost the election. In his years in England, Hawthorne took the opportunity to travel around the country, and his *English Note-books* are full of sharp, interesting – and sometimes unexpected – descriptions and observations.

2nd – Medals for Gallantry

The want of some system of rewards for acts of bravery upon land, and the supplying of this want, being apparently a work closely connected with the objects of the Order – steps were at once taken to act upon the suggestion thus made, and to secure the best means by which it might be practically adopted. It was known that an honorary reward might be obtained for saving life from drowning, and for gallant services in accidents by fire, but it appeared that when casualties occur in our mining and colliery districts, and men expose their lives to the greatest risk to rescue their fellow creatures, no recognition from any public body could be obtained, because it was not within the scope of any existing society to reward such merit. And yet in Great Britain alone about twelve hundred colliers are killed every year by explosions and other accidents in coal mines, in addition to those who lose their lives in other mining operations. This number would be greatly increased if it were not for the bravery of those who, in almost every accident, gallantly volunteer to risk their own lives for the rescue of their unfortunate fellow-workmen in danger and distress. By this means many a valuable life has been saved, the Order of St. John, decided that a system of honorary rewards, by means of medals and certificates, should be established.

The Order of St John

The Order of St John traces its ancestry back to the Knights Hospitallers, the military monks who looked after sick, poor and injured pilgrims in the Holy Land in the Middle Ages. A new version of the Order was established in Britain by a royal charter issued by Queen Victoria in 1888. The Order founded an eye hospital in Jerusalem, as well as the St John Ambulance Brigade. Also, at the end of the nineteenth century there were awards for those who saved people from drowning, or rescued people from fires, but the Order introduced its own gallantry medals for bravery in other disastrous events, particularly accidents in mines and collieries. It also started first-aid courses for members of the public, which was of great help in emergencies.

3rd – The Dog-Whipper

FORTY years ago the "Dog-whipper" was still an institution in this dale. Auld Willy Richardson was then the hereditary holder of the office, his father having been dog-whipper before him; and when Willy himself died, the office, the honour, and the insignia passed to his brother John. For the office was by no means one without outward signs and tokens of its existence. The office-holder held also a whip, and whenever he was on duty the whip was *en évidence*.

Poor old Willy, the first dog-whipper of my acquaintance, was a little man of about five feet four, with legs that were hardly a pair, and which it would have been slander to call straight or well shapen; and, as was natural perhaps, he shambled in his gait. His usual garb on the Sunday was an ancient drab coat, cut—if a tailor had ever been concerned in the making of it—after the fashion described as that of Dominie Sampson's, with broad skirts falling quite below the knee. There were side-pockets in it, opening just upon the hip; capacious and with a sort of suggestiveness about them that they were not simply meant to contain sundries, but were put to such a use by wont and custom. On Sundays, and days when a "burying" was to be—for Willy was sexton also, and kept the depth of his graves religiously to under three feet— the short handle of the whip he bore reposed in the right-hand pocket, but the lainder and lash hung outside; the latter, inasmuch as the bearer's stature was not great, trailing on the ground. Willy was valorous in the execution of his duty, although he may sometimes have seen occasion for the exercise of a wise discretion. I knew of two such instances. In one the intrusive dog was made slowly to recede before the duly-armed official, who was fairly well able to command the whole interspace between the pews which runs the length of the church; but when it came to turning round the corner and backing towards the door, the dog did not see the expediency of the desired course quite so clearly as Willy did; and so, having more room in the crossing in which to attain the necessary impetus, he made a bolt for it, aiming at the archway presented by the dog-whipper's bow-legs. But the archway proved to be less than the dog had assumed it to be; and, in consequence, after riding backwards for a pace or two, poor old Willy came backwards to the pavement, and to grief besides. The dog on the other occasion was more resolute, or else less accommodating; for he met all Willy's advances with a steady refusal to budge an inch in a backward direction. Willy persevered; the dog growled. Willy showed his whip; the dog showed his teeth; and the teeth having a more persuasive look about them than the whip, the man gave way and the dog did not.

J. C. Atkinson, *Forty Years in a Moorland Parish*

The Rev. John Christopher Atkinson (1814–1900) was vicar of Danby in Cleveland from 1847 until he died. He was keenly interested in the folklore, history and antiquities of the parish and the surrounding area, and wrote a number of books and pamphlets about them. *Forty Years in a Moorland Parish* gives a vivid picture of the life and characters found in a remote country village, as well as giving an account of its history, and is now regarded as a classic of its kind. Atkinson walked around his parish – he calculated at one point that he must have covered 'more than 70,000 miles in the prosecution of his clerical work only; and much more than as many again for exercise, relaxation, or recreation.'

4th – The Hospital at Scutari

I am a kind of General Dealer in socks, shirts, knives and forks, wooden spoons, tin baths, tables and forms, cabbage and carrots, operating tables, towels and soap, small tooth combs, precipitate for destroying lice, scissors, bedpans and stump pillows. I will send you a picture of my Caravanserai, into which beasts come in and out. Indeed the vermin might, if they had but 'unity of purpose,' carry off the four miles of beds on their backs, and march with them into the War Office, Horse Guards, S.W.

Florence Nightingale, letter to Sidney Herbert, 1855

When the appalling conditions that wounded soldiers during the Crimean War had to endure were revealed in the British press, Sidney Herbert, then Secretary of State for War, asked his friend Florence Nightingale (1820–1910) to go out and improve things. With thirty-eight female volunteers, she went to Scutari, where she dealt with filth, overcrowding, insanitary conditions, diets and nursing generally. She also insisted on adequate supplies of necessary materials – she bought equipment with funds raised by *The Times* in London. After the war, she reformed many aspects of health care, including the education of nurses, sanitary provisions and the way hospitals were built.

5th – The Jameson Raid

During many an evening of that eventful week we used to sit out after dinner under the rays of a glorious full moon, in the most perfect climatic conditions, and hear heated discussions of the pros and cons of this occurrence, which savoured more of medieval times than of our own. The moon all the while looked down so calmly, and the Southern Cross stood out clear and bright. One wondered what they might not have told us of scenes being enacted on the mysterious veldt, not 300 miles away. It was not till Saturday, January 4, that we knew what had happened, and any hopes we had entertained that the freebooters had either joined forces with their friends in Johannesburg, or else had made good their escape, were dashed to the ground as the fulness of the catastrophe became known. For hours, however, the aghast Kimberleyites refused to believe that Dr. Jameson and his entire corps had been taken prisoners, having been hopelessly outnumbered and outmanoeuvred after several hours' fighting at Krugersdorp; and, when doubt was no longer possible, loud and deep were the execrations levelled at the Johannesburgers, who, it was strenuously reiterated, had invited the Raiders to come to their succour, and who, when the pinch came, never even left the town to go to their assistance. If the real history of the Raid is ever written, when the march of time renders such a thing possible, it will be interesting reading; but, as matters stand now, it is better to say as little as possible of such a deplorable fiasco, wherein the only points which stood out clearly appeared to be that Englishmen were as brave, and perhaps also as foolhardy, as ever; that President Kruger, while pretending to shut his eyes, had known exactly all that was going forward; that the Boers had lost nothing of their old skill in shooting and ambushing, while the rapid rising and massing of their despised forces was as remarkable in its way as Jameson's forced march.

Lady Sarah Wilson, *Book of South African Memories*

Lady Sarah Isabella Augusta Wilson (1865–1929) was Winston Churchill's aunt. She was the first female war correspondent, sending reports on the Siege of Mafeking to the London press. Her diary of some years spent in South Africa describes many adventures, and also gives an interesting view of the personalities and politics of the country. In the preface to her book, Lady Sarah Wilson said that all the most interesting things that had happened to her in her life had happened in South Africa.

6th – Duties of the Footman

Where a single footman, or odd man, is the only male servant, then, whatever his ostensible position, he is required to make himself generally useful. He has to clean the knives and shoes, the furniture, the plate; answer the visitors who call, the drawing-room and parlour bells; and do all the errands. His life is no sinecure; and a methodical arrangement of his time will be necessary, in order to perform his many duties with any satisfaction to himself or his master.

The footman only finds himself in stockings, shoes, and washing. Where silk stockings, or other extra articles of linen are worn, they are found by the family, as well as his livery, a working dress, consisting of a pair of overalls, a waistcoat, a fustian jacket, with a white or jean one for times when he is liable to be called to answer the door or wait at breakfast; and, on quitting his service, he is expected to leave behind him any livery had within six months.

Mrs Isabella Beeton, Mrs Beeton's Book of Household
Management

Isabella Beeton (1836–65) started work on what became the *Book of Household Management* when she was twenty-one – her husband published magazines and wanted material for one of them, *The Englishwoman's Domestic Magazine.* The text originally appeared in twenty-four parts. When these were collected together and published in book form, Mrs Beeton said 'What moved me, in the first instance, to attempt a work like this, was the discomfort and suffering which I had seen brought upon men and women by household mismanagement. I have always thought that there is no more fruitful source of family discontent than a housewife's badly-cooked dinners and untidy ways.'

7th – Hunting for Treasure in Egypt

It is a long and shelterless ride from the palms to the desert; but we come to the end of it at last, mounting just such another sand-slope as that which leads up from the Ghizeh road to the foot of the Great Pyramid. The edge of the plateau here rises abruptly from the plain in one long range of low perpendicular cliffs pierced with dark mouths of rock-cut sepulchres, while the sand-slope by which we are climbing pours down through a breach in the rock, as an Alpine snow-drift flows through a mountain gap from the ice-level above.

And now, having dismounted through compassion for our unfortunate little donkeys, the first thing we observe is the curious mixture of *débris* underfoot. At Ghizeh one treads only sand and pebbles; but here at *Sakkârah* the whole plateau is thickly strewn with scraps of broken pottery, limestone, marble, and alabaster; flakes of green and blue glaze; bleached bones; shreds of yellow linen; and lumps of some odd-looking dark brown substance, like dried-up sponge. Presently some one picks up a little noseless head of one of the common blue-ware funereal statuettes, and immediately we all fall to work, grubbing for treasure—a pure waste of precious time; for though the sand is full of *débris*, it has been sifted so often and so carefully by the Arabs that it no longer contains anything worth looking for. Meanwhile, one finds a fragment of iridescent glass—another, a morsel of shattered vase—a third, an opaque bead of some kind of yellow paste. And then, with a shock which the present writer, at all events, will not soon forget, we suddenly discover that these scattered bones are human—that those linen shreds are shreds of cerement cloths—that yonder odd-looking brown lumps are rent fragments of what once was living flesh! And now for the first time we realise that every inch of this ground on which we are standing, and all these hillocks and hollows and pits in the sand, are violated graves.

Amelia Edwards, *A Thousand Miles up the Nile*, 1877

Amelia Edwards (1831–92) was a novelist, journalist and Egyptologist. With a group of friends, she voyaged up the Nile from 1873 to 1874, becoming fascinated with Egypt, past and present. She became aware that tourism and development threatened many ancient sites, and in 1882 founded the Egypt Exploration Fund (now the Egypt Exploration Society) with Reginald Stuart Poole of the British Museum. *A Thousand Miles up the Nile*, her book about her first Egyptian trip, became a bestseller.

8th – A Crazy Guide

We had got but little way from Jerm, when it was discovered that our guide was ill-qualified for his task, and was, or affected to be, crazy. To every question he replied by a quotation from Hafiz, the purport of which was, that a man in love was the laugh and sport of his acquaintance. Had it not been for the venerable looks of the reciter, I should have been inclined to think that he himself had left his first love behind him in Jerm. He was escorted back, and in his stead Mirza Suliman sent us a much more competent guide. I may here remark that on our return to Jerm the governor's mirza, in the course of conversation, gravely asked me whether I had not conjured the spirit of the poetical guide into a jackass, for, added he, the man is now discovered to be a fool for the first time in his life, and it is known in the bazaar that you left this place with only four donkeys and have brought back five.

Captain John Wood, *A Journey to the Source of the River Oxus*

John Wood (1812–71) was born in Scotland. He joined the British Indian Navy, becoming a surveyor, cartographer and explorer. He commanded the first steamboat to sail up the Indus River, surveying it as he travelled, and later explored the Oxus River (now known as the Amu Darya), finding one of its sources. Sadly, having given local leaders in Afghanistan assurances on behalf of the British government in India, those assurances were ignored. Wood was so upset he resigned from the service. He tried life in New Zealand and in Australia, but eventually returned to India, where he advised on running a flotilla of steamboats on the Indus.

9th – McDermott's War Song, 1877

"The Dogs of War" are loose and the rugged Russian Bear,
Full bent on blood and robbery, has crawl'd out of his lair;
It seems a thrashing now and then, will never help to tame
That brute, and so he's out upon the "same old game."
"The Lion" did his best to find him some excuse,

To crawl back to his den again, all efforts were no use;
He hunger'd for his victim, he's pleased when blood is shed,
But let us hope his crimes may all recoil on his own head.

CHORUS: *We don't want to fight but by jingo if we do,*
We've got the ships, we've got the men, and got the money too!
We've fought the Bear before and while we're Britons true
The Russians shall not have Constantinople.

The misdeeds of the Turks have been "spouted" thro' all lands,
But how about the Russians, can they show spotless hands?
They slaughtered well at Khiva, in Siberia icy cold,
How many subjects done to death will never perhaps be told,
They butchered the Circassians, man, woman, yes and child,
With cruelties their Generals their murderous hours beguiled,
And poor unhappy Poland their cruel yoke must bear,
Whilst prayers for "Freedom and Revenge" go up into the air.

CHORUS

May he who 'gan the quarrel soon have to bite the dust,
The Turk should be thrice armed for "he hath his quarrel just,"
'Tis sad that countless thousands should die thro' cruel war,
But let us hope most fervently ere long it will be o'er;
Let them be warned, Old England is brave Old England still,
We've proved our might, we've claimed our right, and ever, ever
    will,
Should we have to draw the sword our way to victory we'll forge,
With the battle cry of Britons, "Old England and Saint George!"

CHORUS

Written and composed by G. W. Hunt

This song was written at a time of political tension: the Russo-Turkish war of 1877–8 alarmed many European powers. British Prime Minister, Benjamin Disraeli, wished to prop Turkey up, and at the Congress of Berlin he helped to bring peace. Sung by Gilbert Hastings MacDermott ('The Great MacDermott'), one of the major stars of the Victorian music hall, the song became immensely popular. MacDermott bought the song from G. W. Hunt (c. 1839–1904) for one guinea.

10th – Soup for the Poor

"Soup will be given out twice a week, on Wednesdays and Saturdays, and a *fresh ticket* will be required for each occasion.
"Allowance usually given:—
1 quart to a family under 4 persons.
2 quarts   „   from 4 to 6 persons.
3   „   „   above 6 persons.

In this parish our subscriptions amounted in the first year to 38*l*. 3s. 6d., and last year to 38*l*. 19s. 6d.

The expense of starting, including a "copper" (of galvanised iron), in which 32½ gallons may be made, with its furnace and fittings, and bricklayers' and carpenters' bills for putting up, was 7*l*. 1s. 9d.

The copper was put up in the scullery of a cottage belonging to the Vicar and inhabited by the parish clerk. The clerk's daughter makes the soup, and receives 2s. 6d. for each boiling.

The following is our recipe for 32½ gallons of soup:—

40 lb. of meat.	5 gallons of best split peas.
5 lb. of rice.	3 lb. of Scotch barley.
2 gallons of carrots.	2 gallons of turnips.
1½ „ onions.	1 oz. of celery seed.
¼ lb. of black pepper (ground).	3 lb. of salt.
1 lb. of coarse sugar.	1½ gallons of flour.

"Put into the copper at 7 a.m. As soon as boiling begins, *keep stirring* to prevent burning. Serve at 3 p.m. The flour is to be used for thickening, to be added while boiling at the last, mixed with water into a smooth paste, and stirred in by degrees."

The result is an excellent soup, which gives great satisfaction to the recipients.

The meat used for each boiling is 20 lb. of shin of beef and 20 lb. of clads (*i.e.*, the part of the leg between the shoulder and the knee) and necks.

Some of the subscribers should occasionally inspect the meat and other ingredients before they have been put into the copper, so as to ensure their being thoroughly good.

Last winter we distributed, from Dec. 3 to Feb. 21, 3,350 quarts, among 140 families, including a total of 531 persons.

Our expenses were—butcher, 16*l*. 4s.; grocer, 4*l*. 15s. 3d.; vegetables, 9*l*.; fuel, 16s. 10d.; cook for boiling, 3*l*.

F. Darling

In the nineteenth century, many parishes tried to help poor residents in winter by providing soup for them at a very low price. Soup from this recipe was available for twelve weeks, on Wednesdays and Saturdays: a subscription of 5/- entitled the subscriber to two quarts a week. The recipe and details about the distribution system were carefully cut out of an unnamed newspaper, and kept in the personal recipe book of the wife of a Dorset clergyman.

11th – The Dynamics of a Particle

PROP. I. PR.
To find the value of a given Examiner.
Example.—A takes in ten books in the Final Examination and gets a 3rd class; B takes in the Examiners, and gets a 2nd. Find the value of the Examiners in terms of books. Find also their value in terms in which no Examination is held.
PROP. II. PR.
To estimate Profit and Loss.
Example.—Given a Derby Prophet, who has sent three different winners to three different betting-men, and given that none of the three horses are placed. Find the total loss incurred by the three men (*a*) in money, (*b*) in temper. Find also the Prophet. Is this latter usually possible?
PROP. IV. TH.
The end (i.e., '*the product of the extremes*') *justifies* (i.e., '*is equal to*'—see Latin '*aequus*') *the means.*
No example is appended to this Proposition, for obvious reasons.
PROP. V. PR.
To continue a given series.
Example.—A and B, who are respectively addicted to Fours and Fives, occupy the same set of rooms, which is always at Sixes and Sevens. Find the probable amount of reading done by A and B while the Eights are on.
    S. Dodgson Collingwood, *The Life and Letters of Lewis Carroll*

Charles Lutwidge Dodgson (1832–98) is generally thought of as a shy academic mathematician, and it is the brilliantly funny and original work he produced under his pen name, Lewis Carroll, that most people know best. However, he could be funny in his academic field, too! He started writing as a child, producing a magazine, *The Rectory Umbrella*, for his family.

12th – Gladstone speaking

Jan. 1866:—To the House of Commons to hear Gladstone's great speech on redistribution of seats. We stood in a cellar under the floor of the House and all I could see were the two soles of Gladstone's feet above my head, while I heard his wonderful voice coming down like a flood through the ventilator.

Anne Thackeray Ritchie, Letters

Anne Ritchie (1837–1919) was the eldest daughter of William Makepeace Thackeray. She wrote a number of novels which were highly regarded in her day, but it is her biographies and memoirs of notable Victorian literary figures which are most esteemed today.

13th – Justifiable Homicide

Over the north-west frontier, where the writ of the English Raj runs not, the artless Afghan is happy in a code that fully provides for relatives who neglect or misunderstand their obligations. An Afghan it was who found himself compelled to reprove an uncle with an unfortunate habit of squandering the family estate. An excellent relative, this uncle, in all other respects. As a liar, he had few equals; he robbed with taste and discretion; and his murders were all imbued with true artistic feeling. He might have lived to a green old age of spotless respectability but for his one little failing. As it was, justice had to be done, *ruat cælum:* and so it came about that one day the nephew issued forth to correct him with a matchlock. The innocent old man was cultivating his paternal acres; so the nephew was able, unperceived, to get a steady sight on him. His finger was on the trigger, when suddenly there slipped into his mind the divine precept: "Allah is merciful!" He lowered his piece, and remained for a little plunged in thought; meanwhile the unconscious uncle hoed his paddy. Then with a happy smile he took aim once more, for there also occurred to him the precept equally divine: "But Allah is also just." With an easy conscience he let fly, and behold! there was an uncle the more in Paradise.

Kenneth Grahame, Pagan Papers

Kenneth Grahame (1859–1932) was brought up by relatives, and came to dislike them intensely. His objections to relatives in general are expressed in the essay 'Justifiable Homicide'. As a young man, Kenneth Grahame wanted to go to university, but instead was made to go and work at the Bank of England. He left the bank after a strange incident in which he was shot at three times. When he submitted *Pagan Papers,* his first collection of work, to the publisher John Lane, Lane saw the potential for a different kind of writing in his work, and persuaded him to write for children. This eventually resulted in the classic *The Wind in the Willows.*

14th – Cosher Bailey (Crawshay Bailey, Ironmaster)

He was the last and among the first of our great Iron Kings. He helped to develop this country before an iron rail was ever laid down on it. To the very last moment of his life he gave the whole of his energies to increase its manufacture. From the moment he joined his uncle at Cyfartlifa, a boy of twelve, till he died the other day at Llanfoist House, an aged man of 84, he never left the iron country, nor lost sight once of its steam and smoke. No manors, or parks, or aldermanic honours, or castles, or sea side palaces, ever drew him away from the grime and the soot of the smoky "Welsh Hills."

John Griffith, Rector of Merthyr, Funeral Tribute, 1872

Crawshay Bailey (1789–1872) was born in England, but became one of the great Welsh iron-masters and industrialists. He was involved in several iron-works and blast furnaces, and also developed collieries, seeing the importance of coal to Welsh industry. In 1845 he helped set up the Aberdare Railway, and later railways between the Forest of Dean and Pontypool via Monmouth. A popular song was written about him and his exploits: in this his name was corrupted to 'Cosher' Bailey:

> Crawshay Bailey had an Engine
> It was always needin' mendin'
> And dependin' on its power
> It could do four miles an hour
> Did you ever saw
> Did you ever saw
> Did you ever saw
> Such a funny thing before?

15th – A Dog's Sense of Time

It is a curious fact that dogs can count time. I had, when a boy, a favourite terrier, which always went with me to church. My mother, thinking that he attracted too much of my attention, ordered the servant to fasten him up every Sunday morning. He did so once or twice, but never afterwards. Trim concealed himself every Sunday morning, and either met me as I entered the church, or I found him under my seat in the pew. Mr. Southey, in his "Omniana," informs us that he knew of a dog, which was brought up by a Catholic and afterwards sold to a Protestant, but still he refused to eat anything on a Friday.

Edward Jesse, *Anecdotes of Dogs*

Edward Jesse (1780–1868) was the son of a Yorkshire clergyman. He worked as a civil servant (at one point he was commissioner of hackney coaches, and later was involved in the restoration of Hampton Court Palace) but he also wrote about the natural history he loved, as well as producing a number of guidebooks to places such as Windsor Castle and Hampton Court.

16th – Overrating the Virtue of Books

In modern times instruction is communicated chiefly by means of Books. Books are no doubt very useful helps to knowledge, and in some measure also, to the practice of useful arts and accomplishments, but they are not, in any case, the primary and natural sources of culture, and, in my opinion, their virtue is not a little apt to be overrated, even in those branches of acquirement where they seem most indispensable. They are not creative powers in any sense; they are merely helps, instruments, tools; and even as tools they are only artificial tools, superadded to those with which the wise prevision of Nature has equipped us, like telescopes and microscopes, whose assistance in many researches reveals unimagined wonders, but the use of which should never tempt us to undervalue or to neglect the exercise of our own eyes. The original and proper sources of knowledge are not books, but life, experience, personal thinking, feeling, and acting. When a man starts with these, books can fill up many gaps, correct much that is inaccurate, and extend much that is inadequate; but, without living experience to work on, books are like rain and sunshine fallen on unbroken soil.

J. S. Blackie, *On Self-culture*

John Stuart Blackie (1809–95) was from 1860 Professor of Greek at Edinburgh University. He loved German, and was devoted to German songs and culture, and he also had a law degree. John Stuart Blackie worked for educational reform and the Gaelic language, raising the money to endow a Chair of Celtic at Edinburgh University.

17th – The First Training College for Women Teachers

I have already told of the work that Miss Margaret Newman began in 1876, offering to give her services and half her income to train and educate a few girls as teachers in schools for the higher classes,– how she inspired them with that spirit of loving devotion which could alone make their life a blessed one for themselves and their children. At her death in 1877 we felt that it was a sacred duty to carry on her work, and every year saw some further extension of that which she had begun.

In 1884 the first stone of S. Hilda's College was quietly laid by Canon Medd, one of our Council, with prayer and hymns, and on November 27th, 1885, it was formally opened with a special service, at which the Lord Bishop of Gloucester and Bristol, the Very Rev. the Dean of Worcester, the Rural Dean, and others of the clergy assisted.

St. Hilda's as then planned out would hold, besides the twenty Foundationers, nineteen other residents. Mr. Hopkins, the brother of some old pupils, gave a very handsome and beautiful statue of S. Hilda, which adorns the entrance. She holds in her hand the Vulgate, open at the words: "Videmus nunc per speculum in oe nigmate: tunc autem facie ad faciem: nunc cognoseo ex parte, tunc autem cognoscam sicut et cognitus sum." Over the doorway are the words of Plato: "χαλεπα τά καλα," as a warning to those who would enter without counting the cost. On the study walls are these texts: "Shew Thy servants Thy work, and their children Thy glory"; "Knowledge puffeth up, charity buildeth up"; "Let nothing be done through strife or vain-glory."

Dorothea Beale, *St Hilda's*

Dorothea Beale (1831–1906) was the second head of Cheltenham Ladies' College, and the most famous of its principals. Having succeeded in giving girls an excellent education, Dorothea Beale and her associates realised that it would be necessary to train some of those girls to be the next generation of teachers, both in Cheltenham and in the other schools that were being started elsewhere in the country. The college was started in 1876 by her friend Mrs Newman: when she died the following year, Dorothea Beale took over. It was the first residential college for training female teachers at secondary level in the country, eventually becoming incorporated with St Hilda's College Oxford (also started by Miss Beale) in 1901.

18th – A Runaway Engine

Mr. Walker, the superintendent of the telegraphs of the South-Eastern Railway Company, remarks:—"On New Year's Day, 1850, a collision had occurred to an empty train at Gravesend, and the driver having leaped from his engine, the latter darted alone at full speed for London. Notice was immediately given by telegraph to London and other stations; and, while the line was kept clear, an engine and other arrangements were prepared as a buttress to receive the runaway, while all connected with the station awaited in awful suspense the expected shock. The superintendent of the railway also started down the line on an engine, and on passing the runaway he reversed his engine and had it transferred at the next crossing to the up-line, so as to be in the rear of the fugitive; he then started in chase, and on overtaking the other he ran into it at speed, and the driver of the engine took possession of the fugitive, and all danger was at an end. Twelve stations were passed in safety; it passed Woolwich at fifteen miles an hour; it was within a couple of miles of London when it was arrested. Had its approach been unknown, the money value of the damage it would have caused might have equalled the cost of the whole line of telegraph."

Anon, *Railway Adventures and Anecdotes*

From the moment in 1825 when a single carriage for passengers (the only one in the world) ran on the Stockton to Darlington railway, preceded by a man on horseback carrying a flag, trains have not only fascinated people, but made a huge impact on the world. On that first journey, Stevenson, who had built the engine, told the rider to get out of the way, and raised the speed to fifteen miles an hour!

19th – Letter from B Brontë to William Wordsworth

Haworth, near Bradford, Yorkshire, January 19, 1837
SIR, – I most earnestly entreat you to read and pass your judgment upon what I have sent you, because from the day of my birth to this the nineteenth year of my life, I have lived among secluded hills, where I could neither know what I was, or what I could do. I read for the same reason that I ate or drank; because it was a real craving of nature. I wrote on the same principle as I spoke – out of the impulse and feelings of the mind; nor could I help it, for what came, came out, and there was the end of it. For as to self-conceit, that could not receive food from flattery, since to this hour, not half a dozen people in the world know I have ever penned a line.

But a change has taken place now, sir: and I am arrived at an age wherein I must do something for myself: the powers I possess must be exercised to a definite end, and as I don't know them myself I must ask of others what they are worth. Yet there is not one here to tell me; and still, if they are worthless, time will henceforth be too precious to be wasted on them.

Do pardon me, sir, that I have ventured to come before one whose works I have most loved in our literature, and who most has been with me a divinity of the mind, – laying before him one of my writings, and asking of him a judgment of its contents. I must come before some one from whose sentence there is no appeal; and such a one is he who has developed the theory of poetry as well as its practice, and both in such a way as to claim a place in the memory of a thousand years to come.

My aim, sir, is to push out into the open world, and for this I trust not poetry alone – that might launch the vessel, but could not bear her on; sensible and scientific prose, bold and vigorous efforts in my walk in life, would give a farther title to the notice of the world; and then again poetry ought to brighten and crown that name with glory; but nothing of all this can be ever begun without means, and as I don't possess these, I must in very shape strive to gain them. Surely, in this day, when there is not a *writing* poet worth a sixpence, the field must be open, if a better man can step forward.

What I send you is the Prefatory Scene of a much longer subject, in which I have striven to develop strong passions and weak principles struggling with a high imagination and acute feelings, till, as youth hardens towards age, evil deeds and short enjoyments end in mental misery and bodily ruin. Now, to send you the whole of this would be a mock upon your patience; what you see, does not even pretend to be more than the description of an imaginative child. But read it, sir; and, as you would hold a light to one in utter darkness – as you value your own kind-heartedness – *return* me an *answer*, if but one word, telling me whether I should write on, or write no more. Forgive undue warmth, because my feelings in this matter cannot be cool; and believe me, sir, with deep respect,

Your really humble servant,
P. B. BRONTË

Branwell Brontë (1817–48), the brother of Charlotte, Emily and Anne Brontë, had literary ambitions like his sisters, but sadly they did not come to very much: a few poems published in local papers. He wrote to various literary figures hoping for support and encouragement: he got some, but failed to achieve anything.

20th – Swinburne Reads his Poems

When he came back from the country to town he was always particularly anxious to recite or read aloud his own poems ... He would arrive at a friend's house with a breast-pocket obviously bulging with manuscript, but buttoned across his chest. After floating about the room and greeting his host and hostess with many little becks of the head, and affectionate smiles, and light wavings of the fingers, he would settle at last upright on a chair, or, by preference, on a sofa, and sit there in a state of rigid immobility, the toe of one foot pressed against the heel of the other. Then he would say, in an airy, detached way, as though speaking of some absent person, 'I have brought with me my "Thalassius" or my "Wasted Garden" (or whatever it might happen to be), which I have just finished.' Then he would be folded again in silence, looking at nothing. We then were to say, 'Oh, do please read it to us! Will you?' Swinburne would promptly reply, 'I had no intention in the world of boring you with it, but since you ask me ——' and out would come the MS. I do not remember that there was ever any variation in this little ceremony, which sometimes preluded many hours of recitation and reading. His delivery, especially of his own poetry, was delightful as long as he sat quietly in his seat. But sometimes, in reading, he lost control of emotions, the sound became a scream, and he would dance about the room, the paper fluttering from his finger-tips like a pennon in a gale of wind.

Edmund Gosse, *Portraits and Sketches*

Algernon Charles Swinburne (1837–1909) was a hugely prolific poet, playwright and novelist, who scandalised Victorian readers when his revolutionary *Poems and Ballads* was published in 1866: they were thought to be sadistic and blasphemous. At one point he shared a house in Chelsea with Dante Gabriel Rossetti – and a number of wombats. This pen-portrait is by his friend Edmund Gosse (1849–1928), an influential poet, critic and essayist.

21st – A Ride to the Meet

A very nice ride for a lady is to a meet of the hounds, if such should occur within reasonable distance, say from four to eight miles. The sight is a very pretty one, and there is not any reason why you should not thoroughly enjoy it; but having only ridden to see the meet, you must be careful not to interfere with, nor get in the way of those about to ride the run. Nothing is more charming than to see three or four ladies, nicely turned out, arrive to grace the meet with their presence, but nothing is more abominable than the same number of amazons coming galloping up in full hunting toggery, although without the least idea of hunting, and rushing hither and thither, frightening the hounds and getting in everybody's way, as though they were personages of the vastest possible importance, and meant to ride with a skill not second to that of the Nazares. Such women are the horror and spoliation of every hunting-field. They dash off with the hounds the moment the fox is found, but happily the first fence stops them, and a fervent thankfulness is felt by every true lover of the chase as they pause discomfited, look dismally at the yawning chasm, and jog crestfallen away to the road.

Nannie Lambert, *Ladies on Horseback*

Nannie Lambert Power O'Donoghue (1843–1940) was a remarkable Irish journalist and equestrian. She was also a poet, novelist, musician and social activist, often writing about social issues and animal welfare. *Ladies on Horseback*, which gave advice to women on every aspect of horses and riding, was translated into five languages. She is the only person – male or female – to have ridden Ireland's three hardest steeplechase courses without a refusal or a mistake, and she did this riding side-saddle.

22nd – Rorke's Drift

It came about thus. Lieutenant Chard, with one sergeant and six men, had been left in charge of the ponts over the Tugela at this point. Close by was a commissariat *depôt* in charge of Lieutenant Bromhead and a company of the 24th Regiment. About three o'clock on January 22nd news of the disaster at Isandhlwana reached this officer, together with a note, saying that the enemy were advancing in force against his post, which was to be held at all costs. Chard immediately withdrew his small party, and in concert with Bromhead arranged for the loopholing and barricading the store-building and hospital, and for connecting the defences of the two by building walls of mealie-bags. At 3.30 an officer of Durnford's Horse with about 100 men came in, and was asked to send them out as vedettes; these, when pressed, to fall back and assist in the defence of the buildings. It was at once perceived that the line of defence was now too extended for the small force left, and an inner entrenchment of biscuit-boxes was made, and this had been completed to a wall two boxes high, when suddenly 600 of the enemy turned the hill to the south. They advanced at a run against the southern wall, and notwithstanding a tremendous fire reached to within fifty yards of it. Being here encountered by a cross-fire from the store they were stopped.

Taking advantage, however, of some shelter afforded by the cookhouse and ovens, they kept up heavy musketry volleys thence, whilst the main body moved on to the left round the hospital, whence they made a rush upon the north-west wall and breastwork of mealie-bags. Meanwhile the mass of the advancing foe lined a ledge of rocks and filled the caves overlooking the English position at a distance of 100 yards to the south, whence they too kept up a constant fire. Another party to the left occupied a garden in a hollow in the road, and also the bush beyond, which time had not permitted to be cut down. The enemy could thus advance close to the English works, and were soon in possession of one whole side of the wall, whilst on the other in a line extending from the hospital all along the wall to the bush they made a series of determined onsets. But each attack was met and splendidly repulsed with the bayonet, Corporal Schiess (N. N. C.) especially distinguishing himself. The fire from the ledge of rock and caves at length became so galling, that it was necessary to retire behind the inner line of biscuit-boxes.

All this time the enemy had been trying to force the hospital, and at length they did set fire to the roof. The garrison defended the place room by room, bringing out all the sick who could be moved before they retired. Privates Williams, Hook, R. Jones, and W. Jones, 24th Regiment, were the last to leave, holding the doorway against the Zulus with their bayonets, their ammunition being quite expended. Five sick men, owing to the smoke and want of interior communication, had unfortunately to be left to their fates. Two heaps of mealie-bags were now converted into a sort of redoubt, and a second line of fire was thus obtained all round. Darkness now came on, and after several more furious attacks had been repulsed the defenders had ultimately to retire to the middle, and then to the inner wall of the kraal, east of the position they had at first held. The attacks continued all night, the soldiers firing with the utmost coolness, and never wasting a shot. At four a.m., January 23rd, firing ceased, and by daybreak the enemy were disappearing over the hill to the south-west. ... about eight a.m. the British 3rd column began to appear, whereupon the enemy, who had been again advancing, fell back as the troops advanced, and Rorke's Drift Post had been saved.

Waller Asche & E. V. Wyatt-Edgell, *Story of the Zulu Campaign*

Rorke's Drift was a ford over the Buffalo River in South Africa. In 1879, during the Zulu War, it was guarded by 139 British soldiers. When they were attacked by between 3,000 and 4,000 Zulus the men threw up hasty defences. By dint of good rifle fire and extreme courage, they repulsed the Zulu attacks – this was a huge morale-booster to the British, who had been badly beaten at Isandhlwana by the Zulus on the same day. Eleven VCs were awarded to the survivors.

23rd – The Mail Train

The late Sir Hardman Earle suggested that a special compartment should be reserved for the mail guard in which he could sort the letters *en route*. The first vehicle specially set apart for mail purposes was put upon the Grand Junction in 1838. From this humble beginning has gradually developed the express mails, in which the chief consideration is the swift transit of correspondence, and which are therefore limited in the number of the passengers they are allowed to carry. The cost of carrying the mails in 1838 and 1839 between Manchester and Liverpool by rail, including the guard's fare, averaged about £1 a trip, or half of the cost of sending them by coach. The price paid to the Grand Junction for carriage of mails between Manchester and Liverpool and Birmingham was 1d. a mile for the guard and ¾d. per cwt. per mile for the mails. This brought a revenue of about £3,000 a year. When the Chancellor of the Exchequer proposed and carried the imposition of the passenger duty, in 1832, the company intimated to the Post-office that they should advance the mail guard's fare ½d. per mile. In 1840 an agreement was negotiated between the Post-office and railway authorities to convey the mails between Lancashire and Birmingham four times daily for £19 10s. a day, with a penalty of £500 on the railway company in case of bad time keeping. This agreement was not carried into effect.

Manchester Guardian, reprinted in *Railway Adventures and Anecdotes*

Hardman Earle (1792–1877) was a Liverpool businessman: some of his interests included the import of sugar from a plantation which used slave labour. He was one of the original promoters of the Liverpool and Manchester Railway, and continued his railway interests for the rest of his life. The Railways (Conveyance of Mails) Act of 1838 required all railway companies to carry mail as required by the Postmaster General.

24th – The Decline of the Village

One of the most distressing features of modern village life is the continual decrease of the population. The rural exodus is an alarming and very real danger to the welfare of social England. The country is considered dull and life therein dreary both by squire and peasant alike. Hence the attractions of towns or the delights of travel empty our villages. The manor-house is closed and labourers are scarce. To increase the attractions of our villages, to arouse an interest in their past history and social life, is worth attempting; and perhaps this Story may be of some use in fostering local patriotism, and in reconciling those who spend their lives far from the busy hives of men to their lot, when they find how much interest lies immediately around them.

P. H. Ditchfield, *English Villages*

The Rev Peter Hampson Ditchfield (1854–1930) was rector of Barkham in Berkshire from 1886 until he died. An author and historian, he was secretary of the Berkshire Archaeological Society for thirty-eight years, editing their journal until he died, and was also inspector of schools for the Diocese of Oxford. Another of his books was entitled *Books Fatal to their Authors*.

25th – A Landslip at Lyme Regis, 1839

About midnight a great fissure began to form which ran in almost a direct line for three-quarters of a mile. This fissure rapidly widened to 300 feet, descending, as it seemed at first, into the very bowels of the earth, but as the sides fell in it finally was choked at a depth of 150 feet.

One James Robertson and a companion were at that hour crossing the fields which then extended over this tract, and stumbled across a slight ridge of gravel, which at first they thought must have been made by some boys, but one of them stepping on to it, down sank his leg, and his companion had to pull him out of a yawning chasm. Next moment they saw that the whole surface of turf was starred and splitting in all directions, and they fled for their lives. The sound of the rending of the rocks they described as being much like that of the tearing of cloth or flannel. Two other members of the coastguard, who were stationed on the beach, now saw something begin to rise out of the sea like the back of a gigantic whale; at the same time the shore of shingles on which they stood lifted and fell, like the heaving of a breast in sleep. The water was thrown into violent agitation, foaming and spouting, and great volumes of mud rushed up from below. The great back rose higher and ever higher, and extended further till at last it formed a huge reef at a little distance from the beach. This ridge was composed of the more solid matter, chert and other pebbles, that had been in the sand under the chalk, and which by the sinking of the chalk was squeezed out like so much dough. It remained as a reef for some years, but has now totally disappeared, having been carried away by the waves.

As the great chasm was formed, the masses from the sides falling in were, as it were, mumbled and chewed up in the depths, and to the eyes of the frightened spectators sent forth flashes of light; they also supposed that an intolerable stench was emitted from the abyss. But this was no more than the odours given out by the violent attrition of the cherty sandstone and chalk grinding against each other as they descended.

Throughout the 26th the subsided masses of the great chasm continued sinking, and the elevated reef gradually rising; but by the evening of that day everything had settled very nearly into the position in which it remains at present, although edges have since lost their sharpness and minor rents have been choked.

Sabine Baring-Gould, *A Book of the West*

The Reverend Sabine Baring-Gould (1834–1924) was rector (and squire) of Lewtrenchard in Devon for forty years. He was also an archaeologist, a hymn-writer, a folklorist, a travel writer, a biographer and a novelist. When he was a curate in Yorkshire, he met and eventually married a mill girl fifteen years his junior; they were married for forty-eight years, and had fifteen children. He is known to have written more than 1,200 books.

26th – Picture Galleries

If he can get the real air, the real trees, even for an hour, let him take it, in God's name; but how many a man who cannot spare time for a daily country walk, may well slip into the National Gallery in Trafalgar Square (or the South Kensington Museum), or any other collection of pictures, for ten minutes. *That* garden, at least, flowers as gaily in winter as in summer. Those noble faces on the wall are never disfigured by grief or passion. There, in the space of a single room, the townsman may take his country walk—a walk beneath mountain peaks, blushing sunsets, with broad woodlands spreading out below it; a walk through green meadows, under cool mellow shades, and overhanging rocks, by rushing brooks, where he watches and watches till he seems to *hear* the foam whisper, and to *see* the fishes leap; and his hard worn heart wanders out free, beyond the grim city-world of stone and iron, smoky chimneys, and roaring wheels, into the world of beautiful things.

Charles Kingsley, *True World for Brave Men*

The Reverend Charles Kingsley (1819–75) was vicar of Eversley in Hampshire from 1842 until he died. He was also professor of Modern History in Cambridge between 1860 and 1869, and a canon of both Chester and Westminster. He wrote for children and for adults, was a keen naturalist, and was deeply concerned with social problems, to which he applied Christian ethics. His hearty approach to such problems was called 'Muscular Christianity'. Charles Kingsley wrote perhaps his most famous book, *The Water Babies*, as a present for his fourth child, a baby at the time.

27th – V. R. 1819–1901, a Reverie

Moments the mightiest pass uncalendared,
And when the Absolute
In backward Time outgave the deedful word
Whereby all life is stirred:
"Let one be born and throned whose mould shall constitute
The norm of every royal-reckoned attribute,"
No mortal knew or heard.
But in due days the purposed Life outshone –
Serene, sagacious, free;
Her waxing seasons bloomed with deeds well done,
And the world's heart was won ...
Yet may the deed of hers most bright in eyes to be

Lie hid from ours–as in the All-One's thought lay she –
Till ripening years have run.

Thomas Hardy
Sunday Night, 27 January 1901

Queen Victoria died on 22 January 1901. It was truly the end of an era, for she had been on the throne for sixty-four years. Many people had known no other monarch. In her reign technology had made huge advances, and British influence had spread around the globe. Thomas Hardy's thoughtful reflection on the queen's life expressed what many must have felt.

28th – Broken-Winded Horses

I should be glad to know whether the fact of a mare being broken-winded will prevent her being got into good condition. She is an old slave, and was broken-winded in breaking her into harness too soon after being taken up from a long turn out upon grass. She is a good goer, and I would spare no pains or trouble to get her fat, but she does not appear to gain flesh. The liquor arsenicalis does not have the desired effect. She has no worms, and is in good health. I would therefore wish to have the experience of THE FIELD readers as to the best method to get her fat and in hard order, without reference to economy in keep.

'Springbok', *The Field*

By the second half of the nineteenth century, there were large numbers of newspapers and magazines available. Some gave help and advice to readers who wrote in with queries. Broken wind – sometimes called 'heaves' – is a lung disease that affects horses, often caused by dust, mould and other irritants in poorly-ventilated stables. In a society that depended greatly on horses, healthy animals were very important.

29th – An Enterprising Mole

Nothing is more fatal to the mole than excessive rain, which fills their subterranean galleries with water; the following statement made by Mr. A. Bruce in the Linnæan Transactions, shows that the animal is not without enterprise on the water:—"On visiting the Loch of Clunie, which I often did, I observed in it a small island at the distance of one hundred and eighty yards from the nearest land, measured to be so upon the ice. Upon the island, the Earl of Airly, the proprietor, has a castle and small shrubbery. I remarked frequently the appearance of fresh mole casts, or hills. I for some time took them for those of the water mouse, and one day asked the gardener if it was so. No, said he, it was the mole; and that he had caught one or two lately. Five or six years ago, he caught two in traps; and for two years after this he had observed none. But, about four years ago, coming ashore one summer's evening in the dusk, with the Earl of Airly's butler, they saw at a short distance, upon the smooth water, some animal paddling towards the island. They soon closed with this feeble passenger, and found it to be the common mole, led by a most astonishing instinct from the castle hill, the nearest point of land, to take possession of this desert island. It had been, at the time of my visit, for the space of two years quite free from any subterraneous inhabitant; but the mole has, for more than a year past, made its appearance again, and its operations I have since been witness to."

Alfred H. Miles, *Natural History in Anecdote*

Alfred Henry Miles (1848–1929) was a journalist, editor, anthologiser and writer who produced a vast number of books on a wide range of subjects. These included about fifty books retelling exciting stories for children. He also served as a Guardian of the Poor for six years, supervising a workhouse.

30th – English Tourists in Rome

I. Claude to Eustace:
Dear Eustatio, I write that you may write me an answer,
Or at the least to put us again en rapport with each other.
Rome disappoints me much,—St Peter's, perhaps, in especial;
Only the Arch of Titus and view from the Lateran please me:
This, however, perhaps is the weather, which truly is horrid.
Greece must be better, surely; and yet I am feeling so spiteful,
That I could travel to Athens, to Delphi, and Troy, and Mount
  Sinai,

Though but to see with my eyes that these are vanity also.
Rome disappoints me much; I hardly as yet understand it, but
Rubbishy seems the word that most exactly would suit it.
All the foolish destructions, and all the sillier savings,
All the incongruous things of past incompatible ages,
Seem to be treasured up here to make fools of present and future.
Would to Heaven the old Goths had made a cleaner sweep of it!
Would to Heaven some new ones would come and destroy these
　　churches!
However, one can live in Rome as also in London.
It is a blessing, no doubt, to be rid, at least for a time, of
All one's friends and relations,—yourself (forgive me!) included,—
All the *assujettissement* of having been what one has been,
What one thinks one is, or thinks that others suppose one;
Yet, in despite of all, we turn like fools to the English.
Vernon has been my fate; who is here the same that you knew
　　him,—
Making the tour, it seems, with friends of the name of Trevellyn.

A. H. Clough, Amours de Voyage

Arthur Hugh Clough (1819–61) was a British poet who spent part of his life in the United States of America. In Britain, he was a friend of Matthew Arnold (they had met at Rugby) and in America with thinkers such as Ralph Waldo Emerson. For six years he acted as unpaid assistant to Florence Nightingale, who was his wife's cousin. Much of his work, including Amours de Voyage, was only published after his death.

31st – Gun-Room

This term is used to indicate an apartment which is indispensable in a Country-house of any pretensions, as the depository of sporting implements. A room from twelve to fifteen feet square, or sometimes larger, is fitted up round the walls with presses or glass cases and occasional drawers, according to the species and extent of the sporting to be provided for, in which to place the guns, fishing-rods, pouches, bags, baskets, flasks, canisters, nets, and all other appliances in proper order, upon pretty much the same general principles which may be 'discerned in the arrangement of the same articles in the shops of their manufacturers. A table and two or three chairs will complete the furnishing of the room.

The Gun-room ought to be situated either in connexion with the Entrance-Hall, or, in a large house, near a secondary Entrance, as may be most convenient; not, of course, at a Garden-Porch, but perhaps at the Entrance pertaining to the Business-room, or the Luggage-Entrance. The apartment ought to have a good window; and a fireplace is important. It is also essential that precautions should be taken otherwise to secure dryness. The cases must be so made (as described for Library bookcases) as to have a free circulation of air all around and at the back, and the wood used must be thoroughly seasoned.

In small establishments we sometimes find the substitute for the Gun-room to be a suitable locked closet in the Servants' Hall or even in the Butler's-Pantry. In cases of the other extreme, the Gun-room will be in a separate building comprising the keeper's dwelling also. There are likewise some instances where a family of the highest rank and of great ancestral dignity will still be found to keep up an Armoury, in a room or series of rooms designated accordingly, accommodating a stock of various arms for the defence of the peace if occasion should require, as well as a collection of warlike relics.

Robert Kerr, from 'Domestic Offices', *A Gentleman's House*

Robert Kerr (1823–1904) was a Scottish architect, a founder and first president of the Architectural Association. During the years 1861–90 he was professor of the arts of construction at King's College, London. His book *The Gentleman's House, or, How to plan English residences, from the parsonage to the palace* (1864) was a highly influential guide to Victorian house-building.

FEBRUARY

1st – The Law of Nations

What is called the Law of Nations is not properly law, but a part of ethics: a set of moral rules, accepted as authoritative by civilized states. It is true that these rules neither are nor ought to be of eternal obligation, but do and must vary more or less from age to age, as the consciences of nations become more enlightened, and the *exigences* of political society undergo change. But the rules mostly were at their origin, and still are, an application of the maxims of honesty and humanity to the intercourse of states. They were introduced by the moral sentiments of mankind, or by their sense of the general interest, to mitigate the crimes and sufferings of a state of war, and to restrain governments and nations from unjust or dishonest conduct towards one another in time of peace. Since every country stands in numerous and various relations with the other countries of the world, and many, our own among the number, exercise actual authority over some of these, a knowledge of the established rules of international morality is essential to the duty of every nation, and therefore of every person in it who helps to make up the nation, and whose voice and feeling form a part of what is called public opinion. Let not any one pacify his conscience by the delusion that he can do no harm if he takes no part, and forms no opinion. Bad men need nothing more to compass their ends, than that good men should look on and do nothing. He is not a good man who, without a protest, allows wrong to be committed in his name, and with the means which he helps to supply, because he will not trouble himself to use his mind on the subject. It depends on the habit of attending to and looking into public transactions, and on the degree of information and solid judgment respecting them that exists in the community, whether the conduct of the nation as a nation, both within itself and towards others, shall be selfish, corrupt, and tyrannical, or rational and enlightened, just and noble.

John Stuart Mill, Inaugural Address Delivered to the University of St. Andrews, 1 February 1867

John Stuart Mill (1806–73) was a liberal philosopher and economist, who argued for many reforms. He worked for the East India Company for many years, and also sat as an MP – as an Independent – for three years (1865–68). He thought it was a moral duty to promote happiness. Unusually for the period, he was very keen to improve the legal and social position of women.

2nd – The Duke of York's Statue

Enduring is the bust of bronze,
And thine, O flower of George's sons,
Stands high above all laws and duns.

As honest men as ever cart
Convey'd to Tyburn took thy part
And raised thee up to where thou art.

Walter Savage Landor

Walter Savage Landor (1775–1864) was a poet and essayist. He spent much of his life abroad; in 1858 he left Britain to avoid a libel action as, not for the first time, some of his writing had upset someone. He could be touchy and bad-tempered, but also cheerful in a rowdy way. Living in Florence in the last years of his life, the poet Robert Browning, who admired his work, tried to look after him.

3rd – Blue Ruin

Among the lower classes gin was the favourite—the drink of the women as much as of the men. Do you know why they call it 'blue ruin'? Some time ago I saw, going into a public-house, somewhere near the West India Docks, a tall lean man, apparently five-and-forty or there-abouts. He was in rags; his knees bent as he walked, his hands trembled, his eyes were eager. And, wonderful to relate, the face was perfectly blue —not indigo blue, or azure blue, but of a ghostly, ghastly, corpse-like kind of blue, which made one shudder. Said my companion to me, 'That is gin.' We opened the door of the public house and looked in. He stood at the bar with a full glass in his hand. Then his eyes brightened, he gasped, straightened himself, and tossed it down his throat. Then he came out, and he sighed as one who has just had a glimpse of paradise. Then he walked away with swift and resolute step, as if purposed to achieve something mighty. Only a few yards further along the road, but across the way, there stood another public house. The man walked straight to the door, entered, and took another glass, again with the quick gasp of anticipation, and again with that sigh, as of a hurried peep through the gates barred with the sword of fire. This man was a curious object of study. He went into twelve more public houses, each time with greater determination on his lips and greater eagerness in his eyes. The last glass, I suppose, opened these gates for him and suffered him to enter, for his lips suddenly lost their resolution, his eyes lost their lustre, he became limp, his arms fell heavily—he was drunk, and his face was bluer than ever.

Walter Besant, *Fifty Years Ago*, 1888

Sir Walter Besant (1836–1901) was an author, historian and philanthropist. He worked hard to help poor people in the East End of London, and used his literary talents to inform others of the dreadful conditions there. He also helped found the Society of Authors, and argued in favour of an international copyright system to protect writers and their work.

4th – Madame Blavatsky

1887–91:—I found Madame Blavatsky in a little house at Norwood, with but, as she said, three followers left—the Society of Psychical Research had just reported on her Indian phenomena—and as one of the three followers sat in an outer room to keep out undesirable visitors, I was kept a long time kicking my heels. Presently I was admitted and found an old woman in a plain loose dark dress: a sort of old Irish peasant woman with an air of humour and audacious power. I was still kept waiting, for she was deep in conversation with a woman visitor. I strayed through folding doors into the next room and stood, in sheer idleness of mind, looking at a cuckoo clock. It was certainly stopped, for the weights were off and lying upon the ground, and yet, as I stood there the cuckoo came out and cuckooed at me. I interrupted Madame Blavatsky to say, 'Your clock has hooted me.' 'It often hoots at a stranger,' she replied. 'Is there a spirit in it ?' I said. 'I do not know,' she said, 'I should have to be alone to know what is in it.' I went back to the clock and began examining it and heard her say: 'Do not break my clock.' I wondered if there was some hidden mechanism and I should have been put out, I suppose, had I found any, though Henley had said to me, 'Of course she gets up fraudulent miracles, but a person of genius has to do something: Sarah Bernhardt sleeps in her coffin.' Presently the visitor went away and Madame Blavatsky explained that she was a propagandist for women's rights who had called to find out 'why men were so bad.' 'What explanation did you give her?' I said. 'That men were born bad, but women made themselves so,' and then she explained that I had been kept waiting because she had mistaken me for some man, whose name resembled mine and who wanted to persuade her of the flatness of the earth.

When I next saw her she had moved into a house at Holland Park, and some time must have passed—probably I had been in Sligo where I returned constantly for long visits—for she was surrounded by followers. She sat nightly before a little table covered with green baize and on this green baize she scribbled constantly with a piece of white chalk. She would scribble symbols, sometimes humorously explainable, and sometimes unintelligible figures, but the chalk was intended to mark down her score when she played patience. One saw in the next room a large table where every night her followers and guests, often a great number, sat down to their vegetable meal, while she encouraged or mocked through the folding doors. A great passionate nature, a sort of female Dr. Johnson, impressive I think to every man or woman who had themselves any richness, she seemed impatient of the formalism and the shrill abstract idealism of those about her, and this impatience broke out in railing and many nicknames: 'Oh you are a flap-doodle, but then you are a theosophist and a brother.' The most devout and learned of all her followers said to me, 'H. P. B. has just told me that there is another globe stuck on to this at the north pole, so that the earth has really a shape something like a dumb-bell.'

W. B. Yeats, The Trembling of the Veil, 1922

Of Russian and German extraction, Helena Blavatsky (1831–91) was an occultist and medium who founded the Theosophist Society. She claimed to have travelled widely in the East, including studying in Tibet: unfortunately there were no witnesses to corroborate her account so some people think she was a fraud. The Irish poet and Nobel Prize winner William Butler Yeats (1865–1939) was intensely interested in magic, Irish legends and the occult. He knew Madame Blavatsky towards the end of her life, when she settled in London.

5th – Reference for a Music Teacher at Cheltenham Ladies' College

Madam,
One of my pupils, Miss Lee, is inclined to accept a situation as music teacher in your College. She will write to you herself. I can recommend her in every respect.

Yours truly
C. Schumann
5 Febr. 90

Clara Schumann (1819–96) married the composer Robert Schumann, but also had a distinguished international career as a concert pianist. She herself was a composer and taught piano at the Hoch Conservatory in Frankfurt. Cheltenham Ladies' College aimed to give pupils the best education they could: a music teacher recommended by Clara Schumann would definitely be worth considering as a staff member!

6th – Fights in School

Fights might take place anywhere in the court, the field, the school-room, the dormitory; but for more formally arranged encounters Fleuss' Arch [which projected from New Court near Fleuss, the drawing-master's classroom] was recognised as the appropriate spot, unless the principals were leading fellows in the school. In that case the Upper Fifth was sometimes selected. All arrangements would have been made beforehand; a plentiful supply of water and towels would have been brought in; after breakfast the combatants and their personal friends would adjourn to the class-room, and, with the doors securely barricaded, there was no danger of interruption until the school-bell necessitated dispersion. Not a few old Marlburians will recall that famous fight of the early years of the fifties, in which two fellows, strong in limb and of indomitable pluck, met in the Upper Fifth immediately after breakfast until the bell rang for ten o'clock school. One of the combatants was severely punished, but at the close neither was nearer to yielding than in the first round. These two fellows afterwards entered the army, and one died in India. The other is still living, a humble-minded, earnest, Christian man; yet even now, after the lapse of so many years, it is not without a feeling of pride that he hears reference to that famous fight.

J. S. Thomas, Bursar, Marlborough College

John Shearme Thomas was a boy at Marlborough College between 1848 and 1851. Eventually he became Bursar, spending thirty-seven years at the school. He recollected a time when there was a great deal of violence, bullying and lack of discipline in the school, and the staff were often seen by the boys as unjust. Matters improved when a new headmaster came in 1851.

7th – Laws of Nature

AUTHORS of the highest eminence seem to be fully satisfied with the view that each species has been independently created. To my mind it accords better with what we know of the laws impressed on matter by the Creator, that the production and extinction of the past and present inhabitants of the world should have been due to secondary causes, like those determining the birth and death of the individual. When I view all beings not as special creations, but as the lineal descendants of some few beings which lived long before the first bed of the Cambrian system was deposited, they seem to me to become ennobled. Judging from the past, we may safely infer that not one living species will transmit its unaltered likeness to a distant futurity.

And of the species now living very few will transmit progeny of any kind to a far distant futurity; for the manner in which all organic beings are grouped, shows that the greater number of species in each genus, and all the species in many genera, have left no descendants, but have become utterly extinct. We can so far take a prophetic glance into futurity as to foretell that it will be the common and widely-spread species, belonging to the larger and dominant groups within each class, which will ultimately prevail and procreate new and dominant species. As all the living forms of life are the lineal descendants of those which lived long before the Cambrian epoch, we may feel certain that the ordinary succession by generation has never once been broken, and that no cataclysm has desolated the whole world. Hence we may look with some confidence to a secure future of great length. And as natural selection works solely by and for the good of each being, all corporeal and mental endowments will tend to progress towards perfection.

It is interesting to contemplate a tangled bank, clothed with many plants of many kinds, with birds singing on the bushes, with various insects flitting about, and with worms crawling through the damp earth, and to reflect that these elaborately constructed forms, so different from each other, and dependent upon each other in so complex a manner, have all been produced by laws acting around us. These laws, taken in the largest sense, being Growth with Reproduction; Inheritance which is almost implied by reproduction; Variability from the indirect and direct action of the condition of life, and from use and disuse: a Ratio of Increase so high as to lead to a Struggle for Life, and as a consequence to Natural Selection, entailing Divergence of Character and the Extinction of less-improved forms. Thus, from the war of nature, from famine and death, the most exalted object which we are capable of conceiving, namely, the production of the higher animals, directly follows. There is grandeur in this view of life, with its several powers, having been originally breathed by the Creator into a few forms or into one; and that, whilst this planet has gone cycling on according to the fixed law of gravity, from so simple a beginning endless forms most beautiful and most wonderful have been, and are being evolved.

Charles Darwin, *On the Origin of Species*

Charles Darwin (1808–92) went into the church after giving up a medical training. Fascinated by nature, he undertook a five-year journey round the world as captain's companion on HMS *Beagle*. He then spent more than twenty years thinking about what he had seen, studying specimens and organising evidence before publishing *On the Origin of Species* in 1859. It caused a furore, but by the end of his life, most scientists had accepted Darwin's theories.

8th – The House Fire

I had hired a young Irish girl the day before. Her friends were only just located in our vicinity, and she had never seen a stove until she came to our house. After Moodie left, I suffered the fire to die away in the Franklin stove in the parlour, and went into the kitchen to prepare bread for the oven.

The girl, who was a good-natured creature, had heard me complain bitterly of the cold, and the impossibility of getting the green wood to burn, and she thought that she would see if she could not make a good fire for me and the children, against my work was done. Without saying one word about her intention, she slipped out through a door that opened from the parlour into the garden, ran round to the wood-yard, filled her lap with cedar chips, and, not knowing the nature of the stove, filled it entirely with the light wood.

Before I had the least idea of my danger, I was aroused from the completion of my task by the crackling and roaring of a large fire, and a suffocating smell of burning soot. I looked up at the kitchen cooking-stove. All was right there. I knew I had left no fire in the parlour stove; but not being able to account for the smoke and smell of burning, I opened the door, and to my dismay found the stove red hot, from the front plate to the topmost pipe that let out the smoke through the roof.

My first impulse was to plunge a blanket, snatched from the servant's bed, which stood in the kitchen, into cold water. This I thrust into the stove, and upon it I threw water, until all was cool below. I then ran up to the loft, and by exhausting all the water in the house, even to that contained in the boilers upon the fire, contrived to cool down the pipes which passed through the loft. I then sent the girl out of doors to look at the roof, which, as a very deep fall of snow had taken place the day before, I hoped would be completely covered, and safe from all danger of fire.

She quickly returned, stamping and tearing her hair, and making a variety of uncouth outcries, from which I gathered that the roof was in flames.

This was terrible news, with my husband absent, no man in the house, and a mile and a quarter from any other habitation. I ran out to ascertain the extent of the misfortune, and found a large fire burning in the roof between the two stone pipes. The heat of the fires had melted off all the snow, and a spark from the burning pipe had already ignited the shingles. A ladder, which for several months had stood against the house, had been moved two days before to the barn, which was at the top of the hill, near the road; there was no reaching the fire through that source. I got out the dining-table, and tried to throw water upon the roof by standing on a chair placed upon it, but I only expended the little water that remained in the boiler, without reaching the fire. The girl still continued weeping and lamenting.

'You must go for help,' I said. 'Run as fast as you can to my sisters, and fetch your master.'

Susanna Moodie, *Roughing it in the Bush*

Susanna Moodie (1803–85) was a British writer of children's stories and a member of the Anti-Slavery Society. She married in 1831, migrating with her husband and daughter to Ontario in Canada in 1832. Her publisher suggested she write a guide to help British emigrants to Canada: *Roughing it in the Bush* came out in 1852, with a sequel, *Life in the Clearings versus the Bush*, the following year. She did not really enjoy life in the backwoods, and was anxious to warn other middle-class migrants, with no experience of such a life, about the sorts of conditions they would face.

9th – Exams for the Services

I begged my parents to let me leave, offering to go into a London office, Green's Merchant Service, or anywhere, to avoid remaining under the Head Master. My father was negotiating with Green & Co., when shortly after I returned to Marlborough College, in February 1852, I unexpectedly received a nomination for the Royal Navy, being ordered to report for examination at the Royal Naval College, Portsmouth Dockyard, in April. I was placed in charge of

Mr. Eastman, a crammer at Portsea, for three weeks, that I might acquire the necessary amount of arithmetic to satisfy the Examiner; for at Marlborough nearly all my school-time was given to Latin and Greek.

Thirty-eight boys faced Captain (later Admiral) Chads on the 15th April. He read out to us half a page from the *Spectator* deliberately, with clear enunciation, and many repetitions, so that no boy could fail to catch the words. While the Examiner was reading, "And this was a very barren spot, barren, barren," he passed up and down the room, and as he turned his back a boy held up a sheet of paper on which he had written "baron" with a big mark of interrogation. I had time only to shake my head when Captain Chads turned, and that boy did not get into the Navy. We were given a short paper on English history, but this presented no difficulties to me, because I had been taught it by my mother at home before I could read.

The examination for soldiers was often at that time even less formidable, certainly in the case of a distinguished officer who has since risen to command the Army, for on joining at Sandhurst a kindly Colonel asked him his name, and continued, "What! a son of my friend Major —?" and on receiving an affirmative reply, said, "Go on, boy; you have passed."

Evelyn Wood, *From Midshipman to Field Marshal*

Desperate to leave Marlborough College, Evelyn Wood (1838–1919) persuaded his parents to let him try to join the Navy. He was seriously wounded during the Crimean war, and then transferred to the Army. He won the VC during the Indian Mutiny, and then served in Africa during several wars on that continent. He was particularly famous for his heroism during the Zulu War. It's interesting to see what questions a candidate for the Navy was asked!

10th – Refurbishing Buckingham Palace

Pavilion, 10th February 1845

Though the Queen knows that Sir Robert Peel has already turned his attention to the urgent necessity of doing something to Buckingham Palace, the Queen thinks it right to recommend this subject herself to his serious consideration. Sir Robert is acquainted with the state of the Palace and the total want of accommodation for our little family, which is fast growing up. Any building must necessarily take some years before it can be safely inhabited. If it were to be begun this autumn, it could hardly be occupied before the spring of 1848, when the Prince of Wales would be nearly seven, and the Princess Royal nearly eight years old, and they cannot possibly be kept in the nursery any longer. A provision for this purpose ought, therefore, to be made this year. Independent of this, most parts of the Palace are in a sad state, and will ere long require a further outlay to render them *decent* for the occupation of the Royal Family or any visitors the Queen may have to receive. A room, capable of containing a large number of those persons whom the Queen has to invite in the course of the season to balls, concerts, etc., than any of the present apartments can at once hold, is much wanted. Equally so, improved offices and servants' rooms, the want of which puts the departments of the household to great expense yearly. It will be for Sir Robert to consider whether it would not be best to remedy all these deficiencies at once, and to make use of this opportunity to render the exterior of the Palace such as no longer to be a *disgrace* to the country, which it certainly now is. The Queen thinks the country would be better pleased to have the question of the Sovereign's residence in London so finally disposed of, than to have it so repeatedly brought before it.

Queen Victoria, Letter to Sir Robert Peel
Ed. A. C. Benson, *Letters of Queen Victoria*

Queen Victoria (born 1819, reigned 1839–1901) was a prolific writer – letters, memos to members of the government and officials, her diary and her papers allow us to know an enormous amount about her, both as a monarch and as a person. *Leaves from the Journal of our Life in the Highlands* was a bestseller.

11th – The Village Doctor

I may relate a little adventure which happened to my husband and myself, three years ago, at Addingham

We were driving along the street, when one of those ne'er-do-well lads who seem to have a kind of magnetic power for misfortunes, having jumped into the stream that runs through the place, just where all the broken glass and bottles are thrown, staggered naked and nearly covered with blood into a cottage before us. Besides receiving another bad cut in the arm, he had completely laid open the artery, and was in a fair way of bleeding to death – which, one of his relations comforted him by saying, would be likely to "save a deal o' trouble."

When my husband had checked the effusion of blood with a strap that one of the bystanders unbuckled from his leg, he asked if a surgeon had been sent for.

"Yoi," was the answer; "but we dunna think he'll come."

"Why not?"

"He's owd, yo seen, and asthmatic, and it's up-hill."

My husband, taking a boy for his guide, drove as fast as he could to the surgeon's house, which was about three-quarters of a mile off, and met the aunt of the wounded lad leaving it.

"Is he coming?" inquired my husband.

"Well, he didna' say he wouldna' come."

"But tell him the lad may bleed to death."

"I did."

"And what did he say?"

"Why, only, 'D—n him; what do I care?'"

It ended, however, in his sending one of his sons, who, though not brought up to "the surgering trade," was able to do what was necessary in the way of bandages and plasters. The excuse made for the surgeon was, that "he was near eighty, and getting a bit doited, and had had a matter o' twenty childer."

Mrs Gaskell, *The Life of Charlotte Brontë*

Elizabeth Gaskell (1810–65) was the wife of a Unitarian clergyman who worked in the north of England. Her novels were much enjoyed, and her friend Charles Dickens published her work in his magazine *Household Words*. She met Charlotte Brontë in 1850, and the two authors became friends. When Charlotte Brontë died in 1865, Mrs Gaskell wrote her life story. This was factual rather than analytical, and some people objected: some of the parts that described Branwell Brontë's friendship with a married woman had to be withdrawn in the second edition after a lawsuit was threatened.

12th – Family Dinners

1st
Clear Soup.
Roast Leg Mutton.
Harico.
Chicken Curry.
Bread and Butter Pudding.

2nd
Mulligatawny.
Beefsteak Pie.
Cutleis à la Soubise.
Kabob Curry.
Pancakes.

3rd
Vegetable Soup.
Boiled Fowls and Tongue.
Mutton and Cucumber Stew.
Dry Curry.
Custard Pudding.

4th
Pea Soup.
A-la-mode Beef.
Roast Teal.
Prawn Curry.
Sweet Omelette.

5th
Oxtail Soup.
Boiled Mutton and Onion Sauce.
Chicken Cutlets.
Vegetable Curry.
Plum Pudding.

6th
White Soup.
Roast Ducks.
Beefsteak.
Ball Curry.
Sago Pudding.

7th
Hare Soup.
Roast Kid and Mint Sauce.
Mutton Pudding.
Sardine Curry.
Mango Fool.

8th
Turnip Soup.
Roast Fowls.
Irish Stew.
Toast Curry.
Arrowroot Jelly.

A Lady Resident, *The Englishwoman in India*

This book described itself as a guide 'Containing Information for the Use of Ladies Proceeding to, or Residing in, the East Indies, on the Subjects of Their Outfit, Furniture, Housekeeping, the Rearing of Children, Duties and Wages of Servants, Management of the Stables, and Arrangements for Travelling; To Which are Added Receipts for Indian Cookery'. It appeared anonymously in 1864, but the author is now known to have been Maud Diver (1867–1945), a writer born in Pakistan, whose novels, set in India, were once very popular.

13th – Hymn to Commemorate Queen Victoria

Our God, our help in ages past,
Our hope for years to come,
Our shelter from the stormy blast,
And our eternal home:

Beneath the shadow of Thy throne
Thy saints have dwelt secure;
Sufficient is Thine arm alone,
And our defence is sure.

Before the hills in order stood
Or earth received its frame,
From everlasting Thou art God,
To endless years the same.

A thousand ages in Thy sight
Are like an evening gone,
Short as the watch that ends the night
Before the rising sun.

Time, like an ever-rolling stream,
Bears all its sons away;
They fly forgotten, as a dream
Dies at the opening day.

Our God, our help in ages past,
Our hope for years to come,
Be Thou our guard while troubles last,
And our eternal home!

Isaac Watts

When Queen Victoria died, churches up and down the country wanted to remember her. This was the only hymn authorised for such use. Published in 1719, it is a paraphrase of Psalm 90.

14th – The Unlikely Holiday

There was once an old cashier in some ancient City establishment, whose practice was to spend his yearly holiday in relieving some turnpike-man at his post, and performing all the duties appertaining thereunto. This was vulgarly taken to be an instance of mere mill-horse enslavement to his groove – the reception of payments; and it was spoken of both in mockery of all mill-horses and for the due admonishment of others. And yet that clerk had discovered for himself a unique method of seeing Life at its best, the flowing, hurrying, travelling, marketing Life of the Highway; the life of bagman and cart, of tinker, and pig-dealer, and all cheery creatures that drink and chaffer together in the sun. He belonged, above all, to the scanty class of clear-seeing persons who know both what they are good for and what they really want. To know what you would like to do is one thing; to go out boldly and do it is another – and a rarer; and the sterile fields about Hell-Gate are strewn with the corpses of those who would if they could.

Kenneth Grahame, *Pagan Papers*

15th – The Honest Railway Man

On Friday night, a servant of the Birmingham Railway Company found in one of the first-class carriages, after the passengers had left, a pocket book containing a check on a London Bank for £2,000 and £2,500 in bank notes. He delivered the book and its contents to the principal officer, and it was forwarded to the gentleman to whom it belonged, his address being discovered from some letters in the pocket book. He had gone to bed, and risen and dressed himself next morning without discovering his loss, which was only made known by the restoration of the property. He immediately tendered £20 to the party who had found his money, but this being contrary to the regulations of the directors, the party, though a poor man, could not receive the reward. As the temptation, however, was so great to apply the money to his own use, the matter is to be brought before a meeting of the directors.

Anon, *Aris's Gazette*, 1839

Thomas Aris was a London stationer who moved to Birmingham in 1740, and started a newspaper. It was named the *Birmingham Gazette and General Correspondent*, but was known familiarly as *Aris's Gazette*. In 1862 it changed from weekly publication to daily publication, and was eventually taken over by the *Birmingham Post* in 1956.

16th – 'Civil and Uncivil' – Society in India

For the last few days we have been occupied with company again. A regiment passed through, and we had to dine all the officers, including a lady; now they are gone. I perceive the officers' ladies are curiously different from the civilians. The civil ladies are generally very quiet, rather languid, speaking in almost a whisper, simply dressed, almost always ladylike and *comme-il-faut*, not pretty but pleasant and nice-looking, rather dull, and give one very hard work in pumping for conversation. They talk of 'the Governor', 'the Presidency', the Overland', and 'girls' schools at home', and have always daughters of about thirteen in England for education. The military ladies, on the contrary, are always quite young, pretty, noisy, affected, showily dressed, with a great many ornaments, *mauvais ton*, chatter incessantly from the moment they enter the house, twist their curls, shake their bustles, and are altogether what you may call 'Low Toss'. While they are alone with me after dinner, they talk about suckling their babies, the disadvantages of scandal, 'the Officers', and 'the Regiment'; and when the gentlemen come into the drawing room, they invariably flirt with them most furiously.

The military and civilians do not generally get on very well together. There is a great deal of very foolish envy and jealousy between them, and they are often downright ill-bred to each other, though in general the civilians behave much the best of the two. One day an officer who was dining here said to me, 'Now I know very well, Mrs —, you despise us all from the bottom of your heart; you think no one worth speaking to in reality but the Civil Service. Whatever people may really be, you just class them all as civil and military—civil and military; and you know no other distinction. Is it not so?' I could not resist saying, 'No; I sometimes class them as civil and uncivil.' He has made no more rude speeches to me since.

A Lady (Julia Charlotte Maitland), *Letters from Madras*, 1843

Originally published anonymously, the letters in this book were by Julia Maitland (1808–64) when she was living in India with her first husband James Thomas. Together they set up a boys' school, and she also helped to start other schools, assisted with famine relief and investigated the South India slave trade. The introduction to the book said '... first impressions ... are amusing, and may sometimes be useful: such, indeed, constitute the chief feature in these Letters. The reader will also find in them many traits of national character; and some descriptions of the Author's intercourse with the natives of Hindostan, and of the endeavours in which she shared to improve their condition.'

17th – A Foggy Journey ...

15 Clifford's Inn E.C.
Feb. 1882.
Dear Miss Savage,

How did you get home last Saturday? I did not know what a fog it was or I should have come with you. I hope nothing serious happened—if so I shall say it was a judgment upon you because you were trying to curry favour with God by praising his days when no one knew better than he that he ought to be ashamed of them.

You remember you stuck out to me that it was a very fine day when I told you it was nothing of the kind. I don't want to be flattered, but on the other hand I can brook no contradiction. But seriously I shall be very glad to hear that you got home without mishap. Something went up against a good piece of granite coping of Waterloo Bridge and knocked it clean over into the river. I saw the gap next morning, so the fog must have been pretty thick there.

I don't think you were very well on Saturday, and I don't think I asked after you quite enough. I hope are better.

Yours very truly, S. Butler.

Samuel Butler, *Letters between Samuel Butler and Miss E. M. A. Savage, 1871–85*

Samuel Butler (1835–1902) is best known for his humorous satirical novels, though he was also an accomplished artist, a classical scholar, a musician, a poet – and had at one time been a successful sheep farmer in New Zealand. He lived alone, but had one or two close friends – Eliza

Savage was one: he met her in 1867 when she was studying painting on the same course.

18th – ... but All is Well

22 Beaumont Street.
Feb. 1882.
Dear Mr. Butler,
   Thanks for your kind enquiries. You will be glad to hear that I did no damage to anybody or anything, on my way home last Saturday. It was not *I*, as you seem to imply, who knocked that great piece out of Waterloo Bridge. In fact there was no fog at all anywhere that I went to on that day, so that whatever I did by way of propitiation, it was successful.
   But you never need be uneasy about me in a fog—having been accustomed for many generations to the 'hellish and dismal cloud of sea-coal perpetually imminent over our heads', I am quite at home in it, and should not have allowed you to put yourself in peril on my account, for I am as distrustful of other people's power of getting through a fog, as I am comfortably confident in my own ...
Yours very truly, E. M. A. Savage.
Letters between Samuel Butler and Miss E. M. A. Savage,
1871–85

Samuel Butler's friend Eliza Savage may have had romantic hopes about him – but he had been nicknamed 'the incarnate bachelor' at art school. However, he welcomed her encouragement as a writer, and accepted some of her suggestions about his work. The two engaged in a lively correspondence, and he was devastated when she died suddenly in 1885. He published their letters as a tribute to her.

19th – The Birds That Planted Trees

Two years ago, one day in the early spring, I was walking on an extensive down in ... Wiltshire with the tenant of the land, who began there as a large sheep-farmer, but eventually finding that he could make more with rabbits than with sheep turned most of his land into a warren. The higher part of this down was overgrown with furze, mixed with holly and other bushes, but the slopes were mostly very bare. At one spot on a wide bare slope where the rabbits had formed a big group of burrows there was a close little thicket of young elder trees, looking exceedingly conspicuous in the bright green of early April. Calling my companion's attention to this little thicket I said something about the elder growing on the open downs where it always appeared to be out of harmony with its surroundings. "I don't suppose you planted elders here," I said.

"No, but I know who did," he returned, and he then gave me this curious history of the trees. Five years before, the rabbits, finding it a suitable spot to dig in, probably because of a softer chalk there, made a number of deep burrows at that spot. When the wheatears, or "horse-maggers" as he called them, returned in spring two or three pairs attached themselves to this group of burrows and bred in them. There was that season a solitary elder-bush higher up on the down among the furze which bore a heavy crop of berries; and when the fruit was ripe he watched the birds feeding on it, the wheatears among them. The following spring seedlings came up out of the loose earth heaped about the rabbit burrows, and as they were not cut down by the rabbits, for they dislike the elder, they grew up, and now formed a clump of fifty or sixty little trees of six feet to eight feet in height.

Who would have thought to find a tree-planter in the wheatear, the bird of the stony waste and open naked down, who does not even ask for a bush to perch on?

W. H. Hudson, *Afoot in England*

William Henry Hudson (1841–1922) was born and spent his early life in Argentina – his British parents had migrated first to the United States of America, then on to South America. Settling in England in 1869, Hudson loved and studied nature, writing many books about wildlife in South America and England. He also wrote about the countryside in general, and the people he met there. He was also a novelist and a founding member of the Royal Society for the Protection of Birds.

20th – The Very Foolish Sunset (Nature Not According to Ruskin)

Nature contains the elements, in colour and form, of all pictures, as the keyboard contains the notes of all music.

But the artist is born to pick, and choose, and group with science, these elements, that the result may be beautiful—as the musician gathers his notes, and forms his chords, until he bring forth from chaos glorious harmony.

To say to the painter, that Nature is to be taken as she is, is to say to the player, that he may sit on the piano.

That Nature is always right, is an assertion, artistically, as untrue, as it is one whose truth is universally taken for granted. Nature is very rarely right, to such an extent even, that it might almost be said that Nature is usually wrong: that is to say, the condition of things that shall bring about the perfection of harmony worthy a picture is rare, and not common at all.

This would seem, to even the most intelligent, a doctrine almost blasphemous. So incorporated with our education has the supposed aphorism become, that its belief is held to be part of our moral being, and the words themselves have, in our ear, the ring of religion. Still, seldom does Nature succeed in producing a picture.

The sun blares, the wind blows from the east, the sky is bereft of cloud, and without, all is of iron. The windows of the Crystal Palace are seen from all points of London. The holiday-maker rejoices in the glorious day, and the painter turns aside to shut his eyes.

How little this is understood, and how dutifully the casual in Nature is accepted as sublime, may be gathered from the unlimited admiration daily produced by a very foolish sunset.

J. M. Whistler, *The Gentle Art of Making Enemies*

James McNeill Whistler (1834–1903) was an American artist who lived and worked in Britain. He developed a type of painting called 'tonalism' in which he used a very limited range of colours. When the critic Ruskin gave a painting a bad review, Whistler sued him for libel: he won but only received a farthing in damages. The transcript of the trial was the basis for his highly controversial book *The Gentle Art of Making Enemies*, which also included letters of Whistler's expressing grievances against friends and acquaintances.

21st – Crowds in the City

After roaming the streets of the capital a day or two, making headway with difficulty through the human turmoil and the endless lines of vehicles, after visiting the slums of the metropolis, one realizes for the first time that these Londoners have been forced to sacrifice the best qualities of their human nature, to bring to pass all the marvels of civilization which crowd their city; that a hundred powers which slumbered within them have remained inactive, have been suppressed in order that a few might be developed more fully and multiply through union with those of others ... The brutal indifference, the unfeeling isolation of each in his private interest becomes the more repellent and offensive, the more these individuals are crowded together within a limited space. And, however much one may be aware that this isolation of the individual, this narrow self-seeking, is the fundamental principle of our society everywhere, it is nowhere so shamelessly barefaced, so self-conscious as just here in the crowding of the great city. The dissolution of mankind into nomads, of which each one has a separate principle, the world of atoms, is here carried out to its utmost extreme.

Fredrick Engels, *Condition of the Working Class in England in 1844*

Friedrich Engels (1820–95) worked from 1842 in Manchester, in a family-owned cotton mill. He had been involved with liberal and revolutionary groups in Germany before he came to Britain. In Manchester, his close friend Mary Burns showed him some of the worst slums. He also observed child labour, overworked and under-nourished workers and the damaged environment. He sent three articles about these conditions back to Karl Marx, whom he had met just before coming to England, and Marx published them in his newspapers. The articles were later published as the book *Condition of the Working Class in England*.

22nd – English Tourists in Rome

II. Claude to Eustace.
Rome disappoints me still; but I shrink and adapt myself to it.
Somehow a tyrannous sense of a superincumbent oppression
Still, wherever I go, accompanies ever, and makes me

Feel like a tree (shall I say?) buried under a ruin of brickwork.
Rome, believe me, my friend, is like its own Monte Testaceo,
Merely a marvellous mass of broken and castaway wine-pots.
Ye gods! what do I want with this rubbish of ages departed,
Things that Nature abhors, the experiments that she has failed in?
What do I find in the Forum? An archway and two or three
   pillars.
Well, but St. Peter's? Alas, Bernini has filled it with sculpture!
No one can cavil, I grant, at the size of the great Coliseum.
Doubtless the notion of grand and capacious and massive
   amusement,
This the old Romans had; but tell me, is this an idea?
Yet of solidity much, but of splendour little is extant:
'Brickwork I found thee, and marble I left thee!' their Emperor
   vaunted;
'Marble I thought thee, and brickwork I find thee!' the Tourist
   may answer.

A. H. Clough, Amours de Voyage

Clough's poem *Amours de Voyage* is a novel in verse, written in five parts. It takes the form of letters from the various characters in the story. Many are written by Claude, who has a rather lukewarm love affair with Mary, an English tourist in Italy. Various contemporary problems are discussed, often in a mocking, critical tone.

23rd – The Beginnings of the Charity S&SFA

Sir, Ample provision having been made under recent regulations for the relief of widows and orphans of our soldiers and sailors who may be killed or die of disease or of wounds in war, a further responsibility and duty now devolves on the country in seeing that the wives and children of those ordered on active service are not altogether forgotten, or that the cry of poverty and want be not added to that of suspense and anxiety. The Government "separation" allowance, together with that stopped from the pay of the soldier himself, is for this wife 1s. and for each child 3d. per day: whereas no provision whatever is made for the many respectable women, married with or without leave, who are not on the strength of the regiment.

For both I would venture to make an earnest appeal, but

especially for the latter, wholly unprovided for, and who, in a somewhat extended experience in the distribution of former funds, I have invariably found a most deserving class. I shall be glad to receive subscriptions and to hear from any who would be glad to help in this movement.

All amounts received will be acknowledged in the daily Press.

I have the honour to be, Sir, your obedient servant,

James Gildea, Major, late Treasurer and Hon. Sec. Zulu, Afghan, Bombay and Indian Patriotic Funds

Letter to The Times, Monday 23 February, 1885

Colonel Sir James Gildea (1838–1920) was an Anglo-Irish officer in the British Army. He became involved in charitable work during the Franco-Prussian War, when he served with the National Society for Aid to the Sick and Wounded (later the British Red Cross). Following this, he worked for several relief funds set up to help soldiers and their families engaged in various wars, such as those in Afghanistan and South Africa. This letter marks the start of perhaps his greatest achievement: the founding of the charity now known as SSAFA, the Soldiers, Sailors and Airmen's Families Association.

24th – Noisy Neighbours

I am continuing to mend. If I could only get a good sleep, I shall be quite recovered; but, alas! we are gone to the devil again in the sleeping department. That dreadful woman next door, instead of putting away the cock which we so pathetically appealed against, has produced another. The servant has ceased to take charge of them. They are stuffed with ever so many hens into a small hencoop every night, and left out of doors the night long. Of course they are not comfortable, and of course they crow and screech not only from daylight, but from midnight, and so near that it goes through one's head every time like a sword. The night before last they woke me every quarter of an hour, but I slept some in the intervals; for they had not succeeded in rousing *him* above. But last night they had him up at three. He went to bed again, and got some sleep after, the 'horrors' not recommencing their efforts till five; but I, listening every minute for a new screech that would send him down a second time and prepare such wretchedness for the day, could sleep no more.

What is to be done, God knows! If this goes on, he will soon be in Bedlam; and I too, for anything I see to the contrary: and how to hinder it from going on? The last note we sent the cruel woman would not open. I send for the maid and she will not come. I would give them guineas for quiet, but they prefer tormenting us. In the *law* there is no resource in such cases. They may keep beasts wild in their back yard if they choose to do so. Carlyle swears he will shoot them, and orders me to borrow Mazzini's gun. Shoot them with all my heart if the consequences were merely having to go to a police officer and pay the damage. But the woman would only be irritated thereby in getting fifty instead of two. If there is to be any shooting, however, I will do it myself. It will sound better my shooting them on principle than his doing it in a passion.

This despicable nuisance, is not at all unlikely to drive us out of the house after all, just when he had reconciled himself to stay in it. How one is vexed with little things in life! The great evils one triumphs over bravely, but the little eat away one's heart.

Jane Welsh Carlyle, *Letters*

Jane Welsh Carlyle (1801–66) was a well-educated, bright, witty woman, who had a tumultuous and unhappy marriage to Thomas Carlyle. She wrote many letters during her life to a wide variety of acquaintances, including many eminent Victorians. This one, to her mother Grace Welsh, is a lively expression of the problems caused by her neighbour's poultry – not something one would expect to find in Chelsea!

25th – Disaster in the Drawing-Room

It was a very full and long Drawing-room. I had a dreadful misadventure. Tirard (the Coiffeur) had not pinned my cap and veil sufficiently firmly, and when, as I felt the room warm, I asked Louisa Buccleuch to remove the lace scarf I had on my shoulders, happening to turn my head round at the same moment to speak to Lord Lathom, off came the whole thing completely! The ladies rushed to put in on again, but badly of course, and Alice and Lenchen helped, but it was dreadful, though most ludicrous.

Queen Victoria, Journal, recorded in *The Letters of Queen Victoria, Third Series Vol. I (1886–1890)*

26th – The Birkenhead

Amid the loud ebriety of War,
With shouts of 'la Republique' and 'la Gloire,'
The Vengeur's crew, 'twas said, with flying flag
And broadside blazing level with the wave
Went down erect, defiant, to their grave
Beneath the sea.—'Twas but a Frenchman's brag,
Yet Europe rang with it for many a year.
Now we recount no fable; Europe, hear!
And when they tell thee 'England is a fen
Corrupt, a kingdom tottering to decay,
Her nerveless burghers lying an easy prey
For the first comer,' tell how the other day
A crew of half a thousand Englishmen
Went down into the deep in Simon's Bay!
Not with the cheer of battle in the throat,
Or cannon-glare and din to stir their blood,
But, roused from dreams of home to find their boat
Fast sinking, mustered on the deck they stood,
Biding God's pleasure and their chief's command.
Calm was the sea, but not less calm that band
Close ranged upon the poop, with bated breath
But flinching not though eye to eye with Death! Heroes!
Who were those Heroes? Veterans steeled
To face the King of Terrors mid the scaith
Of many an hurricane and trenchèd field?
Far other: weavers from the stocking-frame;
Boys from the plough; cornets with beardless chin,
But steeped in honour and in discipline!
Weep, Britain, for the Cape whose ill-starred name,
Long since divorced from Hope suggests but shame,
Disaster, and thy Captains held at bay
By naked hordes; but as thou weepest, thank
Heaven for those undegenerate sons who sank
Aboard the Birkenhead in Simon's Bay!

Sir Henry Yule

HM Troopship *Birkenhead* was wrecked on 26 February 1852 at Danger
Point, 140 km from Cape Town. There were not enough serviceable

lifeboats, so the women and children were put into the three craft that could be launched, while the troops, mustered on deck, stood firm while the ship sank in shark-infested waters. Of about 640 people on board, only 193 survived. This was the earliest shipwreck in which the principle of 'women and children first' was promoted. The order and discipline of the troops – the *Birkenhead* drill – became famous as an example of courage in desperate conditions. Sir Henry Yule (1820–89) was an Orientalist who published many travel books.

27th – Labour

For there is a perennial nobleness, and even sacredness, in Work. Were he never so benighted, forgetful of his high calling, there is always hope in a man that actually and earnestly works: in Idleness alone is there perpetual despair. Work, never so Mammonish, mean, is in communication with Nature; the real desire to get Work done will itself lead one more and more to truth, to Nature's appointments and regulations, which are truth. The latest Gospel in this world is, Know thy work and do it. 'Know thyself:' long enough has that poor 'self' of thine tormented thee; thou wilt never get to 'know' it, I believe! Think it not thy business, this of knowing thyself; thou art an unknowable individual: know what thou canst work at; and work at it, like a Hercules! That will be thy better plan.

Thomas Carlyle, *Past and Present*

Thomas Carlyle (1795–1881) was a Scottish historian, philosopher, essayist and critic who influenced many Victorians, including Ruskin and Dickens. At a time when many changes were affecting the country, he tried to find moral values that were absolute, such as work and duty. Throughout his life he tried to find a historical figure who could be presented as a true hero.

28th – Celebrating the Golden Jubilee in India

Calcutta, 28th Feb. 1887
All the accounts from every part of India go to show that the celebration of the Jubilee has been an extraordinarily successful as well as a most spontaneous and enthusiastic celebration on the part

of the people. In a previous letter Lord Dufferin communicated to your Majesty the programme for the two days which were set aside as public holidays. Nothing could have been more brilliant than both the fireworks and the illuminations, and Lord Dufferin is sure that it will be a satisfaction to your Majesty to know that in all our arrangements it was the enjoyment and the tastes of the masses of the people that we endeavoured to consult and gratify.

The natives of India are passionately fond of pyrotechnic displays, and on the 16th they were shown fireworks far superior to any that they had ever seen before. The principal feature was the outline of your Majesty's head, traced in lines of fire, which unexpectedly burst on the vision of the astonished crowd. The likeness was admirable, and caused an enormous shout of pleasure and surprise. In the same manner portraits of their Royal Highnesses the Prince and Princess of Wales on the same gigantic scale appeared from out a fiery rose-bush. These were equally like and were similarly recognised. Lord and Lady Dufferin were honoured in the same manner, and the Viceroy thought he had never looked so well. Thirty thousand schoolchildren, both native and European, were entertained in a very successful manner under the superintendence of the wife of one of your Majesty's new Knights, a certain Lady Wilson, a very influential personage in Calcutta.

On the night of the illuminations a procession was formed, and Lord Dufferin with his Council and all the Civil and Military authorities drove through the town. The streets were crowded with thousands and thousands of people, and though an Indian crowd is generally very impassive, on this occasion Lord Dufferin was received with continuous cheers and clappings as he proceeded.

The Earl of Dufferin, letter to Queen Victoria

Frederick Hamilton-Temple-Blackwood, 1st Marquess of Dufferin and Ava (1826–1902), was a very successful diplomat. His appointment as Viceroy of India in 1884 was the climax of his career. He was a good writer (his book *Letters From High Latitudes* had done very well) and his lively and entertaining account of the Jubilee celebrations brings it vividly to life.

MARCH

1st – Household Cures in India

Bites of Wasps, Scorpions, etc. A paste of ipecacuanha and water applied at once over the bite generally acts as a charm. Stimulants if severe symptoms follow.

Of Mad, or even Doubtful Dogs. Cut with a lancet or penknife down to the very bottom of the wound and again across, so as to let it gape and bleed. Then cauterise remorselessly with nitrate of silver, or carbolic acid, or actual hot iron. The object is to destroy the bitten tissue, so see that you get to the *bottom*.

Of a Snake. If in a toe, finger, or end of a limb, apply a ligature with the first thing handy. Whipcord is best, but take the first ligature that comes to hand. Twist with a stick, or any lever, as tight as you can. Apply two or more nearer the heart at intervals of a few inches. Meanwhile, if you have help, get some one else to cut out the flesh round the fang marks, and let it bleed freely. If the snake is known to be deadly, amputate the finger or toe at the next joint, or if you cannot do this, run the knife right round the bone, dividing the flesh completely. Let the bitten person suck the wound till you can burn it with anything at hand—carbolic, nitric acid, nitrate of silver, or actual hot iron. Give one ounce of brandy in a little water. The great object is to prevent the poison getting through the blood to the heart, so every additional pulse beat before the ligatures are on is a danger. If symptoms of poisoning set in, give more stimulants; put mustard plasters over the heart;

rub the limbs; treat, in fact, as for drowning, even to artificial respiration.

Cholera. In cholera seasons check all premonitory diarrhoea with twenty drops of chlorodyne in some *ajwain* water, No. 5. It is easy to give an antibilious pill after, if the diarrhoea turns out to be bilious. The treatment of pronounced cholera is a disputed point, and what is best in one epidemic often fails in the next, but the acid treatment on the whole seems most successful if commenced in time. One tablespoon of vinegar and one teaspoon of Worcester sauce has long been a fairly successful treatment amongst tea coolies, and of late the merits of twenty drops of diluted acetic acid and ten drops of sweet spirits of nitre in a wineglass of water has been greatly extolled. The famous Austrian remedy was diluted sulphuric acid, three drachms; nitric acid, two drachms; syrup, six drachms; water, to make the whole to ten ounces. One tablespoon in very cold water, and repeated in half an hour. Even if collapse sets in, and apparent death, hope should not be given up. Every effort to keep up circulation should be continued, many people having literally been brought back to life by devoted nursing.

Fever (Ordinary Intermittent with Ague). Give hot lime-juice and water, with a little ginger in it to relieve the cold stage. Cold water on the head in the hot, and as soon as the sweating begins, fifteen drops of chlorodyne and six grains of quinine. In long continued hot stages, give fever mixture. Arsenic often succeeds in breaking the fever when quinine fails. *Dose.* Five drops of Fowler's solution twice a day. *In simple continued fever* give small doses of quinine and ipecacuanha, and fever mixtures; for the debility after fevers, give chiretta infusion No. 8.

Headache. Give an aperient. If nervous, try a mustard plaster at the pit of the stomach and strong coffee. Eno's fruit salt is good.

Hiccough. Hold the right ear with the left forefinger and thumb, bringing the elbow as far across the chest as possible. An unreasonable but absolutely effective cure.

> Flora Steel and Grace Gardiner, *The Complete Indian Housekeeper and Cook*, 1890

Flora Annie Steel (1847–1929) lived in India for many years. She was interested in Indian society at all levels, and also education, particularly that of women. Exceptionally, she became an inspector of schools. She wrote novels, history and books for children, as well as making a collection of Indian folk-tales. Together with Grace Gardiner, another long-term resident, she wrote a very comprehensive guide to living in India for British women, which now gives an entertaining and far-reaching view of what life for a memsahib in the Raj must have been like. As the authors said, 'an Indian household can no more be governed peacefully, without dignity and prestige, than an Indian Empire.'

2nd – Mother Wept

Mother wept, and father sighed;
With delight a-glow
Cried the lad, 'To-morrow,' cried,
'To the pit I go.'

Up and down the place he sped, –
Greeted old and young;
Far and wide the tidings spread;
Clapt his hands and sung.

Came his cronies; some to gaze
Wrapt in wonder; some
Free with counsel; some with praise;
Some with envy dumb.

'May he,' many a gossip cried,
'Be from peril kept;'
Father hid his face and sighed,
Mother turned and wept.

Joseph Skipsey

Joseph Skipsey (1832–1903) was known as 'the Pitman Poet' as he started work in the mines aged just seven. During the long shifts, he taught himself to read and write, and then started writing his own poetry. After publishing his third collection of poems, he was awarded a small Civil List pension. Although he tried other jobs, he went back to mining until 1882, when he became a school caretaker. In 1889, his literary friends secured him an appointment as caretaker of Shakespeare's House in Stratford-upon-Avon, but after two years he resigned and returned to the north of England.

3rd – Eating Locusts

Locusts are now a regular portion of the day's provision with us, and are really an excellent article of diet. After trying them in several ways, we have come to the conclusion that they are best plain boiled. The long hopping legs must be pulled off, and the locust held by the wings, dipped into salt and eaten. As to flavour this insect tastes of vegetable rather than of fish or flesh, not unlike green wheat in England, and to us it supplies the place of vegetables, of which we are much in need. The red locust is better eating than the green one. Wilfrid considers that it would hold its own among the *hors d'oeuvres* at a Paris restaurant; I am not so sure of this, for on former journeys I have resolved that other excellent dishes should be adopted at home, but afterwards among the multitude of luxuries, they have not been found worth the trouble of preparation. For catching locusts, the morning is the time, when they are half benumbed by the cold, and their wings are damp with the dew, so that they cannot fly; they may then be found clustered in hundreds under the desert bushes, and gathered without trouble, merely shovelled into a bag or basket. Later on, the sun dries their wings and they are difficult to capture, having intelligence enough to keep just out of reach when pursued. Flying, they look extremely like May flies, being carried side-on to the wind. They can steer themselves about as much as flying fish do and can alight when they like; in fact, they very seldom let themselves be drifted against men or camels, and seem able to calculate exactly the reach of a stick. This year they are all over the country, in enormous armies by day, and huddled in regiments under every bush by night. They devour everything vegetable; and are devoured by everything, animal: desert larks and bustards, ravens, hawks, and buzzards. We passed to-day through flocks of ravens and buzzards, sitting on the ground gorged with them. The camels munch them in with their food, the greyhounds run snapping after them all day long, eating as many as they can catch.

The Bedouins often give them to their horses, and Awwad says that this year many tribes have nothing to eat just now but locusts and camels' milk; thus the locust in some measure makes amends for being a pestilence, by being himself consumed.

Lady Anne Blunt, A *Pilgrimage to Nejd*, 1881

Lady Anne Blunt (1837–1917) was the brilliant daughter of Ada Lovelace, the mathematician who worked with Charles Babbage on the first computer. Lady Anne Blunt was an artist and musician, spoke several languages, and was an outstanding horsewoman. She married the poet and Arabist Wilfred Scawen Blunt, but the marriage was unhappy, and eventually they separated. However, in 1878 they started a stud, to breed Arab horses, and in 1882 started a second stud, Shaykh 'Ubayd, outside Cairo. Lady Anne made three important trips to central Arabia, looking for good horses to preserve the pure Arabian strain: the first European woman to be recorded as doing so. After the marriage breakdown, she spent the winters in Egypt, eventually moving there permanently.

4th – Save Jumbo!

The Council of the Zoological Society of London having decided to dispose of the large African elephant Jumbo, and a purchaser at £2,000 having been found in Mr. Barnum, public excitement against the animal's removal to New York took a very strong turn, which increased when the real or pretended unwillingness of the animal to enter his travelling cage became better known. On the part of the Zoological Society, the secretary has written that the huge animal's temper had of late been a source of great anxiety. The excuse, however, did not carry conviction to every mind. In consequence, Mr. Barnum telegraphed: 'Reconsidered. Will return Jumbo next December, if Zoological Society desires. Jumbo advertised here so extensively, irreparable loss and disappointment should he fail to arrive.'

Annual *Register*: 4 March 1882

Jumbo was the first African elephant to be seen alive in Europe. Originally put on show in a Paris zoo, he was traded for a rhinoceros and came to live in London Zoo, where he gave rides and was extremely popular.

As the biggest elephant in captivity, he attracted the attention of P. T. Barnum, the American circus owner, who eventually bought him in 1882 for £2,000. This caused outrage and distress in Britain, and a campaign was launched to stop the sale. However, Barnum succeeded in making his purchase and Jumbo went to America. He died in 1885, as a result of a railway accident in Canada. 'Jumbomania' produced all manner of goods relating to the elephant, and his name was subsequently used to mean 'huge'.

5th – Villon's Straight Tip to All Cross Coves

"Tout aux tavernes et aux filles"

Suppose you screeve? or go cheap-jack?
Or fake the broads? or fig a nag?
Or thimble-rig? or knap a yack?
Or pitch a snide? or smash a rag?
Suppose you duff? or nose and lag?
Or get the straight, and land your pot?
How do you melt the multy swag?
Booze and the blowens cop the lot.

Fiddle, or fence, or mace, or mack;
Or moskeneer, or flash the drag;
Dead-lurk a crib, or do a crack;
Pad with a slang, or chuck a fag;
Bonnet, or tout, or mump and gag;
Rattle the tats, or mark the spot;
You can not bank a single stag;
Booze and the blowens cop the lot.

Suppose you try a different tack,
And on the square you flash your flag?
At penny-a-lining make your whack,
Or with the mummers mug and gag?
For nix, for nix the dibbs you bag!
At any graft, no matter what,
Your merry goblins soon stravag:
Booze and the blowens cop the lot.

THE MORAL
It's up the spout and Charley Wag
With wipes and tickers and what not.
Until the squeezer nips your scrag,
Booze and the blowens cop the lot.

W. E. Henley

William Ernest Henley (1849–1903) was a poet and editor. He lost a part of his leg in childhood due to an illness. When he met and became friends with Robert Louis Stevenson during a three-year stay in an Edinburgh hospital he became the model for Long John Silver in *Treasure Island*. With a colleague he edited a seven-volume dictionary of slang, which inspired this poem. It is a translation into thieves' slang of a ballade by the fifteenth-century French poet François Villon. Other poems include a number he wrote in hospital, including his most famous, *Invictus*.

6th – The True Blue Independent Stagecoach

Whatever disadvantages old stage coaches possessed, and their name certainly was legion, it must be admitted that in a case of this sort their slowness was a recommendation. The old True Blue Independent did not profess to travel or trail above eight miles an hour, and this it only accomplished under favourable circumstances, such as light loads, good roads, and stout steeds, instead of the top-heavy cargo that now ploughed along the woolly turnpike after the weak, jaded horses, that seemed hardly able to keep their legs against the keen careering wind. If, under such circumstances, the wretched concern made the wild-beast-show looking place in London, called an inn, where it put up, an hour or an hour and a half or so after its time, it was said to be all very well, "considering,"—and this, perhaps, in a journey of sixty miles.

Posterity will know nothing of the misery their forefathers underwent in the travelling way; and whenever we hear—which we often do—unreasonable grumblings about the absence of trifling luxuries on railways, we are tempted to wish the parties consigned to a good long ride in an old stage coach. Why the worst third class that ever was put next the engine is infinitely better than the inside of the best of them used to be, to say nothing of the speed. As to the outsides of the old coaches, with their roastings, their soakings, their freezings, and their smotherings with dust, one cannot but feel that the establishment of railways was a downright prolongation of life. Then the coach refreshments, or want of refreshments rather; the turning out at all hours to breakfast, dine, or sup, just as the coach reached the house of a proprietor "wot oss'd it," and the cool incivility of every body about the place. Any thing was good enough for a coach passenger.

R. S. Surtees, Ask Mamma

Robert Smith Surtees (1805–64) trained as a lawyer, but spent most of his time hunting and writing about sport. When his father died in 1838, he took over the family estate in County Durham, and continued hunting and writing, though he wrote for pleasure rather than profit. His novels are loosely written, but his observation of a wide variety of characters and their speech is very acute and his views of the countryside and of hunting are extremely realistic.

7th – Young and Old

When all the world is young, lad,
And all the trees are green;
And every goose a swan, lad,
And every lass a queen;
Then hey for boot and horse, lad,
And round the world away;
Young blood must have its course, lad,
And every dog his day.

When all the world is old, lad,
And all the trees are brown;
And all the sport is stale, lad,
And all the wheels run down:
Creep home and take your place there,
The spent and maimed among:
God grant you find one face there,
You loved when all was young.

Charles Kingsley, The Water Babies

8th – Mary Kingsley Changes Her Mind

One by one I took my old ideas derived from books and thoughts based on imperfect knowledge and weighed them against the real life around me, and found them either worthless or wanting. The greatest recantation I had to make I made humbly before I had been three months on the Coast in 1893. It was of my idea of the traders. What I had expected to find them was a very different thing to what I did find them; and of their kindness to me I can never sufficiently speak, for on that voyage I was utterly out of touch with the governmental circles, and utterly dependent on the traders, and the most useful lesson of all the lessons I learnt on the West Coast in 1893 was that I could trust them. Had I not learnt this very thoroughly I could never have gone out again and carried out the voyage I give you a sketch of in this book.

Thanks to "the Agent," I have visited places I could never otherwise have seen; and to the respect and affection in which he is held by the native, I owe it that I have done so in safety. When I have arrived off his factory in a steamer or canoe unexpected, unintroduced, or turned up equally unheralded out of the bush in a dilapidated state, he has always received me with that gracious hospitality which must have given him, under Coast conditions, very real trouble and inconvenience – things he could have so readily found logical excuses against entailing upon himself for the sake of an individual whom he had never seen before – whom he most likely would never see again – and whom it was no earthly profit to him to see then. He has bestowed himself – Allah only knows where – on his small trading vessels so that I might have his one cabin. He has fished me out of sea and fresh water with boat-hooks; he has continually given me good advice, which if I had only followed would have enabled me to keep out of water and any other sort of affliction; and although he holds the meanest opinion of my intellect for going to such a place as West Africa for beetles, fishes and fetish, he has given me the greatest assistance in my work. The value of that work I pray you withhold judgment on, until I lay it before you in some ten volumes or so mostly in Latin. All I know that is true regarding West African facts, I owe to the traders; the errors are my own.

Mary Kingsley, *Travels in West Africa*

Mary Kingsley (1862–1900) was an explorer and scientist, the niece of Charles Kingsley. Free to travel after the death of her parents, she went alone to countries in West and Central Africa, such as Sierra Leone, Angola and Gabon, living with the people there and studying their ways of life and religions. Her first book, *Travels in West Africa*, was very popular – but also very controversial, as she opposed some of the practices of Europeans in West Africa.

9th – Donkey-Barrows at Covent Garden

The donkey-barrows, from their number and singularity, force you to stop and notice them. Every kind of ingenuity has been exercised to construct harness for the costers' steeds; where a buckle is wanting, tape or string make the fastening secure; traces are made of rope and old chain, and an old sack or cotton handkerchief is folded up as a saddle-pad. Some few of the barrows make a magnificent exception, and are gay with bright brass; while one of the donkeys may be seen dressed in a suit of old plated carriage-harness, decorated with coronets in all directions. At some one of the coster conveyances stands the proprietor, arranging his goods, the dozing animal starting up from its sleep each time a heavy basket is hoisted on the tray. Others, with their green and white and red load neatly arranged, are ready for starting, but the coster is finishing his breakfast at the coffee-stall. On one barrow there may occasionally be seen a solitary sieve of apples, with the horse of some neighbouring cart helping himself to the pippins while the owner is away. The men that take charge of the trucks, whilst the costers visit the market, walk about, with their arms full of whips and sticks. At one corner a donkey has slipped down, and lies on the stones covered with the cabbages and apples that have fallen from the cart.

Henry Mayhew, *London Labour and the London Poor*

Henry Mayhew (1812–87) was a journalist who first started writing comic material – he was one of the founders of *Punch*, but he left that magazine in 1846. Changing direction entirely, in 1849 he started publishing an enormous survey of 'Labour and the Poor'. He researched widely, going into great detail about working conditions, and his material was often controversial. The survey began as a series of articles in the *Morning Chronicle*, then from 1850 Henry Mayhew began to publish his articles independently. They were collected into three books, which also included biographical sketches and oral accounts.

10th – Carrot Jam

The following recipe for carrot jam or French preserve, I know to be very good when properly made: – Take 5 lb of carrots, clean them, and boil until quite soft, as for dinner. Mash them very fine, rub through a wire-sieve, boil the pulp again with 5 lb. of sugar twenty minutes, add the juice of two lemons whilst boiling. Then take it off the fire, and stir in 1 oz. of tartaric acid and half a pint of orange wine.

Eliza, *The Field*

11th – Milking

The hour of milking, which used to be pretty general everywhere, varies now in different places, to suit the necessities of the milk trade. The milk has, perhaps, to travel three or four miles to the railway station; near great towns, where some of the farmers deliver milk themselves from house to house, the cows are milked soon after noonday. What would their grandfathers have said to that? But where the old customs have not much altered, the milker sits down in the morning to his cow with the stars still visible overhead, punching his hat well into her side—a hat well battered and thickly coated with grease, for the skin of the cow exudes an unctuous substance. This hat he keeps for the purpose. A couple of milking pails—they are of large size—form a heavy load when filled. The milker, as he walks back to the farmhouse, bends his head under the yoke—whence so many men are round-shouldered—and steps slowly with a peculiar swaying motion of the body, which slight swing prevents it from spilling.

Richard Jefferies, *The Book of Hodge and His Master*

Richard Jefferies (1848–87) was a farmer's son who studied journalism. He wrote many books about country life, or with a country setting: these describe it in a detailed and unsentimental way, and show his real understanding of how rural life was lived, as well as conveying his love of nature. *Hodge and His Masters* is a collection of the articles he had written for the *Wiltshire and Gloucestershire Standard* in his early days as a local reporter.

12th – A Penny Plain, Twopence Coloured

There stands, I fancy, to this day (but now how fallen!) a certain stationer's shop at a corner of the wide thoroughfare that joins the city of my childhood with the sea. When, upon any Saturday, we made a party to behold the ships, we passed that corner; and since in those days I loved a ship as a man loves Burgundy or daybreak, this of itself had been enough to hallow it. But there was more than that. In the Leith Walk window, all the year round, there stood displayed a theatre in working order, with a "forest set," a "combat," and a few "robbers carousing" in the slides; and below and about, dearer tenfold to me! the plays themselves, those budgets of romance, lay tumbled one upon another. Long and often have I lingered there with empty pockets. One figure, we shall say, was visible in the first plate of characters, bearded, pistol in hand, or drawing to his ear the clothyard arrow; I would spell the name: was it Macaire, or Long Tom Coffin, or Grindoff, 2d dress? O, how I would long to see the rest! how—if the name by chance were hidden—I would wonder in what play he figured, and what immortal legend justified his attitude and strange apparel! And then to go within, to announce yourself as an intending purchaser, and, closely watched, be suffered to undo those bundles and breathlessly devour those pages of gesticulating villains, epileptic combats, bosky forests, palaces and war-ships, frowning fortresses and prison vaults—it was a giddy joy. That shop, which was dark and smelt of Bibles, was a loadstone rock for all that bore the name of boy. They could not pass it by, nor, having entered, leave it.

Robert Louis Stevenson

Robert Louis Stevenson (1850–94) is best known today for his historical novels, his children's books and his travel writing. He also wrote short stories and many essays. His health was poor, but in spite of that in his twenties he explored the Cevennes region of France with the donkey Modestine. Skelt's, the firm that made the toy theatres of his childhood, was taken over several times, and is now Pollock's toy theatres.

13th – The Cats' Good Deed

So far as I know, the park cats can only be credited with one good deed. Two or three years ago a number of rabbits were introduced into Hyde Park, and quickly began to increase and multiply, as rabbits will. For a time the cats respected them, being unaccustomed to see such animals, and possibly thinking that they would be dangerous to tackle. But they soon found out that these strangers were the natural prey of a carnivore, and, beginning with the little ones, then going on to those that were grown up, eventually devoured them all. Two big old buck rabbits survived the others for a couple of months, but even these were finally conquered and eaten. I for one am very glad at the result, for it really seemed too ridiculous that our great national park should be turned into a rabbit warren as well as a duck-breeding establishment.

W. H. Hudson, *Birds in London*

14th – A Visit to Windsor

To-day Aunt Barclay, Edith, Hugh, Ada, Alice, Papa, Lisa, Edward & Emily and myself all went by train to see the chapel and state rooms at Windsor, which are now open so that anybody may go and see them without tickets, and special trains to Windsor were running every half hour. Just before we got to the Windsor station we quite stopped as there was a train just in front of us, and then Aunt Barclay found out that she had left all her tickets behind with Mr. Frederick Barclay, so she screamed out of the window to Martin who was several carriages off and gave him full directions as to what he was to say when she sent the guard to him to explain about the tickets so that the whole train heard what she was saying. When we got to the castle there were a great number of people, and we were let in by hundreds into the chapel. We had first to go through a large sort of house, erected just for the wedding, which consisted of a sort of large hall in the middle, and smaller rooms all round it, for the different people, there was one for the Bride, one for the Bridegroom, & so on for lots of other people, and they were all most beautifully decorated. We went through the chapel and saw the places where Aunt and Uncle Bunsen, and Fowell and Lady Victoria had sat. In the chapel there were no decorations except for scarlet carpets and footstools. Then we walked about in the castle gardens a little and went and saw the stables and then came home.

Ellen Buxton, Journal

Ellen Buxton was born in 1848, the second of twelve surviving children of a prosperous brewer, and part of a large extended family who were Quakers or evangelical Anglicans, with many philanthropic interests. Her grandfather was a leader of the campaign to abolish slavery, and a great-aunt was Elizabeth Fry, the prison reformer. She kept a diary for four years from the age of twelve: a wonderful insight into family life, expeditions, and comments on social affairs and national events as they appeared to her.

15th – Cui Bono?

What is hope? A smiling rainbow
Children follow through the wet.
'Tis not here—still yonder, yonder;
Never urchin found it yet.
What is life? A thawing iceboard
On a sea with sunny shore.
Gay we sail; it melts beneath us;
We are sunk, and seen no more.
What is man? A foolish baby;
Vainly strives, and fights, and frets;
Demanding all, deserving nothing,
One small grave is what he gets!

Thomas Carlyle

Thomas Carlyle (1795–1881) was a Scottish historian, philosopher and critic. He is not generally thought of as a poet: if this rather pessimistic poem is a reflection of his style, perhaps it is just as well he concentrated on other writing.

16th – Letter from Charlotte Brontë to Robert Southey

March 16th.

SIR, – I cannot rest till I have answered your letter, even though by addressing you a second time I should appear a little intrusive; but I must thank you for the kind and wise advice you have condescended to give me. I had not ventured to hope for such a reply; so considerate in its tone, so noble in its spirit. I must suppress what I feel, or you will think me foolishly enthusiastic.

At the first perusal of your letter, I felt only shame and regret that I had ever ventured to trouble you with my crude rhapsody; I felt a painful heat rise to my face when I thought of the quires of paper I had covered with what once gave me so much delight, but which now was only a source of confusion; but, after I had thought a little and read it again and again, the prospect seemed to clear. You do not forbid me to write; you do not say that what I write is utterly destitute of merit. You only warn me against the folly of neglecting real duties, for the sake of imaginative pleasures; of writing for the love of fame; for the selfish excitement of emulation. You kindly allow me to write poetry for its own sake, provided I leave undone nothing which I ought to do, in order to pursue that single, absorbing, exquisite gratification. I am afraid, sir, you think me very foolish. I know the first letter I wrote to you was all senseless trash from beginning to end; but I am not altogether the idle dreaming being it would seem to denote. My father is a clergyman of limited, though competent, income, and I am the eldest of his children. He expended quite as much in my education as he could afford in justice to the rest. I thought it therefore my duty, when I left school, to become a governess. In that capacity I find enough to occupy my thoughts all day long, and my head and hands too, without having a moment's time for one dream of the imagination. In the evenings, I confess, I do think, but I never trouble any one else with my thoughts. I carefully avoid any appearance of pre-occupation and eccentricity, which might lead those I live amongst to suspect the nature of my pursuits. Following my father's advice – who from my childhood has counselled me just in the wise and friendly tone of your letter – I have endeavoured not only attentively to observe all the duties a woman ought to fulfil, but to feel deeply interested in them. I don't always succeed, for sometimes when I'm teaching or sewing I would rather be reading or writing; but I try to deny myself; and my father's approbation amply rewarded me for the privation. Once more allow me to thank you with sincere gratitude. I trust I shall never more feel ambitious to see my name in print; if the wish should rise I'll look at Southey's letter, and suppress it. It is honour enough for me that I have written to him, and received an answer. That letter is consecrated; no one shall ever see it, but papa and my brother and sisters. Again I thank you. This incident, I suppose, will be renewed no more; if I live to be an old woman, I shall remember it thirty years hence as a bright dream. The signature which you suspected of being fictitious is my real name. Again, therefore, I must sign myself,

C. BRONTË

P.S. – Pray, sir, excuse me for writing to you a second time; I could not help writing, partly to tell you how thankful I am for your kindness, and partly to let you know that your advice shall not be wasted; however sorrowfully and reluctantly it may be at first followed. C. B.

Charlotte Brontë (1816–55) had been writing since childhood, as had her brother and sisters. She sent her poems to Southey while she was at Roe Head, a school where she was first a pupil then a governess. Southey gave her sensible advice, but it was not until 1845 that she persuaded her sisters Emily and Anne to add their poems to hers: *Poems by Currer, Ellis and Acton Bell* came out in 1846, but was ignored.

17th – The Bodleian: A Dead Sea of Books

Few places affected me more than the Libraries, and especially the Bodleian Library, reputed to have half a million printed books and manuscripts. I walked solemnly and reverently among the alcoves and through the halls, as if in the pyramid of embalmed souls. It was their life, their heart, their mind, that they treasured in these book-urns. Silent as they are, should all the emotions that went to their creation have utterance, could the world itself contain the various sound? They longed for fame? Here it is—to stand silently for ages, moved only to be dusted and catalogued, valued only as units in the ambitious total, and gazed at, occasionally, by men as ignorant as I am, of their name, their place, their language, and their worth. Indeed, unless a man can link his written thoughts with the everlasting wants of men, so that they shall draw from them as from wells, there is no more immortality to the thoughts and feelings of the soul than to the muscles and the bones. A library is but the soul's burial-ground. It is the land of shadows.

Yet one is impressed with the thought, the labour, and the struggle, represented in this vast catacomb of books. Who could dream, by the placid waters that issue from the level mouths of brooks into the lake, all the plunges, the whirls, the divisions, and foaming rushes that had brought them down to the tranquil exit? And who can guess through what channels of disturbance, and experiences of sorrow, the heart passed that has emptied into this Dead Sea of books?

Henry Ward Beecher, *Star Papers*

Henry Ward Beecher (1813–87) was an American nonconformist clergyman and social reformer, who supported the abolition of slavery. His sister, Harriet Beecher Stowe, wrote the influential Abolitionist novel *Uncle Tom's Cabin*. After the American Civil War he supported causes such as temperance and women's suffrage. He was also involved in a famous scandal in which he was tried for adultery, but the jury could not reach a verdict. Later, a church hearing exonerated him.

18th – Clipping the Church

A curious custom—one hesitates whether to count it a game or not—once obtained in several Midland parishes, under the name of "clipping the church." It existed at Ellesmere till nearly 1820; at Wellington it lasted until about 1860; at Birmingham it was in vogue until about a century since; and at Edgmond was revived as recently as 1867 with certain modern modifications. The point of the whole performance consists in a number of people joining hand in hand, and so completely surrounding the church in this fashion as to "clip," or embrace, it. In the two first-named parishes this used to be done by the school children, with a good deal of tumult and shouting, every Shrove Tuesday. In its revived form at Edgmond it constitutes part of the annual "feast" of the parish schools. The charity children clipped the church in Birmingham. At Bradford-on-Avon, also, this custom only died out within the last half-century.

George Smith Tyack, *Lore and Legend of the English Church*

19th – Golden Rules for the Kitchen

Without *cleanliness* and *punctuality* good Cooking is *impossible*.
Leave nothing *dirty; clean and clear as you go*.
A time for everything, and *everything in time*.
A good Cook *wastes nothing*.
An hour *lost in the morning* has to be run after *all day*.
Haste *without hurry* saves worry, fuss and flurry.
Stew *boiled* is Stew *spoiled*.
Strong fire for *Roasting; clear* fire for *Broiling*.
Wash Vegetables in *three* waters.
Boil fish *quickly*, meat *slowly*.

Mrs Isabella Beeton, *Mrs Beeton's Book of Household Management*

20th – Pugin at Sea

Pugin was pursuing a rather eccentric mode of life; it has been previously remarked that he was fond of the sea: he now frequently made cruises along the coast, sometimes extending them to the opposite shores of France, and in fair weather reaching the coast of Holland. In this way he was frequently afloat for many days together; yet, amidst this seeming neglect of his legitimate demands on his time, he contrived to give sufficient attention to what was in progress at home. The following incident is somewhat characteristic. After an absence of some weeks Pugin unexpectedly called at his publisher's, who observed that his dress, which usually was untidy, appeared more strange than ever. He was enveloped in a huge pilot-coat, large enough for a man twice his size. On this strange exhibition Mr. Weale, his publisher, remarked:

'Why, you appear to have made a mistake, and have got a coat belonging to somebody else.'

'Oh,' observed Pugin, 'it is of no consequence—I caught up the first garment that came in my way, getting into harbour after a stiff gale off Calais; but here are the plates for my book:' —at the same time pulling out a heap of copper-plates from under the ample folds of his coat. 'They are all ready for proving.'

'But how and where did you finish the etchings?'

'Oh,' said Pugin, 'I finished them in the boat.'

'Impossible,' replied Mr, Weale.

'Not a bit of it,' retorted Pugin; 'the motion of the sea makes no difference to me and, truly, many of the outlines illustrating the 'Apology' were etched under these apparently impossible circumstances.'

Benjamin Ferrey, *Recollections of A. N. Welby Pugin and His Father*

Augustus Welby Pugin (1812–52) was an architect who was passionate about Gothic architecture, and in promoting it – particularly for church work – triggered the Gothic Revival. He believed the gothic style was the only Christian one. Sadly his religious fanaticism turned to madness, and he died young. The Gothic details and decorations he added to the new Houses of Parliament, in the Perpendicular style, are world-famous.

21st – English Tourists in Rome

III. Georgina Trevellyn to Louisa —.
At last, dearest Louisa, I take up my pen to address you.
Here we are, you see, with the seven-and-seventy boxes,
Courier, Papa and Mamma, the children, and Mary and Susan:
Here we all are at Rome, and delighted of course with St. Peter's,
And very pleasantly lodged in the famous Piazza di Spagna.
Rome is a wonderful place, but Mary shall tell you about it;
Not very gay, however; the English are mostly at Naples;
There are the A.'s, we hear, and most of the W. party.
George, however, is come; did I tell you about his mustachios?
Dear, I must really stop, for the carriage, they tell me, is waiting;
Mary will finish; and Susan is writing, they say, to Sophia.
Adieu, dearest Louise,—evermore your faithful Georgina.
Who can a Mr. Claude be whom George has taken to be with?
Very stupid, I think, but George says so VERY clever.

A. H. Clough, *Amours de Voyage*

22nd – Ave Imperatrix!

(Written on the occasion of the attempt to assassinate Queen Victoria in March 1882)

From every quarter of your land
They give God thanks who turned away
Death and the needy madman's hand,
Death-fraught, which menaced you that day.

One school of many made to make
Men who shall hold it dearest right
To battle for their ruler's sake,
And stake their being in the fight,

Sends greeting humble and sincere—
Though verse be rude and poor and mean—
To you, the greatest as most dear—
Victoria, by God's grace Our Queen!

Such greeting as should come from those
Whose fathers faced the Sepoy hordes,
Or served you in the Russian snows,
And, dying, left their sons their swords.

And some of us have fought for you
Already in the Afghan pass—
Or where the scarce-seen smoke-puffs flew
From Boer marksmen in the grass;

And all are bred to do your will
By land and sea—wherever flies
The Flag, to fight and follow still,
And work your Empire's destinies.

Once more we greet you, though unseen
Our greeting be, and coming slow.
Trust us, if need arise, O Queen,
We shall not tarry with the blow!

Rudyard Kipling, *Early Verse*

Rudyard Kipling (1865– 1933) began his working life as a journalist in India. He was interested in every aspect of the community, and the stories and poems he began to write were fresh and vigorous, and showed his curiosity about people of all sorts. Returning to London in 1889, his poems and short stories were highly regarded, but two full-length novels did not do so well. With his American wife, he went to live in the United States for four years before he returned to England and settled in Sussex. He also wrote wonderful tales for children. He received the Nobel Prize for Literature in 1907, the first English writer to do so.

23rd – Fire at Covent Garden

You should have seen the ruins of Covent Garden Theatre. I went in the moment I got to London – four days after the fire. Although the audience part and the stage were so tremendously burnt out that there was not a piece of wood half the size of a lucifer-match for the eye to rest on, though nothing whatever remained but bricks and smelted iron lying on a great black desert, the theatre still looked so wonderfully like its old self grown gigantic that I never saw so strange a sight. The wall dividing the front from the stage still remained, and the iron pass-doors stood ajar in an impossible and inaccessible frame. The arches that supported the stage were there, and the arches that supported the pit; and in the centre of the latter lay something like a Titanic grape-vine that a hurricane had pulled up by the roots, twisted, and flung down there; this was the great chandelier. Gye had kept the men's wardrobe at the top of the house over the great entrance staircase; when the roof fell in it came down bodily, and all that part of the ruins was like an old Babylonic pavement, bright rays tesselating the black ground, sometimes in pieces so large that I could make out the clothes in the "Trovatore".

Charles Dickens, *Letters*

Charles Dickens (1812–70) was a novelist, journalist, magazine editor, theatre-lover and letter-writer. Spotting early talent, a schoolmaster encouraged him, and he read widely. However, his father's imprisonment for debt meant he had to go to work, aged 12, in a shoe-blacking factory. The serialisation of *The Pickwick Papers* brought him success, which continued through the rest of his life. His output was enormous, though he also had to cope with domestic problems, including separation from his wife.

24th – The University Boat Race

But the end had not come, for in a couple more strokes the Oxford bowman ceased rowing, and the others perceiving this redoubled their efforts. The last three-quarters of a mile was the scene of the wildest excitement, for the disabled oar in the Oxford boat could not be used except for the purpose of keeping time, and thus Oxford had to row home with seven oars against eight, and, besides, carry a "dead bowman." Shoot by shoot the Cantabs crept up, and, amid the yells and deafening shouts of countless thousands, the judge declared it a "dead heat." Time 24min. 4 secs.

Some of the Oxford people were not satisfied with the decision of the judge, and it was questioned before the umpire, but Phelps [the judge] was not moved by anybody, and adhered to his verdict that it was so close he could not say which came in first.

Morning Post, Monday, March 26, 1877

In the long history of the boat race between Oxford and Cambridge (it started in 1829) only one race resulted in a draw – this one.

25th – The Stag Hunt

All of a sudden the wild outcry before them seemed to stop and concentrate, thrown back, louder and louder as they rode, off the same echoing crag; till at a sudden turn of the road there stood the stag beneath them in the stream, his back against the black rock with its green cushions of dripping velvet, knee-deep in the clear amber water, the hounds around him, some struggling and swimming in the deep pool, some rolling and tossing and splashing in a mad, half-terrified ring, as he reared into the air on his great haunches, with the sparkling beads running off his red mane, and dropping on his knees, plunged his antlers down among them, with blows which would have each brought certain death with it if the yielding water had not broken the shock. Do you think that he does not remember the death? The huge carcass dragged out of the stream, followed by dripping, panting dogs; the blowing of the mort, and the last wild halloo, when the horn-note and the voices rang through the autumn woods, and rolled up the smooth flat mountain sides.

Charles Kingsley, *Prose Idylls*

26th – A Delicious Day

A delicious day upon Clyro Hill. It was sunny and warm under the sheltering bank and woods of Wern Vawr and pleasant walking along the low road leading to the old farm house with its large projecting and high-gabled porch. There was a stir about the house and yard. They had killed a fat stall-fed heifer yesterday and a party of people much interested in the matter, among them old Jones and his wife, were busy cutting up the carcase in the barn. A man went to and fro from the barn to the house with huge joints of beef having first weighed them on the great steelyard which hangs at the barn door. In the house Mrs. Jones of New Building, an old daughter of the house, was engaged in the great kitchen taking the joints up into an inner room or larder to put them in salt. By the fire sat a young woman who hid her face and did not look up. She had a baby lying across her lap.

I decided to explore the lane running parallel with the brook towards Painscastle and discover the old Rhos-Goch Mill. There was a good deal of water and suddenly I came upon the mill pond and the picturesque old mill with an overshot wheel. I crossed one of the streams on a larch felled across the water for a bridge and came back round the front of the cosy old picturesque ivy-grown mill house with its tall chimney completely covered with ivy. A handsome young man with a fine open face, fresh complexion and dressed as a miller was having a romp with a little girl before the door. He said his name was Powell, his father was dead and he carried on the business and with the most perfect politeness and well bred courtesy asked me to come in and sit down. So this is the place that I have heard old Hannah Whitney talk of so often, the place where the old miller sleeping in the mill trough used to see the fairies dancing of nights upon the mill floor.

At Rhos Goch Lane House no one was at home so I stuck an ivy leaf into the latch hole.

Francis Kilvert, *Diary*

Francis Kilvert (1840–79) was a clergyman, working in Wiltshire and on the Welsh border of Herefordshire. He kept a voluminous diary, but sadly after his death his wife destroyed two sections of it, and then a niece destroyed another 19 books. Only three volumes remain, all given to other people. Kilvert died suddenly from peritonitis five weeks after his marriage.

27th – A Visit to the British Museum

March 27, Friday To-day we all went to see the British Museum. Aunt Bunsen knows Professor Owen, a man who gives his whole life to studying antiquities particularly fossils and skeletons, & so she asked him to let us all go with him to see some of the things there, & he said he would explain it. We went to see the great bones and he explained a great many of them, but he spoke in such a low voice that some could not hear, the principal thing that we had come to see was a most remarkable fossil bird which had been found imbedded in stone, & only discovered last year, but it lived such a long time ago, that when it was alive none of the chalk was made, and as all the chalk is made of old animals ground to powder who lived long before the Deluge, it must have lived millions of years ago. But it was most remarkably perfect and we could see each feather and each bone, but the head was gone, probably it had been eaten by some wild beast ... Louisa is going to school on Easter Tuesday at Miss Clarence's near Brighton where there are 27 girls.

Ellen Buxton, *Journal*

28th – Death of John Brown

We have to record the death of Mr. John Brown, the Queen's personal attendant, which took place at Windsor Castle at a quarter-past 11 o'clock on Tuesday evening, the 27th inst. of erysipelas. This melancholy event has caused the deepest regret to the Queen, the Royal Family, and all the members of the Royal household. To Her Majesty the loss is irreparable; and the death of this truly faithful and devoted servant has been a grievous shock to the Queen.

In 1849 Mr. John Brown entered the Queen's service as one of the Balmoral gillies; and, by his careful attention, steadiness, and intelligence, he rose in 1858 to the position of the Queen's personal servant in Scotland, which, in 1864, was extended to that of constant personal attendant on Her Majesty on all occasions. During the last eighteen years and a half he served Her Majesty constantly, and never once absented himself from his duty for a single day. He has accompanied the Queen in her daily walks and drives, and on all her journeys and expeditions, as well as personally waiting on her at banquets, etc. An honest, faithful and devoted follower, a trustworthy, discreet and straightforward man, and possessed of strong sense, he filled a position of great and anxious responsibility, the duties of which he performed with such constant and unceasing care as to secure for himself the real friendship of the Queen.

Court Circular, 28 March 1882

29th – The Decline of Humour

How very singular has been the history of the decline of humour. Is there any profound psychological truth to be gathered from consideration of the fact that humour has gone out with cruelty? A hundred years ago, eighty years ago—nay, fifty years ago—we were a cruel but also a humorous people. We had bull-baitings, and badger-drawings, and hustings, and prize-fights, and cock-fights; we went to see men hanged; the pillory and the stocks were no empty 'terrors unto evil-doers,' for there was commonly a malefactor occupying each of these institutions. With all this we had a broad blown comic sense. We had Hogarth, and Bunbury, and George Cruikshank, and Gilray; we had Leech and Surtees, and the creator of Tittlebat Titmouse; we had the Shepherd of the 'Noctes,' and, above all, we had *you*.

From the old giants of English fun—burly persons delighting in broad caricature, in decided colours, in cockney jokes, in swashing blows at the more prominent and obvious human follies—from these you derived the splendid high spirits and unhesitating mirth of your earlier works. Mr. Squeers, and Sam Weller, and Mrs. Gamp, and all the Pickwickians, and Mr. Dowler, and John Browdie—these and their immortal companions were reared, so to speak, on the beef and beer of that naughty, fox-hunting, badger-baiting old England, which we have improved out of existence. And these characters, assuredly, are your best; by them, though stupid people cannot read about them, you will live while there is a laugh left among us. Perhaps that does not assure you a very prolonged existence, but only the future can show.

The dismal seriousness of the time cannot, let us hope, last for ever and a day. Honest old Laughter, the true *lutin* of your inspiration, must have life left in him yet, and cannot die.

Andrew Lang, from 'Letter to Charles Dickens', *Letters to Dead Authors*

Andrew Lang (1844–1912) was a Scottish scholar and writer. As a scholar, he worked on Homer publishing with colleagues translations of the *Odyssey* and the *Iliad*. As a writer, he published poetry, history (mostly Scottish), biography and anthropology, and it was this interest that led to the collections of fairy stories for which he is particularly famous. He also worked as a journalist.

30th – Dressed and Loaded for Bear-Shooting

The winter of 1890–91 was as exceptionally severe in the Himalayas as in Europe. Snow fell heavily, even in March, and consequently bear-shooting did not commence till a month later than usual …
Our canvas home for the next few months consisted of one Kashmir sleeping-tent, with bath-room and verandah; one field-officer's Cabul tent, for dining and sitting in, with bath-room for keeping stores in; three shouldari tents, single-fly, for our servants and cook-house. The total cost of our camp equipment was some four hundred rupees. D. carried a D. B. .500 Express, by Lancaster, and a hammerless D. B. gun by Tolley. I was armed with a 400 D. B. Express by Holland, and a D. B. .410 gun by Green of Cheltenham.

For those who desire to try a shooting trip in these grand mountains, a few words as to the dress I affected myself, and which I consider most suitable for ladies, will be found useful, and even for those who have no thought of such an undertaking, it may prove of interest to know the kind of dress that is absolutely necessary for the work that I went through.

To commence with, I wore a very short plain skirt of the strong *karkee* drill, such as soldiers wear in India, and a Norfolk jacket of the same material. The skirt was not too narrow, or it would have interfered with the jumping and climbing over rocks that is so often necessary. On the legs I wore stockings with the feet cut off; on the feet short worsted socks with *puttoo* (homespun) over-socks, and grass shoes. Bound round the legs I wore the grey *putties* of India, which are strips of *puttoo* four and a half inches long, by four and a half inches wide.

The advantage of wearing *karkee* is, that the colour is so admirably suited for sport, and that it never tears. Although it sounds cold, and undoubtedly *is* cold, that difficulty can be overcome by wearing plenty of underclothing. A further advantage is that *karkee* can be easily washed, which was a consideration, as I had often to wash part of my own clothing. My rifle coolie carried across his shoulder, in a leather bag, a grey *puttoo* jacket, small cap and pair of warm gloves, which I put on when sitting in the snow. I myself carried my own cartridges in a leather pouch round my waist; but the coolie was intrusted with my field-glasses, and also, unless in the vicinity of game, always carried my rifle, though I never allowed him to touch it when loaded. As head covering when the sun was hot, I preferred an old double Terai hat of grey felt to anything else, on account of its portability, and because my hair was unsuited to the wearing of a puggaree. For camp I had a couple of short *puttoo* skirts, and *chapties* (leather sandals) for the feet, and a cardigan jacket, which I often found very useful.

Mrs R. H. Tyacke, *How I Shot My Bears*, 1893

31st – Easter Sunday, April Eve

A soft warm spring morning of changing sunshine and shower. I never was so hard put to it as in Church this morning to resist untimely and inextinguishable laughter. It was almost irresistible. The sun was beating fiercely through the southern windows upon the heads and books of the devout Hodgson party in the Cabalva seat. Mrs. Chinnock tried to draw down the blind, but the blind was broken and would not draw or be drawn. Mrs. Venables then signed to the clerk to come and pull the blind down. The little man came and pulled and pulled till at last with a more violent tug smash went the wooden bar with a loud report and hung in ruins in the air with a broken back. I knew the crash was coming when I saw the clerk pulling, and when it came it was almost too much. I was nearly choked. There came into my mind suddenly my Father's old story of the clergyman waiting for the hymn before the sermon to be finished and meanwhile looking through the church window and seeing an old woman pulling up a stubborn carrot. At last up came the carrot all at once, over went the old woman on her back head over heels. 'I thought so!' exclaimed the delighted clergyman aloud, to the astonishment of the expectant congregation who had finished the hymn and were waiting for him to begin the prayer.

Francis Kilvert, *Diary*

APRIL

1st – Ladies' Clothes for India

A lady will not require more linen than she had for the long sea voyage, with the exception of a set of trimmed night dresses to wear in case of illness. Stockings wear out very quickly, and cotton ones in India cost nearly as much as silk at home; four dozen thread and two dozen silk would be a good supply, including two or three pairs of black silk ones.

The country leather shoes and boots are not presentable for any lady. Half a dozen pairs of thin boots, the same of kid shoes, with one or two pairs of kid riding and walking boots, and a large supply of white ones for evening, should be brought from England. White kid wears better than satin for dancing, and white jean or coutil is nice morning wear. Spare elastic should be provided, and if a skin of morocco, or kid and satin, with the necessary binding, be brought out, the native shoemakers will often make very decently from a good pattern. Gentlemen sometimes bring a last, which is an excellent plan, as the sambur skin makes far better racket shoes and shooting boots than English materials.

Petticoats should be made of fine cambric calico, with a few stouter ones for morning or travelling use; where economy is studied it would be well to leave the worked borders to be put on in India, as embroidery is about a quarter the price, and if the cotton and fine long cloth are given to work it upon, it is very little inferior.

Under-linen should not be bought ready-made, unless warranted to be done in a *lock-stitch* sewing-machine, for, as the dhobies beat the clothes on stones, ordinary work soon unrips; it is both more lasting and better done when given to be made at a school, or a penitentiary, to say nothing of its aiding a charity.

Stays require constant washing, and several pairs should be brought—not the ones with elastic, which are ruined at once by the heat, but light coutil ones with few steels; they are very expensive in India, from 30s. to £2.

The most economical morning dresses are nice white ones, as the dhoby cannot take out the colour. Some people fancy India too hot to wear anything but muslin, but this is a great mistake. Flannel is so generally left off that the heat of the dress is of less consequence. All rich silks should have the high body down to the shoulders lined with thin flannel, as otherwise they are apt to change colour; and if they are at all damp from perspiration they should be carefully turned inside out and dried, or they are certain to mildew in the box ...

For evening and dinner dress, silk, moiré, even velvet is worn; in fact, exactly what is worn at home; but light blue always spots and turns yellow, and every shade of lilac and mauve looks dreadful in the light of the oil lamps. A white and a black lace dress are a *sine qua non*; and a plentiful stock of tarlatane, tulle, and sarsnet for slips should not be omitted, as well as some dresses unmade, as the tailors make beautifully from a pattern. But it is necessary to be very particular in taking every requisite in the way of trimming, fringe, lace, buttons, blonde, sewing silk, &c., that is likely to be wanted, as anything omitted is often not to be had, and, if procurable, is certain to be very far dearer than at home.

A Lady Resident, *The Englishwoman in India*, 1864

2nd – The Schoolboy at Home

The pony's lamed, the cat is dead,
The pigs are in the tulip bed;
The flue with rubbish has been filled,
And all my lady's plants are killed;
A strange wet cur of low degree
Is planted on the rich settee;
The grave mackaw has lost his tail,

And slowly tears a Brussels veil;
The pistol's cleaned with sister's shawl,
For midday practice in the hall;
And little Jane, so prim and good,
Is scampering wild about the wood;
The maids are whimpering with affright,
Because a ghost was seen last night;
The linen's burnt, the roller's split,
The tangled chain won't turn the spit;
The ale is running all about,
And in the urn's a ragged clout;
And all around, at every pass,
Is smash and clash and broken glass;
And here's a neighbour come to fret,
And, mercy! there's a hive upset!

Richard Hill Sandys

Richard Hill Sandys (1801–92) went to Cambridge and was then called to the bar. He wrote books on legal and religious subjects, as well as publishing poetry.

3rd – A Sore Throat

10 Downing Street, 3rd April 1886
Madam,
I am venturing to appeal to your Majesty's kindness. My husband's throat, I grieve to say, requires so much rest, that I had arranged to take him a few miles from London, where he would have perfect quiet. The extraordinary effort upon the 8th being so great, Sir Andrew Clark has enforced the utmost quiet and watching on my part, with all the special care a wife can give to contrive absence of talking and the rest.
Under these circumstances, I appeal to your Majesty, whose kindness is unbounded, to forbid my husband obeying your Majesty's gracious command just received to go to Windsor Castle. I know you will forgive my writing, for no one will enter into a wife's anxieties so much as your Majesty can.
I remain, dear Madam, your Majesty's humble and devoted servant,

Catherine Gladstone

Catherine Gladstone (1812–1900), was married to the politician and four times Prime Minister William Ewart Gladstone for fifty-nine years. Hawarden Castle, where the Gladstones lived for many years, was her family home. Unlike her husband, she was extremely untidy – she is recorded as saying to him 'What a bore you would have been if you had married someone as tidy as you are.' She was concerned about other people, and founded such things as convalescent homes and orphanages.

4th – The Conservative Party Programme

Gentlemen, there seems at first something incongruous that one should be addressing the population of so influential and intelligent a county as Lancashire who is not locally connected with them, and, gentlemen, I will frankly admit that this circumstance did for a long time make me hesitate in accepting your cordial and generous invitation. But, gentlemen, after what occurred yesterday, after receiving more than 200 addresses from every part of this great country, after the welcome which then greeted me, I feel that I should not be doing justice to your feelings, I should not do duty to myself, if I any longer considered my presence here tonight to be an act of presumption. Gentlemen, though it may not be an act of presumption, it still is, I am told, an act of great difficulty. Our opponents assure us that the Conservative party have no political programme; and, therefore, they must look with much satisfaction to one whom you honour tonight by considering him the leader and representative of your opinions when he comes forward, at your invitation, to express to you what that programme is. The Conservative party are accused of having no programme of policy. If by a programme is meant a plan to despoil churches and plunder landlords, I admit we have no programme. If by a programme is meant a policy which assails or menaces every institution and every interest, every class and every calling in the country, I admit we have no programme. But if to have a policy with distinct ends, and these such as most deeply interest the great body of the nation, be a becoming programme for a political party, then, I contend, we have an adequate programme, and one which, here or elsewhere, I shall always be prepared to assert and to vindicate.

Gentlemen, the programme of the Conservative party is to maintain the Constitution of the country.

Benjamin Disraeli
From a speech given in Manchester, 1872

Benjamin Disraeli, 1st Earl of Beaconsfield (1804–81) started writing in an effort to pay off debts and continued writing for a number of years for the same reason. Entering Parliament in 1837 after several attempts, he eventually led the Conservative party, being twice Prime Minister.

5th – Punishment for Drunkenness

There were few, if any means out there for our men having any innocent recreation when off duty. While a fair percentage of steady men saved most of their pay by entrusting it to their officers, or the pay sergeant for safe-keeping, there was always a certain number who cared for nothing but spending it on grog, and though excessive drinking entailed a very severe punishment it failed as a deterrent. The penalty for habitual drinking in those days was flogging (thank heaven it is now a thing of the past). Nothing, I believe, could be devised that would more degrade a man and be more likely to make him a brute than to tie him up to be lashed on the bare back with the cat o' nine tails in the presence of the whole regiment. It was always a revolting sight. Once having undergone corporal punishment the man often became utterly reckless and was seldom out of trouble.

I remember a splendidly made fellow in our Grenadier Company, considerably over six feet in height, a terrible fellow when in liquor but a good soldier otherwise—that I saw flogged twice within very short time.

Punishment parade was always held early in the morning and on occasion the air was frosty and a keen wind was blowing as the grenadier was stripped of his shirt, his wrists and ankles tied to the triangle of stretcher poles, and his bare back exposed. A drummer plied the cat o' nine tails and the drum major counted the strokes. The man received fifty lashes, and he took them without a murmur, though the blood came before he had received them all.

After it was all over, and he was released, he pulled down his shirt, adjusted his stock, buttoned up his tunic, and saluting the Colonel, who stood by, said, 'That's a warm breakfast you gave me, your honour, this morning,' and again saluting, faced about, and was marched away to hospital.

Vieth, F. H. D., *Recollections of the Crimea Campaign & the Expedition to Kinburn*

6th – A Reclusive Neighbour

London is a place of mystery. Looking out of one of the windows at the back of Dr. Fothergill's house, I saw an immense wooden blind, such as we have on our windows in summer, but reaching from the ground as high as the top of the neighbouring houses. While admitting the air freely, it shut the property to which it belonged completely from sight. I asked the meaning of this extraordinary structure, and learned that it was put up by a great nobleman, of whose subterranean palace and strange seclusion I had before heard. Common report attributed his unwillingness to be seen to a disfiguring malady with which he was said to be afflicted. The story was that he was visible only to his valet.

Oliver Wendell Holmes, *One Hundred Days in Europe*, 1887

The American Oliver Wendell Holmes (1809–94) trained as a doctor, and from 1847–82 was the Parkman Professor of Anatomy and Physiology at Harvard, and proposed some important medical reforms; he coined the term 'anasthesia'. He was also a novelist, poet and essayist. Much of his literary work is conversational, light-hearted and funny.

7th – A Recollection of Wordsworth

The first person interviewed by Mr. Rawnsley was an old lady who had been once in service at Rydal Mount, and was, in 1870, a lodging-house keeper at Grasmere. She was not a very imaginative person, as may be gathered from the following anecdote:—Mr. Rawnsley's sister came in from a late evening walk, and said, 'O Mrs. D—, have you seen the wonderful sunset?' The good lady turned sharply round and, drawing herself to her full height, as if mortally offended, answered: 'No, miss; I'm a tidy cook, I know, and "they say" a decentish body for a landlady, but I don't knaw nothing about sunsets or them sort of things, they've never been in my line.' Her reminiscence of Wordsworth was as worthy of tradition as it was explanatory, from her point of view, of the method in which Wordsworth composed, and was helped in his labours by his enthusiastic sister. 'Well, you know,' she said, 'Mr. Wordsworth went humming and booing about, and she, Miss Dorothy, kept close behint him, and she picked up the bits as he let 'em fall, and tak' 'em down, and put 'em together on paper for him. And you may be very well sure as how she didn't understand nor make sense out of 'em, and I doubt that he didn't know much about them either himself, but, howivver, there's a great many folk as do, I dare say.'

Oscar Wilde, 'Some Literary Notes', *Woman's World*, April 1889
Reprinted in *A Critic in Pall Mall*

Oscar Wilde (1854–1900) wrote plays, novels and essays, and was renowned for his wit. At the start of the 1890s his society comedies were extremely popular in London. He scandalised society by his behaviour: dressing extravagantly, collecting peacocks' feathers and looking down on sport. His relationship with Lord Alfred Douglas led to a court case for gross indecency: he was imprisoned and upon being freed went to France, where he lived for the last three years of his life.

8th – The South Devon Railway

The south of Devon had for several years demanded railway accommodation, and at the period now under review, Mr. Brunel projected what was called the coast line. This line, while it best accommodated the population of the district, passed through a very difficult country. If it was to be constructed at a moderate cost, curves of a quarter of a mile radius had to be admitted; and above 30 miles of its entire length traversed a district involving the adoption of gradients steeper than had been elsewhere used for such considerable distances. The Act for this railway was obtained in the Session of 1844.

The South Devon Railway, on leaving Exeter, crosses the flat country on the right bank of the river Exe, as far as Starcross, a village nearly opposite to Exmouth. From this point it runs down to the coast and along the seashore, by Dawlish, to Teignmouth; being protected by a sea-wall for the greater part of the distance, and passing through several headlands by short tunnels. Beyond Teignmouth it follows the left bank of the river Teign, which it crosses a short distance before reaching the station at Newton Abbott. The portion of the line from Exeter to Newton—20¼ miles in length—is very nearly level, the steep inclines for which the railway is noted being west of Newton. Between Newton and Totnes, for the first mile and a half the line is almost level, and in the next two miles it rises 200 feet, with gradients of 1 in 100, 1 in 60, and nearly a mile of 1 in 43. At the summit is a short tunnel; and thence the line descends 170 feet in a mile and three-quarters, with gradients of 1 in 40 and 1 in 43 for about three-quarters of a mile, and gradients of 1 in 57 and 1 in 88 for the rest of the incline. It then runs with more moderate gradients and about a mile and a half of level line to Totnes.

From the valley of the Dart at Totnes the line rises at once by a rapid ascent of 350 feet in four miles and a half, with gradients varying from 1 in 48 to 1 in 90, more than a mile and a half averaging 1 in 50. Thence it runs, with easy up and down gradients, for a distance of 12 miles along the skirts of Dartmoor, crossing by lofty viaducts the deep valleys which penetrate the moor. It then descends to Plympton, in the valley of the Plym, falling 273 feet in a little more than two miles, with a gradient of 1 in 42½. From Plympton the line for two miles is level, and then rises on an incline of 1 in 80 for a mile and a half, and descends by a similar gradient into the Plymouth station.

The main characteristics of the railway are that, while it traverses a very heavy country, its principal changes of level are concentrated into four long and steep inclines. These four inclines were intended to be worked by auxiliary power.

Isambard Brunel, *The Life of Isambard Kingdom Brunel,*
Civil Engineer

Isambard Kingdom Brunel (1806–59) was the son of a French engineer working in Britain, and an English mother. He trained in Paris, which was rare for a British engineer at the time, and first worked with his father. Convalescing in Bristol after an illness, he was appointed engineer to the Clifton Bridge project, the Great Western Railway, and a floating harbour, which stimulated him to design and build important steamships. His works were ground-breaking and revolutionary, and although during his life investors did not necessarily appreciate his ingenuity, he has subsequently been recognised by all as a giant in his field.

9th – Conundrums

Why was the sculptor of the Greek Slave a dishonest man?
A. Because he chiselled her out of her clothes.
Why does a sculptor die the worst of deaths?
A. Because he makes faces and bu(r)sts.
Why is a postage-stamp like a naughty boy?
A. Because it gets licked and put in the corner.
When is a ship in love?
A. When she is attached to a (buoy) boy.
Why is 'St Paul's Cathedral' like a bird's nest?
A. Because it was built by a Wren.
Why is Hobart Town like a battle-field?
A. Because it is guarded by Nelson, and looked over by Wellington.
Why is a boy, in the act of getting thrashed, like the eye?
A. Because it is a pupil under the lash.
Why is the letter F like a cow's tail?
A. Because it is the end of beef.
Why is a grandmother a soldier?
A. Because she is a granny dear (grenadier.)
What book would a man wish his wife to be like?
A. An almanac, so that he might have a new one every year.

> Contributed to *The Albatross*, newsletter published on
> SS *Great Britain*

The SS *Great Britain* sailed from Melbourne in Australia on 18 September 1862, heading for England. The voyage took over two months, so one of the passengers, Colonel Sir James Alexander, started a weekly newspaper, *The Albatross*, to which all passengers and the captain contributed. The contents of the newsletters were published in book form in 1863.

10th – The White Poppy

A riot of scarlet on gold, the red poppy of our native fields tosses heavy tresses with gipsy *abandon;* her sister of the sea-shore is golden, a yellow blossom that loves the keen salt savour of the spray. Of another hue is the poppy of history, of romance, of the muse. White as the stark death-shroud, pallid as the cheeks of that queen of a silent land whose temples she languorously crowns, ghost-like beside her fuller-blooded kin, she droops dream-laden, *Papaver somniferum,* the poppy of the magic juice of oblivion. In the royal plenitude of summer, the scarlet blooms will sometimes seem but a red cry from earth in memory of the many dews of battle that have drenched these acres in years gone by, for little end but that these same "bubbles of blood" might glow to-day; the yellow flower does but hint of the gold that has dashed a thousand wrecks at her feet around these shores: for happier suggestion we must turn to her of the pallid petals, our white Lady of Consolation. Fitting hue to typify the crowning blessing of forgetfulness! Too often the sable robes of night dissemble sleeplessness, remorse, regret, self-questioning. Let black, then, rather stand for hideous memory: white for blessed blank oblivion, happiest gift of the gods! For who, indeed, can say that the record of his life is not crowded with failure and mistake, stained with its petty cruelties of youth, its meannesses and follies of later years, all which storm and clamour incessantly at the gates of memory, refusing to be shut out? Leave us alone, O gods, to remember our felicities, our successes: only aid us, ye who recall no gifts, aptly and discreetly to forget.

Kenneth Grahame, Pagan Papers

11th – Bird's-Nesting around Marlborough

Ap. 11 [1851] Went to Region with S. 1., B. 1. and B. 3. took 4 robins and 1 blackbird. S. 1. took a thrush, 2 robins were broken in the nest ... Kept in ½ hr. for being late in chap ...

Ap. 18 ... Went out from 12–1 with B. 3. to Gundry's bridge. Got caught by his keeper ...

Ap. 21 ... Went out 1st to sweet briar pit with M. and B.3. Only got 6 black-birds. After 4–6 with Hutch, to Ash. rookery and got 5 rooks from S. 1's tree, one of which fell from tree, neither being broken ...

May 2 Went out from 1.45–4 with B. 3. to Ash. Rookery and Gales. Got 2 rooks and 4 starlings. Bought jackdaws.

May 3 Got some Dabchicks, House sparrows, mavis's, Tree-climbers, Redstarts and Linnets.

Boscawen Somerset, Diary (1847–52)

12th – The Threat of Chartist Riots

Monday passed off with surprising quiet, and it was considered a most satisfactory demonstration on the part of the Government, and the peaceable and loyal part of the community. Enormous preparations were made, and a host of military, police, and special constables were ready if wanted; every gentleman in London was sworn, and during a great part of the day, while the police were reposing, they did duty. The Chartist movement was contemptible; but everybody rejoices that the defensive demonstration was made, for it has given a great and memorable lesson which will not be thrown away, either on the dis-affected and mischievous, or the loyal and peaceful; and it will produce a vast effect in all foreign countries, and show how solid is the foundation on which we are resting. We have displayed a great resolution and a great strength, and given unmistakable proofs, that if sedition and rebellion hold up their heads in this country, they will be instantly met with the most vigorous resistance, and be put down by the hand of authority, and by the zealous co-operation of all classes of the people. The whole of the Chartist movement was to the last degree contemptible from first to last.

Charles Greville, *Diary*

Charles Greville (1794–1865) was Clerk to the Council from 1821 to 1859. His brother was the Duke of Wellington's private secretary. Charles Greville was a friend of Wellington, and knew every prominent politician of his day. His *Memoirs*, published after he died in three parts to cover the three different monarchs he served, are an important record of the history and politics of the century.

13th – Famine

To his Excellency Lord Heytesbury,
the Lord Lieutenant and Governor General of Ireland
The humble petition of the farm labourers
residents in the parish of Killeeneen, Barony of Dunkellon and County of Galway.

Sheweth

That the price of potatoes in the district is over five pence per stone.

That a day's wages, without food and now in the busiest season, is eight pence.

That many of us have wives and families — the number in each family is placed opposite our names herento affixed: that a stone of potatoes is the allowance to daily support one man, that some of us having families require two stones, others require three stones daily. That manifestly our wages and with constant employment, would not enable us to feed ourselves and families: that our potatoes are nearly run out, with some of us already exhausted.

That year after year we see wages having a tendency to fall lower and lower: that from the abundance of labourers, the rate of wages is kept down, whilst the price of food rises from scarcity and other causes: That annually new mouths are added and fresh hands from boyhood are able to join us, encreasing our numbers, still the land, that is the source of our food, is the same in quantity.

That we feel our remedy is cheap food, so as to bring the price along side the rate of wages; because, if wages cannot keep up to the price of food, food should keep pace in price with the rate of wages, — for, wages is the measure of food to feed the labourer: if not, the labourer would be cut out of his share of the fruits of the Earth.

That we have heard that Indian corn meal, from foreign parts, has been brought over to this country by the Government, and to be sold at such prices as would enable poor men (earning *free* wages and obliged to buy *protected* price food, and now encreased in price from the failure of the potato crop) to feed themselves & families: That we seek no charity, we only want to get enough of food in exchange for all we can obtain by hard and honest labour: we ask our measure of food, that wages merely represents. That we want no relief by Poor Laws — that the whole world beholds our distress, and yet these laws require (us) to prove our distress, ere aid be afforded, by submitting to imprisonment and separation from our wives and children; and where are the work houses to hold our numbers.

That we never before petitioned Government to look to us: that we do so now, because we are assured our necessities shall be cared for.

Petitioners humbly pray that your Excellency may order that an immediate supply of Indian Corn Meal be sent to this district and sold to us at prices our wages can reach.

Craughwell

13 April 1846

Petition of Galway farm labourers to the Lord Lieutenant and Governor General

From 1845–51 the potato crop in Ireland failed. The majority of the population depended on the potato, a cheap crop, as a food staple, and about a million people died of starvation or related diseases. In the 25 years following the start of the famine, at least 3 million people emigrated. At first the British government tried to help by providing maize meal, but a change of government produced a change of policy, and in 1847 all relief was stopped. Imported wheat was heavily taxed to protect English farmers, and although the Corn Laws were repealed, it did not help the Irish poor. The Great Famine remains a highly sensitive issue in folk memory.

14th – A Teenager's View of the Cotton Famine

We went on a drive with Aunt Sarah to see the working classes of poor women who have nothing to do because of the cotton famines all about Carlisle and Lancashire. I do not think I have mentioned the Cotton Famine before but during the last winter the people of Lancashire & Cumberland have been in fearful distress and would have been starving if it were not for the relief fund which comes in to the managers from all parts of England—it is all caused by the dreadful civil war in America, the Northern against the Southern States, and so if the people are fighting they cannot plant cotton, and so all the mills are stopped and so all the poor people are thrown out of work.

Ellen Buxton, *Journal*

15th – Presentation of the Chartist Petition

The petition was brought down piecemeal and presented in the afternoon. Since that there has been an exposure of the petition itself, covering the authors of it with ridicule and disgrace. It turns out to be signed by less than two millions, instead of by six as Feargus stated; and of those, there were no end of fictitious names, together with the insertion of every species of ribaldry, indecency, and impertinence. The Chartists are very crestfallen, and evidently conscious of the contemptible figure they cut; but they have endeavoured to bluster and lie as well as they can in their subsequent gatherings, and talk of other petitions and meetings, which nobody cares about.

Charles Greville, *Diary*

From 1837 to 1854, there were demands for Parliamentary reform by a group known as Chartists. They were mostly working people who did not have the vote and who wanted a government in which they could be represented. They had six main objectives, which formed their 'charter' – universal suffrage for men, secret ballots, annual parliaments, pay for MPs, no property qualifications for those standing as MPs, and constituencies with equal-sized populations. The Chartists proposed to use force if they could not get their demands legally. Support for the movement eventually dwindled, and it became more interested in such things as education and civic reform.

16th – The Origin of Cook's Railway Excursions

Mr. Thomas Cook, the celebrated excursionist, in an article in the *Leisure Hour* remarks: ... "The beginning was very small, and was on this wise. I believe that the Midland Railway from Derby to Rugby *via* Leicester was opened in 1840. At that time I knew but little of railways, having only travelled over the Leicester and Swannington line from Leicester to Long Lane, a terminus near to the Leicestershire collieries. The reports in the papers of the opening of the new line created astonishment in Leicestershire, and I had read of an interchange of visits between the Leicester and Nottingham Mechanics' Institutes. I was an enthusiastic temperance man ... A great meeting was to be held at Leicester, over which Lawrence Heyworth, Esq., of Liverpool—a great railway as well as temperance man—was advertised to preside. From my residence at Market Harborough I walked to Leicester (fifteen miles) to attend that meeting. About midway between Harborough and

Leicester—my mind's eye has often reverted to the spot—a thought flashed through my brain, what a glorious thing it would be if the newly-developed powers of railways and locomotion could be made subservient to the promotion of temperance. That thought grew upon me as I travelled over the last six or eight miles. I carried it up to the platform, and, strong in the confidence of the sympathy of the chairman, I broached the idea of engaging a special train to carry the friends of temperance from Leicester to Loughborough and back to attend a quarterly delegate meeting appointed to be held there in two or three weeks following. The chairman approved, the meeting roared with excitement, and early next day I proposed my grand scheme to John Fox Bell, the resident secretary of the Midland Counties Railway Company. Mr. Paget, of Loughborough, opened his park for a gala, and on the day appointed about five hundred passengers filled some twenty or twenty-five open carriages—they were called 'tubs' in those days—and the party rode the enormous distance of eleven miles and back for a shilling, children half-price. We carried music with us, and music met us at the Loughborough station. The people crowded the streets, filled windows, covered the house-tops, and cheered us all along the line, with the heartiest welcome. All went off in the best style and in perfect safety we returned to Leicester; and thus was struck the keynote of my excursions, and the social idea grew upon me."

Thomas Cook, *The Leisure Hour*, reprinted in *Railway Adventures and Anecdotes*

17th – A Riding-Habit

For your outfit you will require ... a nice well-made habit of dark cloth. If you are a very young girl, grey will be the most suitable; if not, dark blue. If you live in London, pay a visit to Mayfair, and get Mr. Wolmershausen to make it for you; if in Dublin, Mr. Scott, of Sackville Street, will do equally well; indeed, for any sort of riding-gear, ladies' or gentlemen's, he is not to be excelled. If you are not within easy distance of a city, go to the best tailor you can, and give him directions, which he must not be above taking. Skirt to reach six inches below the foot, well shaped for the knee, and neatly shotted at end of hem just below the right foot; elastic band upon inner side, to catch the left toe, and to retain the skirt in its place. It should be made tight and spare, without *one inch* of superfluous cloth; jacket close-fitting, but sufficiently easy to avoid even the suspicion of being squeezed; sleeves perfectly tight, except at the setting on, where a slight puffiness over the shoulder should give the appearance of increased width of chest. No braiding nor ornamentation of any sort to appear. A small neat linen collar, upright shape, with cuffs to correspond, should be worn with the habit, no frilling nor fancy work being admissible—the collar to be fastened with a plain gold or silver stud.

Nannie Lambert, *Ladies on Horseback*

18th – Aristotle at Afternoon Tea

In a *tête-à-tête* one should talk about persons, and in general Society about things. The state of the weather is always an excusable exordium, but it is convenient to have a paradox or heresy on the subject always ready so as to direct the conversation into other channels. Really domestic people are almost invariably bad talkers as their very virtues in home life have dulled their interest in outer things. The very best mothers will insist on chattering of their babies and prattling about infant education. In fact, most women do not take sufficient interest in politics, just as most men are deficient in general reading. Still, anybody can be made to talk, except the very obstinate, and even a commercial traveller may be drawn out and become quite interesting. As for Society small talk, it is impossible … for any sound theory of conversation to depreciate gossip, 'which is perhaps the main factor in agreeable talk throughout Society.' The retailing of small personal points about great people always gives pleasure, and if one is not fortunate enough to be an Arctic traveller or an escaped Nihilist, the best thing one can do is to relate some anecdote of 'Prince Bismarck, or King Victor Emmanuel, or Mr. Gladstone.' In the case of meeting a genius and a Duke at dinner, the good talker will try to raise himself to the level of the former and to bring the latter down to his own level. To succeed among one's social superiors one must have no hesitation in contradicting them.

Oscar Wilde, review of *The Principles of the Art of Conversation: A Social Essay*, by J. P. Mahaffy, *Pall Mall Gazette*, 1887

19th – Lighthouses

Of all the vessels, great and small, that annually seek and leave our ports, a large proportion meet their doom, and, despite all our lighthouses, beacons, and buoys, lay their timbers and cargoes in fragments, on our shores. This is a significant fact, for if those lost ships be—as they are—a mere fraction of our commerce, how great must be the fleet, how vast the wealth, that our lighthouses guide safely into port every year? If all our coast-lights were to be extinguished for only a single night, the loss of property and life would be terrible beyond conception. But such an event can never happen, for our coast-lights arise each evening at sunset with the regularity of the sun himself. Like the stars, they burst out when darkness begins to brood upon land and sea like them, too, their action and aspect are varied. Some, at great heights, in exposed places, blaze bright and steady like stars of the first magnitude. Others, in the form of revolving lights, twinkle like the lesser stars—now veiling, now flashing forth their beams.

One set of lights shine ruby-red like Mars; another set are white, like Venus; while those on our pier-heads and at our harbour mouths are green; and, in one or two instances, if not more, they shine, (by means of reflecting prisms), with borrowed light like the moon; but all—whether revolving or fixed, large or small, red or white or green—beam forth, like good angels, offering welcome and guidance to the mariner approaching from beyond seas; with God-like impartiality shedding their radiance on friend and foe, and encircling—as with a chaplet of living diamonds, rubies, and emeralds—our highly favoured little islands of the sea.

R. M. Ballantine, *Personal Reminiscences in Book Making*

Robert Michael Ballantine (1825–94) was born in Scotland, but went to Canada to work for the Hudson's Bay Company. Returning to Britain, he used his experiences to write a story for boys, *The Young Fur-traders*. He subsequently wrote over eighty books, many of them based on personal experiences. After getting the thickness of a coconut shell wrong in his most famous title, *Coral Island*, he researched backgrounds carefully so as not to make any other mistakes. He was one of the most popular adventure writers, for both children and adults.

20th – Death of Benjamin Disraeli, Lord Beaconsfield

Lord Beaconsfield has been removed at a time when he was still the foremost statesman of the Conservative party, and while he attracted the attention of the country only in a less degree than Mr. Gladstone himself. This is not the occasion for a cold and critical examination of Lord Beaconsfield's course in politics during half a century. Few leaders of parties have been the objects of so much denunciation and suspicion, and scarcely one can be named who, in the face of many and great obstacles, so steadily advanced to a commanding place in the state. But to-day censure will be generously silent. There was much that was dignified and still more that was brilliant in Lord Beaconsfield's career, and on those parts of it even his enemies, not always chivalrous in their attacks upon him, will prefer to dwell at the hour of his death. The doubts which sometimes tried the allegiance of his followers— though when the time for action came no leader was ever more loyally obeyed by a proud and powerful party—will be forgotten in regret for the loss of a chief who, whatever his faults, added many remarkable pages to the history of English conservatism. No dissentient voice will break in upon the tribute of admiration, in which foes, we are sure, will cordially join with friends, that must be paid to Lord Beaconsfield's high courage, his unswerving purpose, his imperturbable temper, and his versatile mastery of parliamentary tactics. His oratorical gifts, though not comparable for artistic effect and passionate power with those of Mr. Bright, or even with the accomplished fluency and skilful command of facts in which Mr. Gladstone is unrivalled, were, perhaps, rarer than either, and will not soon be matched again in the House of Commons.

The Times, 20 April 1881

21st – Home-Thoughts, from the Sea

Nobly, nobly Cape Saint Vincent to the North-West died away;
Sunset ran, one glorious blood-red, reeking into Cadiz Bay;
Bluish 'mid the burning water, full in face Trafalgar lay;
In the dimmest North-East distance, dawned Gibraltar grand and
    gray;

"Here and here did England help me: how can I help
   England?"—say,
Whoso turns as I, this evening, turn to God to praise and pray,
While Jove's planet rises yonder, silent over Africa.

Robert Browning

Robert Browning (1812–89) wrote poetry from his youth, some of
it being inspired by visits to Italy. He admired the poems of Elizabeth
Barrett, and started to write to her; this correspondence led to their
marriage. They lived in Italy for many years, but when Elizabeth died,
he returned to England. By this time Robert Browning had become a
dramatist, as well as a popular poet. He died in Italy, and wanted to be
buried there, but this was not possible so he was buried in Westminster
Abbey instead.

22nd – A Partridge's Nest

A curious provision of nature, conducing to the preservation of
the species, may be here mentioned as interesting; the partridge,
while sitting on her eggs, has no scent. On one occasion a man
was consulting me about a tombstone at St. Andrew's Church,
Woodhall. We walked into the churchyard together, and stood
conversing opposite the grave in question. I was aware that a
partridge was sitting on her nest concealed in the grass between
that grave and the next, and therefore would not approach very
near. Suddenly I perceived that he had a terrier with him, which
was very busily hunting over the churchyard. I begged him to
keep it in. He was rather indignant, and replied that it could do
no harm in the churchyard. I remarked that he was not aware
that within eight or ten feet of us a partridge was on her nest,
and I did not wish her to be disturbed. He thereupon called in his
dog, but that only brought his dog nearer to the nest, hunting the
while; and the dog actually passed over the nest without scenting
the bird. The eggs were hatched the next day, and that doubtless
accounted for her sitting so closely. Whether or not from an
instinctive consciousness of this safeguard is not for me to say,
but the partridge is rather given to selecting her nesting place near
a highway or a footpath. I have known several instances of this,
and only last year I repeatedly saw both the parent birds sitting on

their nest together, on a bank close to a public footpath which was daily traversed.

J. Conway Walter, *Woodhall Spa and Neighbourhood*

The Reverend James Conway Walter (1831–1913) was a naturalist and historian, writing about the area of Lincolnshire in which he lived and worked.

23rd – An Undergraduate's First Impressions

The chapel-clock is *in* my bedroom, and woke me with its vibration every time it struck the hour. However, I suppose I shall get used to it. But I was up long before the scout came to call me at seven, and was in such fear of being late for chapel, that I was ten minutes too early, and had to walk about in the cold and stare at the extraordinary stained windows—Jonah and the whale swimming about side by side; Abraham dragging Isaac to the sacrifice by his hair; Mary and Martha attending upon Christ, each with a brass ladle in her hand, only that Mary holds hers suspended, and Martha goes on dipping hers in the pot while He is talking. At last the Master entered statelily, and the troop of undergraduates in black gowns and scholars in white ones came clattering in; and Mr. Hedley read the service, and we all responded, and a scholar read the lessons; and then there was a general rush into Quad, and a great shaking of hands, at which I, having no hand to shake, felt very blank, and escaped to my rooms, and afterwards to breakfast with Mr. Jowett ... I am to go to him every night with a hundred lines of Sophocles, some Latin composition, and a piece of Cicero by heart—a great addition to my eighteen lectures a week, but the greatest advantage; and really he could not have done a more true kindness: I do not know how to say enough of it.

Augustus Hare, *The Story Of My Life*

Augustus Hare (1834–1903) was given away to his aunt by his parents, and his aunt brought him up. He wrote two sorts of books: biographies and travel books including descriptive and historical details. His six-volume autobiography contains a number of ghost stories.

24th – Against Slavery

My Dear E—. I return you Mr. —'s letter. I do not think it answers any of the questions debated in our last conversation at all satisfactorily: the *right* one man has to enslave another, he has not the hardihood to assert; but in the reasons he adduces to defend that act of injustice, the contradictory statements he makes appear to me to refute each other. He says, that to the continental European protesting against the abstract iniquity of slavery, his answer would be, 'the slaves are infinitely better off than half the continental peasantry.' To the Englishman, 'they are happy compared with the miserable Irish.' But supposing that this answered the question of original injustice, which it does not, it is not a true reply. Though the negroes are fed, clothed, and housed, and though the Irish peasant is starved, naked, and roofless, the bare name of freeman—the lordship over his own person, the power to choose and will—are blessings beyond food, raiment, or shelter; possessing which, the want of every comfort of life is yet more tolerable than their fullest enjoyment without them. Ask the thousands of ragged destitutes who yearly land upon these shores to seek the means of existence—ask the friendless, penniless foreign emigrant, if he will give up his present misery, his future uncertainty, his doubtful and difficult struggle for life, at once, for the secure, and as it is called, fortunate dependance of the slave: the indignation with which he would spurn the offer will prove that he possesses one good beyond all others, and that his birthright as a man is more precious to him yet than the mess of pottage for which he is told to exchange it because he is starving.

Fanny Kemble, *Journal of a Residence on a Georgian Plantation*
1838–1839

Fanny Kemble (1809–93) was born into a theatrical family, and became a leading actress on the London stage. She married the American land-owner Pierce Butler – but she supported the abolition of slavery, and her husband owned slaves. As well as describing the people she met in Georgia, and the flora and fauna there, her diary describes some of the horrors of slavery, and unusually includes accounts of women slaves. Fanny Kemble tried to stop her husband treating slaves harshly, but they could not agree. After many quarrels, the couple separated in 1845, and divorced in 1849. She was urged to publish her diary, but did not do so (her husband had the care of their daughters) until the American Civil War broke out. When the book came out in 1863, it caused a sensation.

25th – Mafeking Before the Siege

Colonel Baden-Powell did not look on my presence with great favour, neither did he order me to leave, and I had a sort of presentiment that I might be useful, considering that there were but three trained nurses in the Victoria Hospital to minister to the needs of the whole garrison. Therefore, though I talked of going South every day by one of the overcrowded trains to Cape Town, in which the Government was offering free tickets to any who wished to avail themselves of the opportunity, I secretly hoped to be allowed to remain. We had taken a tiny cottage in the town, and we had all our meals at Dixon's Hotel, where the food was weird, but where certainly no depression of spirits reigned. I even bought a white pony, called Dop, from a Johannesburg polo-player, and this pony, one of the best I have ever ridden, had later on some curious experiences. One day Dr. Jameson arrived on his way to Rhodesia, but he was hustled away with more haste than courtesy by General Baden-Powell, who bluntly told him that if he meant to stay in the town a battery of artillery would be required to defend it; and of field-guns, in spite of urgent representations, not one had reached us from Cape Town. We used to ride morning and evening on the flat country which surrounds Mafeking, where no tree or hill obscures the view for miles; and one then realized what a tiny place the seat of government of the Bechuanaland Protectorate really was, a mere speck of corrugated iron roofs on the brown expanse of the burnt-up veldt, far away from everywhere. I think it was this very isolation that created the interest in the siege at home, and one of the reasons why the Boers were so anxious to reduce it was that this town was practically the jumping-off place for the Jameson Raid. So passed the days till October 13, and then the sword, which had been suspended by a hair, suddenly fell.

Lady Sarah Wilson, *Book of South African Memories*

26th – Brahma

If the wild bowler thinks he bowls,
Or if the batsman thinks he's bowled,
They know not, poor misguided souls,
They too shall perish unconsoled.
I am the batsman and the bat,
I am the bowler and the ball,
The umpire, the pavilion cat,
The roller, pitch, and stumps, and all.

Andrew Lang

27th – Children's Reading

Never take a book away from a child unless it is positively vicious; that they should learn how to read a book and read it quickly is the great point; that they should get a habit of reading, and feel a void without it, is what should be cultivated. Never mind if it is trash now; their tastes will insensibly alter. I like a boy to cram himself with novels; a day will come when he is sick of them, and rejects them for the study of facts. What we want to give a child is 'bookmindedness,' as some one calls it. They will read a good deal that is bad, of course; but innocence is as slippery as a duck's back; a boy really fond of reading is generally pure-minded enough. When you see a robust, active, out-of-door boy deeply engrossed in a book, then you may suspect it if you like, and ask him what he has got; it will probably have an animal bearing.

A. C. Benson, *Memoirs of Arthur Hamilton, B.A.*

Arthur Christopher Benson (1862–1925) was a teacher, academic and author, the older brother of the novelist E F Benson. A poet and hymn-writer, perhaps his most famous work is 'Land of Hope and Glory', the words for Elgar's first Pomp and Circumstance march.

28th – Considering Species

In considering the Origin of Species, it is quite conceivable that a naturalist, reflecting on the mutual affinities of organic beings, on their embryological relations, their geographical distribution, geological succession, and other such facts, might come to the conclusion that each species had not been independently created, but had descended, like varieties, from other species. Nevertheless, such a conclusion, even if well founded, would be unsatisfactory, until it could be shown how the innumerable species inhabiting this world have been modified, so as to acquire that perfection of structure and coadaptation which most justly excites our admiration. Naturalists continually refer to external conditions, such as climate, food, &c., as the only possible cause of variation. In one very limited sense, as we shall hereafter see, this may be true; but it is preposterous to attribute to mere external conditions, the structure, for instance, of the woodpecker, with its feet, tail, beak, and tongue, so admirably adapted to catch insects under the bark of trees. In the case of the misseltoe, which draws its nourishment from certain trees, which has seeds that must be transported by certain birds, and which has flowers with separate sexes absolutely requiring the agency of certain insects to bring pollen from one flower to the other, it is equally preposterous to account for the structure of this parasite, with its relations to several distinct organic beings, by the effects of external conditions, or of habit, or of the volition of the plant itself.

The author of the 'Vestiges of Creation' would, I presume, say that, after a certain unknown number of generations, some bird had given birth to a woodpecker, and some plant to the missletoe, and that these had been produced perfect as we now see them; but this assumption seems to me to be no explanation, for it leaves the case of the coadaptations of organic beings to each other and to their physical conditions of life, untouched and unexplained.

It is, therefore, of the highest importance to gain a clear insight into the means of modification and coadaptation. At the commencement of my observations it seemed to me probable that a careful study of domesticated animals and of cultivated plants would offer the best chance of making out this obscure problem. Nor have I been disappointed; in this and in all other perplexing cases I have invariably found that our knowledge, imperfect though it be, of variation under domestication, afforded the best and safest clue. I may venture to express my conviction of the high value of such studies, although they have been very commonly neglected by naturalists.

Charles Darwin, Introduction, *On the Origin of Species*

29th – The Butler's-Pantry

The ancient Buttery or Butlery was the place of the Butler or Bottler, the dispenser of drink. The place of the Server or Sewer was the Sewery, the depository of napery, plate, and the like. The modern butler is both butler and chief sewer; and his Pantry, so called, accommodates both the service of wine and the service and stowage of plate,—chiefly the latter nowadays when drinking is in decadence and wealth increasing daily.

A position ought to be chosen for the Butler's-Pantry which shall answer several purposes. It must be as near as possible to the Dining-room for convenience of service. It ought to be removed from general traffic (and especially from the Back door), for the safety of the plate. The communication with the Wine and Beer Cellars must be ready. When there is a Housekeeper's-room, the butler (if there be no Steward) ought to be within easy reach of it, although apart; if there be a Steward, the butler must have ready access to his office; in both cases the transaction of hourly business being in question. With the Kitchen the butler may be said to have no intercourse whatever.

A proper Butler's-Pantry will be of fair size, say from 12 or 14 feet square up to twice that size. A fireplace is essential. The fittings consist of a small dresser containing a pair of lead sinks with folding covers (for hot and cold water respectively, that is to say, for washing and rinsing), a washbasin (for dressing), large closets for glass, &c., a moveable table, perhaps a napkin-press, drawers for table-linen, shelving, and hat-pegs, and a closet for plate with sliding trays lined with baize. When the plate is of much value, it is usual to attach to the pantry a fire-proof plate-safe with brick enclosure and iron door. Hot and cold water is to be laid on to the sinks; and if necessary the plate-safe may be warmed to expel damp.

A separate room for cleaning the plate, called the plate scullery, is useful where there is much of such work to do. It will open of course from the pantry alone, and will contain the usual pair of sinks and a dresser.

The butler's-bedroom is best placed in immediate connection with the pantry, whereby the plate is under guard at night. Frequently, however, a closet-bedstead is provided for a subordinate in the pantry itself; but this is obviously a makeshift. It is not unusual to place the door of the platesafe within the butler's bedroom. In fact, one of the most essential points in respect of the butler's-rooms is to provide against the theft of the articles under his charge; and this idea must govern every question of plan.

In a very large establishment the charge of the plate will devolve upon the under butler, and a separate butler's-room will have to be provided for the superior servant (who may be valet also), but still close at hand for business.

Robert Kerr, 'Domestic Offices', *The Gentleman's House*

30th – The Chimney Sweep

Once upon a time there was a little chimney-sweep, and his name was Tom. That is a short name, and you have heard it before, so you will not have much trouble in remembering it. He lived in a great town in the North country, where there were plenty of chimneys to sweep, and plenty of money for Tom to earn and his master to spend. He could not read nor write, and did not care to do either; and he never washed himself, for there was no water up the court where he lived. He had never been taught to say his prayers. He never had heard of God, or of Christ, except in words which you never have heard, and which it would have been well if he had never heard. He cried half his time, and laughed the other half. He cried when he had to climb the dark flues, rubbing his poor knees and elbows raw; and when the soot got into his eyes, which it did every day in the week; and when his master beat him, which he did every day in the week; and when he had not enough to eat, which happened every day in the week likewise. And he laughed the other half of the day, when he was tossing halfpennies with the other boys, or playing leap-frog over the posts, or bowling stones at the horses' legs as they trotted by, which last was excellent fun, when there was a wall at hand behind which to hide. As for chimney-sweeping, and being hungry, and being beaten, he took all that for the way of the world, like the rain and snow and thunder, and stood manfully with his back to it till it was over, as his old donkey did to a hail-storm; and then shook his ears and was as jolly as ever; and thought of the fine times coming, when he would be a man, and a master sweep, and sit in the public-house with a quart of beer and a long pipe, and play cards for silver money, and wear velveteens and ankle-jacks, and keep a white bull-dog with one gray ear, and carry her puppies in his pocket, just like a man. And he would have apprentices, one, two, three, if he could. How he would bully them, and knock them about, just as his master did to him; and make them carry home the soot sacks, while he rode before them on his donkey, with a pipe in his mouth and a flower in his button-hole, like a king at the head of his army. Yes, there were good times coming; and, when his master let him have a pull at the leavings of his beer, Tom was the jolliest boy in the whole town.

Charles Kingsley, *The Water-Babies*

MAY

1st – May Morning on Magdalen Tower

I am writing at half-past six a.m., for at four o'clock I got up, roused Milligan (now my chief friend and companion), and we went off to Magdalen. A number of undergraduates were already assembled, and when the door was opened, we were all let through one by one, and up the steep winding staircase to the platform amid the pinnacles on the top of the tower. Here stood the choristers and chaplains in a space railed off, with bare heads, and white surplices waving in the wind. It was a clear morning, and every spire in Oxford stood out against the sky, the bright young green of the trees mingling with them. Below was a vast crowd, but in the high air the silence seemed unbroken, till the clock struck five, and then, as every one took off their caps, the choristers began to sing the Latin hymn, a few voices softly at first, and then a full chorus bursting in. It was really beautiful, raised above the world on that great height, in the clear atmosphere of the sky. As the voices ceased, the bells began, and the tower rocked so that you could *see* it swaying backwards and forwards. Milligan and I walked round Magdalen walks afterwards, and when my scout found me dressed on coming to call me, he asked if I had been 'out a-Maying.' Yesterday afternoon I rowed with Milligan on the river to Godstowe. It was so shallow, that if we had upset, which was exceedingly probable, we could have walked to shore.

Augustus Hare, *The Story of My Life*

2nd – The Opening of the Great International Exhibition

Of the hundreds and thousands who lined the streets and thronged the building, few forgot the Prince by whom the great work of the day was encouraged and helped on – who sowed, but reaped not; and many were the kindly and regretful words spoken of the Royal lady who would have been so gladly welcomed, and who yesterday was so sorely missed.

The Times, 2 May 1862

3rd – Outback Adventure

In the infant days of Port Phillip – say 1841 – I had then been in the colony upwards of a year, and was residing in Bunninyong, not far from the now celebrated Ballarat, which, I need scarcely add, was at that time bush of the wildest description. A neighbour of mine, Mr H. Anderson, who came in the early days of the settlement from Western Australia, was settled as a sheep farmer at Winter's Flat, rode over to my place to tell me that he had lost a colt which he had just taken in hand to break in, with a tether rope attached, and he feared he would get tied up in the bush, and so perish.

I had fixed to go the following morning, at day-break, with a Mr Cartwright, a nephew of the celebrated dentist of that name, who was forming a station at the foot of Warrenheip Hill, to the Messrs Learmonth's station, to procure some sheep for killing, which we obtained, and started with a horse and dray to my place with them, a distance of about three miles, by a bush track. Having my kangaroo dogs with me, I returned by the side of the range, a little to the left of the track, hoping to fall in with a 'dingo.'

I had not gone far when I saw Mr Anderson's colt in company with a second which had just completed its education. I approached them carefully and caught the one with the rope attached, which was a three-inch coir, and which I coiled upon my arm, managing the horse with my eye more than by any other power which I had over him, as the rope was only round his neck.

I had not gone far when the second horse, which kept close to the colt I was so intent on managing, suddenly galloped off to, as I afterwards found out, a small herd of cattle,—imagining, I doubt not, that it was the mob of horses they were accustomed to run with. The colt, an immensely powerful animal, over sixteen hands, followed suit, and now picture my position. In the excitement of managing the unbroken animal, I had imperceptibly allowed the end of the rope to coil round my left leg, and in an instant I was being dragged over a rough and thickly timbered country, about twelve feet from the horse's heels, as fast as he, now much alarmed as well as I, could go, and after the first effort to shake myself clear of the rope, with the certain knowledge that I could not extricate myself, and more, that even if any one saw me, which was not likely, and attempted to follow the mad career of the horse, my chance of escape would be less. At each bound of the horse I was thrown about like a cork, the right leg being free to strike anything that was in the way. Fortunately I was light and young, so that the blows which I received all over my body did not deprive me of my senses. There was, however, more in my favour than that; there was a watchful Providence (who watches over all, and who suffers not a sparrow to fall to the ground without His willing it) guiding the wild steps of the animal. I expected each moment would be my last. I did not feel great fear, but my mind was filled with anxiety for those from whom I, a joyous boy of sixteen, had so recently parted in England, and who would hear of my sad end. I was impotent to help myself, and I trusted in the Almighty to save if He so willed it.

I never committed an account of this to paper before, but even at the risk of being tedious, I cannot close without bearing my evidence to the wonderful power of the mind in cases of extreme danger. I can truly say that, in a few moments, all which I had done from my infancy to that moment passed in quick review before me, and so do I believe will it be with all of us when we are called to judgment at the last great day.

To return, the horses finding their mistake when they got amongst the cattle, and seeing the horse in Cartwright's Dray in the distance, they continued their gallop towards it. Cartwright saw my danger, although he at first thought it was only my dogs which were hunting the horses; they, poor brutes, were keeping, with their accustomed faithfulness, as near as they could to their master. He (Cartwright) stopped his horse, and the others checked for a moment when they arrived near the dray, upon which he instantly caught the slack of the rope and released me from my perilous position. I had been dragged, we afterwards found out, nearly a mile and a-half, at a pace which scarcely enabled me to breathe ; and, excepting that my clothes were torn to shreds, and my shoulder-blades literally skinned, I was not much hurt. Even to this day I feel nervous when I see any one leading a horse with a long rope.

H. C.

Published in *The Albatross*, the newsletter of SS *Great Britain*

4th – New Money

We have received from a country bookseller an order for some copies of our journal, for payment of which he enclosed some twenty-four penny post stamps. This is perhaps the first time that ever a money payment was made in sticking-plaster.

Gloucester Journal

5th – A Meeting of Authors

On the 4th of May a meeting, consisting chiefly of authors, was held at the house in the Strand, for the purpose of hastening the removal of the trade restrictions on the Commerce of Literature, and it is thus described in the following letter:

The meeting last night went off triumphantly, and I saluted Mr. Chapman with "See the Conquering Hero Comes" on the piano at 12 o'clock; for not until then was the last magnate, except Herbert Spencer, out of the house. I sat at the door for a short time, but soon got a chair within it, and heard and saw everything.

Dickens in the chair—a position he fills remarkably well, preserving a courteous neutrality of eyebrows, and speaking with clearness and decision. His appearance is certainly disappointing— no benevolence in the face, and, I think, little in the head; the anterior lobe not by any means remarkable. In fact, he is not distinguished-looking in any way—neither handsome nor ugly, neither fat nor thin, neither tall nor short. Babbage moved the first resolution—a bad speaker, but a great authority. Charles Knight is a beautiful, elderly man, with a modest but firm enunciation; and he made a wise and telling speech which silenced one or two vulgar, ignorant booksellers who had got into the meeting by mistake. One of these began by complimenting Dickens—"views held by such worthy and important gentlemen, *which is your worthy person in the chair*." Dickens looked respectfully neutral. The most telling speech of the evening was Prof. Tom Taylor's—as witty and brilliant as one of George Dawson's. Prof. Owen's, too, was remarkably good. He had a resolution to move as to the bad effect of the trade restrictions on scientific works, and gave his own experience in illustration. Speaking of the slow and small sale of scientific books of a high class, he said, in his silvery, bland way— alluding to the boast that the retail booksellers *recommended* the works of less known authors—"for which limited sale we are doubtless indebted to the kind recommendation of our friends, the retail booksellers"—whereupon these worthies, taking it for a *bona fide* compliment, cheered enthusiastically. Dr. Lankester, Prof. Newman, Robert Bell, and others, spoke well. Owen has a tremendous head, and looked, as he was, the greatest celebrity of the meeting. George Cruikshank, too, made a capital speech, in an admirable moral spirit. He is the most homely, genuine-looking man; not unlike the pictures of Captain Cuttle.

George Eliot, Letter to the Brays, 5 May 1852

George Eliot – the pen name of Mary Anne Evans (1819–80) was one of the foremost women writers of the nineteenth century. She was a novelist, poet and critic, and also an excellent letter-writer. She used a male name for her novels because she wanted to be taken seriously, and also to separate this kind of writing from her other work. A free-thinker, she lived for over twenty years with the philosopher George Lewes.

6th – Comments on the Potato Famine

If blight and famine fell upon the South of France, the whole common revenue of the kingdom would certainly be largely employed in setting the people to labour upon works of public utility; in purchasing and storing for sale, at a cheap rate, such quantities of foreign corn as might be needed, until the season of distress should pass over, and another harvest should come. If Yorkshire and Lancashire had sustained a like calamity in England, there is no doubt such measures as these would have been taken promptly and liberally. And we know that the English Government is not slow to borrow money for great public objects, when it suits British policy so to do. They borrowed twenty million sterling to give away to their slaveholding colonists for a mischievous whim.

It will be easy to appreciate the feelings which then prevailed in the two islands — in Ireland, a vague and dim sense that we were somehow robbed; in England, a still more vague and blundering idea, that an impudent beggar was demanding their money, with a scowl in his eye and a threat upon his tongue.

In addition to the proceeds of the new Poor law, Parliament appropriated a further sum of £50,000, to be applied in giving work in some absolutely pauper districts where there was no hope of ever raising rates to repay it. £50,000 was just the sum which was that same year voted out of the English and Irish revenue to improve the buildings of the British Museum.

In this year (1847) it was that the Irish famine began to be a world's wonder, and men's hearts were moved in the uttermost ends of the earth by the recital of its horrors. The London *Illustrated News* began to be adorned with engravings of tottering windowless hovels in Skibbereen, and elsewhere, with naked wretches dying on a truss of wet straw; and the constant language of English ministers and members of Parliament created the impression abroad that Ireland was in need of alms, and nothing but *alms*; whereas Irishmen themselves uniformly protested that what they required was a repeal of the Union, so that the English might cease to devour their substance.

John Mitchel, *History of Ireland*

7th – An Escape

Sailing up the Gulf of St Lawrence in a transport, I was walking the deck at eleven o'clock at night, with the chief officer, previous to 'turning in,' when I felt an unusual chill in the air, and it was the month of May. I said to the mate, 'We must be near ice;' he answered, 'I think we're long past it.' The soldiers of the watch on deck feeling as I did, began to stamp their feet to keep themselves warm; and as they were disturbing those below, I sent them down, and to remain, if required, at the bottom of the ladder. The deck was no sooner clear of them, and we could see well for'ard, than the mate suddenly ran to the forecastle, and called aft, 'Hard a-port!'

I looked to the steersman and saw he was nodding over the wheel; I roused him and called, 'Hard a-port!' and looking to the bows, I saw a line of fire, as it were, on the deep; it was the sea breaking on an immense iceberg, towards which we had been directly steering. The captain, hearing a commotion on deck, now came out in his shirt, a card party of officers below was suddenly broken up, and we were close under the lee of the great berg. The sails were aback, and the captain anxiously watched them; at last the top-gallant sails filled, and we slowly passed the iceberg, which disappeared like a great mass of ground glass, and presenting altogether an appearance of solemn grandeur, which was heightened by our providential escape.

J. E. A.

Published in *The Albatross*, newsletter of SS *Great Britain*

8th – A Concert with Yvette Guilbert

May 8, 1896:—To-night I heard Yvette Guilbert sing five songs—including 'La Soularde', Béranger's 'Grand'mère', 'Her Golden Hair was hanging down her back', and I want you, ma Honey' (alternate verses in French and English). The performance took about 23 minutes, and she receives £70 per night (ten nights). My father, who had seen her on the previous evening, said to me at dinner at Gatti's, 'I don't see £70 in what she does.' 'No,' I said, 'perhaps *you* can't; but you can see it in the audience which pays to listen to her.'

I think I never saw the Empire so full. Yvette wore a gown of bluish green flowered silk, and the unchangeable black gloves. To the back of the pit, where I stood, her voice came as if from an immense distance, attenuated, but clear and crisp.

Arnold Bennett, *Journals*

Yvette Guilbert (1865–1944) was a French cabaret singer who caused a sensation with her suggestive songs and innocent appearance. She liked 'patter songs', writing some of them herself. The artist Henri de Toulouse-Lautrec made many portraits and sketches of her. She became an international star; later in life she appeared in films and published two novels.

9th – The Drawbacks of Marriage

Looking at a woman's position both as wife and mother, it is impossible not to recognise the fact that marriage is a direct disadvantage to her. In an unlegalised union the woman retains possession of all her natural rights, she is mistress of her own actions, of her body, of her property; she is able to legally defend herself against attack; all the Courts are open to protect her; she forfeits none of her rights as an Englishwoman; she keeps intact her liberty and her independence; she has no master; she owes obedience to the laws alone.

Anne Besant, *An Autobiography*

Annie Besant (1847–1933) was interested in socialism, women's rights, theosophy, and self-rule for India and Ireland. Her early marriage to a clergyman failed because of her anti-religious views: she supported the National Secular Society with speeches and writing, as well as supporting union activities and the Fabian Society. Meeting Helena Blavatsky in 1890, her anti-religious ideas changed as she became interested in theosophy. This took her to India, where she helped set up colleges. She gave speeches and lectures throughout her life, as well as writing many books and pamphlets on the subjects she was passionate about.

10th – Derby Day

Visitors to the Exhibition of the Royal Academy will note with surprise that a police-constable stands before a certain picture in the big room; and that this picture is further guarded by a barrier, to prevent interested members of the public coming too near.

W. P. Frith, *Morning Herald*, 10 May 1858

11th – Prince Albert's Title

Windsor Castle, May 1856.
It is a strange omission in our Constitution that while the wife of a King has the highest rank and dignity in the realm after her husband assigned to her by law, the *husband* of a *Queen regnant* is entirely ignored by the law. This is the more extraordinary,

as a husband has in this country such particular rights and such great power over his wife, and as the Queen is married just as any other woman is, and swears to obey her lord and master, as such, while by law he has no rank or defined position. This is a strange anomaly. No doubt, as is the case now—the Queen can give her husband the highest *place* by *placing* him *always near her person*, and the Nation would give it him as a *matter of course*. Still, when I first married, we had much difficulty on this subject; much bad feeling was shown, and several members of the Royal Family showed bad grace in giving precedence to the Prince, and the late King of Hanover positively resisted doing so. I gave the Prince precedence by issuing Letters Patent, but these give no rank in Parliament—or at the Council Board—and it would be far better to put this question beyond all doubt, and to secure its settlement for *all future Consorts of Queens*, and thus have this omission in the Constitution rectified. Naturally my own feeling would be to give the Prince the same title and rank as I have, but a Titular King is a complete novelty in this country, and might be productive of more inconveniences than advantages to the individual who bears it. Therefore, upon mature reflection, and after considering the question for nearly *sixteen years*, I have come to the conclusion that the title which is now by universal consent given him of "Prince Consort," with the highest rank in and out of Parliament immediately after the Queen, and before every other Prince of the Royal Family, should be the one assigned to the husband of the Queen regnant *once and for all*. This ought to be done before our children grow up, and it seems peculiarly easy to do so *now* that none of the old branches of the Royal Family are still alive.

Queen Victoria, *Memorandum*

12 – Arrangement in Grey and Black

Portrait of Whistler's Mother –
Before such pictures as the full-length portraits by Mr. Whistler, critic and spectator are alike puzzled. Criticism and admiration seem alike impossible, and the mind vacillates between a feeling that the artist is playing a practical joke upon the spectator, or that the painter is suffering from some peculiar optical delusion. After all, there are certain accepted canons about what constitutes

good drawing, good colour, and good painting, and when an artist deliberately sets himself to ignore or violate all of these, it is desirable that his work should not be classed with that of ordinary artists.

Times review of J. M. Whistler, *The Gentle Art of Making Enemies*

13th – The Ruined Maid

"O 'Melia, my dear, this does everything crown!
Who could have supposed I should meet you in Town?
And whence such fair garments, such prosperi-ty?" —
"O didn't you know I'd been ruined?" said she.

— "You left us in tatters, without shoes or socks,
Tired of digging potatoes, and spudding up docks;
And now you've gay bracelets and bright feathers three!" —
"Yes: that's how we dress when we're ruined," said she.

— "At home in the barton you said 'thee' and 'thou,'
And 'thik oon,' and 'theäs oon,' and 't'other'; but now
Your talking quite fits 'ee for high compa-ny!" —
"Some polish is gained with one's ruin," said she.

— "Your hands were like paws then, your face blue and bleak
But now I'm bewitched by your delicate cheek,
And your little gloves fit as on any la-dy!" —
"We never do work when we're ruined," said she.

— "You used to call home-life a hag-ridden dream,
And you'd sigh, and you'd sock; but at present you seem
To know not of megrims or melancho-ly!" —
"True. One's pretty lively when ruined," said she.

— "I wish I had feathers, a fine sweeping gown,
And a delicate face, and could strut about Town!" —
"My dear — a raw country girl, such as you be,
Cannot quite expect that. You ain't ruined," said she.

Thomas Hardy

Thomas Hardy (1840–1928) was trained as an architect, but was already beginning to write. His novels and short stories brought him success, but he is best remembered for poetry. Most of his work is set in Wessex.

14th – Hedgers and Ditchers

Hedgers and ditchers often work by the piece, and so take their own time for meals; the ash woods, which are cut in the winter, are also usually thrown by the piece. Hedging and ditching, if done properly, is hard work, especially if there is any grubbing. Though the arms get warm from swinging the grub-axe or billhook, or cleaning out the ditch and plastering and smoothing the side of the mound with the spade, yet feet and ankles are chilled by the water in the ditch. This is often dammed up and so kept back partially, but it generally forces its way through. The ditcher has a board to stand on; there is a hole through it, and a projecting stick attached, with which to drag it into position. But the soft soil allows the board to sink, and he often throws it aside as more encumbrance than use. He has some small perquisites: he is allowed to carry home a bundle of wood or a log every night, and may gather up the remnants after the faggoting is finished. On the other hand, he cannot work in bad weather.

Richard Jefferies, *Book of Hodge and His Masters*

15th – Dogs

The great pleasure of a dog is that you may make a fool of yourself with him and not only will he not scold you, but he will make a fool of himself too.

Samuel Butler, 'Higgledy-Piggledy', *Notebooks of Samuel Butler*

16th – Photographic Portraiture

Photographic portraiture is the best feature of the fine arts for the million that the ingenuity of man has yet devised. It has in this sense swept away many of the illiberal distinctions of rank and wealth, so that the poor man who possesses but a few shillings can command as perfect a lifelike portrait of his wife or child as Sir Thomas Lawrence painted for the most distinguished sovereigns of Europe.

Photographic News, 1861

17th – The Relief of Mafeking

As the sun set came a helio-message: "Diamond Fields Horse.—All well. Good-night." We went to dinner at seven, and just as we were sitting down I heard some feeble cheers. Thinking something must have happened, I ran to the market-square, and, seeing a dusty khaki-clad figure whose appearance was unfamiliar to me, I touched him on the shoulder, and said: "Has anyone come in?" "We have come in," he answered—"Major Karri-Davis and eight men of the Imperial Light Horse." Then I saw that officer himself, and he told us that, profiting by an hour's dusk, they had ridden straight in before the moon rose, and that they were now sending back two troopers to tell the column the way was clear. Their having thus pushed on at once was a lucky inspiration, for, had they waited for daylight, they would probably have had a hard fight, even if they had got in at all. This plucky column of 1,100 men had marched nearly 300 miles in twelve days, absolutely confounding the Boers by their rapidity.

We heard weeks afterwards how that same day of the relief of Mafeking was celebrated in London with jubilation past belief, everyone going mad with delight. The original event in the town itself was a very tame if impressive affair—merely a score or so of people, singing "Rule, Britannia," surrounding eight or nine dust-begrimed figures, each holding a tired and jaded horse, and a few women on the outskirts of the circle with tears of joy in their eyes. Needless to say, no one thought of sleep that night. At 3.30 a.m. someone came and fetched me in a pony-cart, and we drove out to the polo-ground, where, by brilliant moonlight, we saw the column come into camp. Strings and strings of waggons were soon drawn up; next to them black masses, which were the guns; and beyond these, men, lying down anywhere, dead-tired, beside their horses. The rest of the night I spent at the hospital, where they were bringing in those wounded in the action of the previous afternoon.

Lady Sarah Wilson, *Book of South African Memories*

18th – Public Notice

A HANDSOME REWARD will be given to any person who can furnish such information as will discover the fate of ROGER CHARLES TICHBORNE. He sailed from the port of Rio Janeiro on the 20th April, 1854, in the ship La Bella, and has never been heard of since, but a report reached England to the effect that a portion of the crew and passengers was picked up by a vessel bound to Australia (Melbourne, it is believed); it is not known whether the said Roger Charles Tichborne was amongst the drowned or saved. He would at the present time be about 32 years of age, is of a delicate constitution, rather tall, with very light brown hair and blue eyes. Mr. Tichborne is the son of Sir James Tichborne, Bart. (now deceased), and is heir to all his estates. The advertiser is instructed to state that a most liberal reward will be given for any information that may definitely point out his fate. Gentlemen in a position to refer to the shipping reports may be able to find some record of the saving of the shipwrecked persons from La Bella, and a very careful search, if with a successful result, will amply repay any one who will take the trouble to investigate the matter. All replies to be addressed to Mr. Arthur Cubitt, Missing Friends' office, Bridge-street, Sydney, New South Wales.

The Tichborne case was a Victorian cause célèbre. Roger Tichborne, the heir to a baronetcy and a fortune, disappeared in South America. It was assumed he had perished in a shipwreck, as he was known to have booked a passage to Jamaica on a ship that did not arrive. Only some wreckage was found. His mother refused to believe he was dead, and advertised extensively for information. Eventually a butcher from Wagga Wagga in Australia claimed to be Roger Tichborne. Lady Tichborne believed that the claimant was her son, but many others did not. The case dragged on for years, but after two trials it was proved that the claimant was in fact Arthur Orton, a butcher from Wapping.

19th – The Metropolitan Underground Railway

Here were a goodly place wherein to die;–
Grown latterly to sudden change averse,

All violent contrasts fain avoid would I
On passing from this world into a worse.

Sir William Watson

Sir William Watson (1858–1935) wrote poems that commented on the politics of the day, as well as more traditional verse. He was twice considered for the position of Poet Laureate, but was unsuccessful.

20th – The Death of Mr Gladstone

In truth religion was for Mr. Gladstone the first and the most permanent interest, as personal piety lay at the root of his character; but whereas he began his career by publishing a book to prove that Church and State must be united, he honestly passed to the belief that in many cases they both flourish better apart. If it were necessary to prove his ever-present interest in religion, we might refer to a multitude of books not long published, such as the lives of Manning Hope-Scott, and Lord Blachford, and any of the countless volumes that describe the Oxford Movement. It is obvious that, in a country where seriousness is a great force, this must have proved to Mr. Gladstone a source of strength if of weakness also. Given beliefs as intense as those of Mr. Gladstone, together with his gifts of mind; and the history of his life, of his influence, and of the passionate antagonisms which he aroused, becomes intelligible. For to a profound persuasion of the essential rightness of his aims and methods he added gifts which have never in English history been found in combination—extraordinary physical strength and endurance, an absolutely unrivalled memory, dialectic of the highest order, and a copiousness of speech which on occasions could rise to eloquence of the most impressive kind. To these add a boundless capacity for work, a power of rapid acquisition beyond anything of which his colleagues had had experience, a personal magnetism which, when he chose to exercise it, was irresistible, and that rare combination, an equal grasp of principles and of details. At last, at eighty-four years of age, he laid down the burden of power, and after four years more he has died in that beautiful home at Hawarden which he loved so well and which, thanks to him, has become a familiar name wherever our language is spoken.

The Times, 20 May 1898

21st – Trees About Town

Planes are much planted now, with ill effect; the blotches where the bark peels, the leaves which lie on the sward like brown leather, the branches wide apart and giving no shelter to birds—in short, the whole ensemble of the plane is unfit for our country.

It was selected for London plantations, as the Thames Embankment, because its peeling bark was believed to protect it against the deposit of sooty particles, and because it grows quickly. For use in London itself it may be preferable: for semi-country seats, as the modern houses surrounded with their own grounds assume to be, it is unsightly. It has no association. No one has seen a plane in a hedgerow, or a wood, or a copse. There are no fragments of English history clinging to it as there are to the oak.

If trees of the plane class be desirable, sycamores may be planted, as they have in a measure become acclimatised. If trees that grow fast are required, there are limes and horse-chestnuts; the lime will run a race with any tree. The lime, too, has a pale yellow blossom, to which bees resort in numbers, making a pleasant hum, which seems the natural accompaniment of summer sunshine. Its leaves are put forth early.

Horse-chestnuts, too, grow quickly and without any attention, the bloom is familiar, and acknowledged to be fine, and in autumn the large sprays of leaves take orange and even scarlet tints. The plane is not to be mentioned beside either of them. Other trees as well as the plane would have flourished on the Thames Embankment, in consequence of the current of fresh air caused by the river. Imagine the Embankment with double rows of oaks, elms, or beeches; or, if not, even with limes or horse-chestnuts! To these certainly birds would have resorted—possibly rooks, which do not fear cities. On such a site the experiment would have been worth making.

If in the semi-country seats fast-growing trees are needed, there are, as I have observed, the lime and horse-chestnut; and if more variety be desired, add the Spanish chestnut and the walnut. The Spanish chestnut is a very fine tree; the walnut, it is true, grows slowly. If as many beeches as cedar deodaras and laurels and planes were planted in these grounds, in due course of time the tap of the woodpecker would be heard: a sound truly worth ten thousand laurels. At Kew, far closer to town than many of the semi-country seats are now, all our trees flourish in perfection.

Hardy birches, too, will grow in thin soil. Just compare the delicate drooping boughs of birch—they could not have been more delicate if sketched with a pencil—compare these with the gaunt planes!

Richard Jefferies, *Nature Near London*

22nd – The Ten Hours Bill

It must then, I think, be admitted that, where health is concerned, and where morality is concerned, the State is justified in interfering with the contracts of individuals. And, if this be admitted, it follows that the case with which we now have to do is a case for interference.

Will it be denied that the health of a large part of the rising generation may be seriously affected by the contracts which this bill is intended to regulate? Can any man who has read the evidence which is before us, can any man who has ever observed young people, can any man who remembers his own sensations when he was young, doubt that twelve hours a day of labour in a factory is too much for a lad of thirteen?

Or will it be denied that this is a question in which public morality is concerned? Can any one doubt,—none, I am sure, of my friends around me doubts,—that education is a matter of the highest importance to the virtue and happiness of a people? Now we know that there can be no education without leisure. It is evident that, after deducting from the day twelve hours for labour in a factory, and the additional hours necessary for exercise, refreshment, and repose, there will not remain time enough for education.

I have not touched the strongest part of our case. I hold that, where public health is concerned, and where public morality is concerned, the State may be justified in regulating even the contracts of adults. But we propose to regulate only the contracts of infants. Now, was there ever a civilised society in which the contracts of infants were not under some regulation? Is there a single member of this House who will say that a wealthy minor of thirteen ought to be at perfect liberty to execute a conveyance of his estate, or to give a bond for fifty thousand pounds? If anybody were so absurd as to say, "What has the Legislature to do with the matter? Why cannot you leave trade free? Why do you pretend to understand the boy's interest better than he understands it?"—you would answer; "When he grows up, he may squander his fortune away if he likes: but at present the State is his guardian; and he shall not ruin himself till he is old enough to know what he is about." The minors whom we wish to protect have not indeed large property to throw away: but they are not the less our wards. Their only inheritance, the only fund to which they must look for their subsistence through life, is the sound mind in the sound body. And is it not our duty to prevent them from wasting their most precious wealth before they know its value?

Thomas Babington Macaulay
From a speech in favour of the Ten Hours Bill, House of Commons, 22 May 1846

Thomas Babington Macaulay (1800–59) was a poet, historian, essayist and politician. He excelled in every field. As a politician he was a supporter of reforms, and at different times he was appointed to the Supreme Council for India and served as Paymaster General and Secretary of State for War. The first two volumes of his *History of England* sold 13,000 copies in four months, and his *Lays of Ancient Rome* was enormously popular.

23rd – Plea for Officers' Widows and Orphan Daughters

Sir,

Of the many works initiated and carried on during the last fifty years for the benefit of those connected with the Navy and Army there is, I venture to think, still a missing link, namely, a home or homes for the widows and orphan daughters of Officers of the two Services. None but those who have to do with Naval and Military Funds and Institutions know the distressing cases which are continually coming to light of Officers' widows and daughters who, with very limited incomes, are bravely battling against altered circumstances, and who, from the natural delicacy of their position, seldom make their wants known. To these a home, rent free, would make all the difference in their advancing years. A few are, by the never-failing thought of Queen Victoria, provided with apartments in Hampton Court Palace and elsewhere, but these are exceptional cases. It is on the system of separate apartments in a home that, I venture to think, some steps might be taken. The object should be, in the first instance at least, to provide unfurnished rooms, say three or four, rent free, subject to certain limitations, for those who have a small but sufficient income for maintenance, but who cannot afford to pay rent and taxes. Later on, if sufficient funds were available, this might, in some special cases, be supplemented by a small allowance. It might be advisable that the home or homes should be established in or near London, but, in any case, not far from shops, where the necessaries of life can be easily and cheaply obtained. I would therefore earnestly appeal to Officers, both Naval and Military, and all interested in the Services, to co-operate in this movement. A Fund, entitled "Homes for Officers' Widows and Daughters," has been opened at Messrs. Coutts & Co., 59, Strand, to which subscriptions may be paid, and I shall be glad to receive and acknowledge any such that may be sent to me direct, or to supply any further information that may be desired.

Yours, etc.

JAMES GILDEA, *Colonel.*

23, Queen Anne's Gate,

24th May, 1899

24th – Degrees for Women

This year [1879], the Ordinary Degree Examinations were opened to women by the University of London.

During the nine years that the Special Examinations of the London University for Women had existed, 139 women passed, 53 taking Honours; of these 44 were from Cheltenham, 16 in Honours, *i.e.*, almost exactly one-third of the whole number. The next in rank was the North London Collegiate School, with 28 passes and 12 in Honours. Of special certificates 100 were granted; of these Cheltenham took 51, or more than half.

Minutes of Special Meeting of the Board, *The History of the Cheltenham Ladies' College*

25th – Persicos Odi

Dear Lucy, you know what my wish is, –
I hate all your Frenchified fuss:
Your silly *entrées* and made dishes
Were never intended for us.
No footman in lace and in ruffles
Need dangle behind my arm-chair;
And never mind seeking for truffles,
Although they be ever so rare.

But a plain leg of mutton, my Lucy,
I pr'ythee get ready at three:
Have it smoking, and tender, and juicy,
And what better meat can there be?
And when it has feasted the master,
'Twill amply suffice for the maid;
Meanwhile I will smoke my canaster,
And tipple my ale in the shade.

William Makepeace Thackeray

William Makepeace Thackeray (1811–63) studied law and art before the need to make money to support his family meant he had to write more seriously than he had previously done. He wrote sketches, satires and reviews for various periodicals. His first novel, *Barry Lyndon*, was serialised in Fraser's Magazine in 1844. At the same time, he produced three travel books. More novels, including his most famous, *Vanity Fair*, and his humorous writing for the new periodical, *Punch*, established him as one of the foremost authors of the century. This is a translation of Horace, *Oder*, 1.38.

26th – Owls in Kensington Gardens

It is certainly curious to find that in these gardens, where, as we have seen, birds are not encouraged, two such species as the jackdaw and owl are still resident, although long vanished from all their other old haunts in London. Of so important a bird as the owl I should have preferred to write at some length in one of the earlier chapters, but there was very little to say, owing to its rarity and secrecy. Nor could it be included in the chapters on recent colonists, since it is probable that it has always been an inhabitant of Kensington Gardens, although its existence there has not been noticed by those who have written on the wild bird life of London. It is unfortunate that we have no enjoyment of our owls: they hide from sight in the old hollow trees, and when they occasionally exercise their voices at night we are not there to hear them. Still, it is a pleasure to know that they are there, and probably always have been there. It is certain that during the past year both the brown and white owl have been living in the gardens, as the night-watchers hear the widely different vocal performances of both birds, and have also seen both species. Probably there are not more than two birds of each kind. Owls have the habit of driving away their young, and the stray white owls occasionally seen or heard in various parts of London may be young birds driven from the gardens. Some time ago the cries of a white owl were heard on several nights at Lambeth Palace, and it was thought that the bird had made its home in the tower of Lambeth Church, close by. In the autumn of 1896 a solitary white owl frequented the trees at Buckhurst Hill. An ornithological friend told me that he had seen an owl, probably the same bird, one evening flying over the Serpentine; and on inquiring of some of the park people, I was told that they knew nothing about an owl, but that a cockatoo had mysteriously appeared every evening at dusk on one of the trees near the under-ranger's lodge! After a few weeks it was seen no more. I fancy that this owl had been expelled from the gardens by its parents.

W. H. Hudson, *Birds in London*

27th – The Whitsun Cricket Match

We ourselves are to have a cricket-match on Monday, not played by the men, who, since a certain misadventure with the Beech-hillers, are, I am sorry to say, rather chop-fallen, but by the boys, who, zealous for the honour of their parish, and headed by their bold leader, Ben Kirby, marched in a body to our antagonists' ground the Sunday after our melancholy defeat, challenged the boys of that proud hamlet, and beat them out and out on the spot. Never was a more signal victory. Our boys enjoyed this triumph with so little moderation that it had like to have produced a very tragical catastrophe. The captain of the Beech-hill youngsters, a capital bowler, by name Amos Stone, enraged past all bearing by the crowing of his adversaries, flung the ball at Ben Kirby with so true an aim that if that sagacious leader had not warily ducked his head when he saw it coming, there would probably have been a coroner's inquest on the case, and Amos Stone would have been tried for manslaughter. He let fly with such vengeance, that the cricket-ball was found embedded in a bank of clay five hundred yards off, as if it had been a cannon shot. Tom Coper and Farmer Thackum, the umpires, both say they never saw so tremendous a ball. If Amos Stone live to be a man (I mean to say if he be not hanged first) he'll be a pretty player. He is coming here on Monday with his party to play the return match, the umpires having respectively engaged Farmer Thackum that Amos shall keep the peace, Tom Coper that Ben shall give no unnecessary or wanton provocation—a nicely worded and lawyer-like clause, and one that proves that Tom Coper hath his doubts of the young gentleman's discretion; and, of a truth, so have I. I would not be Ben Kirby's surety, cautiously as the security is worded—no! not for a white double dahlia, the present object of my ambition.

Mary Russell Mitford, *Our Village*

Mary Russell Mitford (1787–1855) was the daughter of a Hampshire doctor. When he was ruined because of his extravagance, she supported him by her writing. The family had to move from a house in Reading (paid for with money she had won, aged ten, in a lottery) to a labourer's cottage in the village of Three Mile Cross. She produced poems, plays and a novel, but she succeeded best with the sketches of village life she wrote which first appeared in *The Ladies Magazine*, and then came out in book form. Her last book, *Recollections of a Literary Life*, was a series of amusing chats about her favourite books and literary contemporaries.

28th – Half-Yearly Report of the Liverpool Branch of the Hospital Work Society

I am sorry to say that we have, during the past six months, lost two kind workers by death: two others have resigned, but three new members, Mrs. H. H. Hornby, Mrs. Rome, and Mrs. St. Clare Byrne, have joined the Work Society, so that I hope the supply of work will not fall off, for we could readily distribute more than we receive. Clothes never come in as well during the summer as in the winter months, but those things which have been received were all very welcome. I shall be grateful if our members will make as many nightgowns and nightshirts as they conveniently can, the demand for them is continual, they are needed in such numbers at all the hospitals. Boys' suits are also still much wanted. Some flannel cricket caps for the boys and gingham hoods for the girls which were sent during the summer have been much liked at the Children's Infirmary, they are much cooler for summer wear for the convalescent children than the flannel hoods and Tam O'Shanter caps which we have had before. The clothes have been as usual distributed among the various hospitals.

H. M. Crosfield, 43, Aigburth Road

The Hospital Work Society had branches across the country: members made clothes for children in hospital, and sometimes provided other things, such as sheets, old linen and even scrapbooks. The London branch of the Society stipulated that 'each member is required to make four garments a year and to supply her own materials'.

29th– Bullying At Boys' Schools

Bullying must be fought with in other ways,—by getting not only the Sixth to put it down, but the lower fellows to scorn it, and by eradicating mercilessly the incorrigible; and a master who really cares for his fellows is pretty sure to know instinctively who in his house are likely to be bullied, and, knowing a fellow to be really victimised and harassed, I am sure that he can stop it if he is resolved. There are many kinds of annoyance—sometimes of real cutting persecution for righteousness' sake—that he can't stop; no more could all the ushers in the world; but he can do very much in many ways to make the shafts of the wicked pointless.

But though, for quite other reasons, I don't like to see very young boys launched at a public school, and though I don't deny (I wish I could) the existence from time to time of bullying, I deny its being a constant condition of school life, and still more, the possibility of meeting it by the means proposed ...

I don't wish to understate the amount of bullying that goes on, but my conviction is that it must be fought, like all school evils, but it more than any, by *dynamics* rather than *mechanics*, by getting the fellows to respect themselves and one another, rather than by sitting by them with a thick stick.

Letter from friend, quoted by Thomas Hughes in the Preface to
Tom Brown's Schooldays

Thomas Hughes (1822–96) trained as a lawyer and ended his career as a circuit judge in Chester, having also been an MP. He was a friend of Charles Kingsley, and, like Kingsley, was an advocate of 'muscular Christianity', which he had met while a schoolboy at Rugby. *Tom Brown's Schooldays* is largely based on his own time at school: his other writings were nowhere near so successful.

30th – Library Boundaries

As the Free Library Acts have been adopted, and are likely to become operative in Belfast, and as it has been openly proposed that the books and other property belonging to this society should be handed over to the Free Library, the committee think it right to state that no such power as that suggested is vested in them. In any case they consider that the Free Library will not interfere in any way with the working of this library, and that within their respective lines there will be found ample room for both institutions in this town and neighbourhood. It is, therefore, their intention to give a cordial welcome to the Belfast Free Library as a fellow agent and helper in the cause for which this society was founded ninety-five years ago – viz. 'that of Promoting Knowledge'.

J. J. Murphy, President of the Belfast Society for Promoting
Knowledge

31st – Under Siege in Lucknow

About 7, Sir Henry came down from Cantonments with a large escort, and was received with great cheering; four more guns came down with him; every preparation was made, expecting an attack that night; every man was at his gun, and the slow matches lighted in readiness. There was no chance of sleeping down in this hot Babel, so I and several other ladies took our bedding up on the roof and slept there; it was a lovely moonlit night, and never shall I forget the scene. The panorama of Lucknow, from the top of the Residency, is splendid; and down immediately below us, in the compound, we could see the great guns and all the military preparations; all, every instant, expecting an attack, and firing going on in the distance. However, I was so worn out with the previous night that I lay down and was asleep in a second; of course I did not undress, nor had I done so the night before. I started frequently, fancying I heard the tramp of the mob coming; we had the two Padres up with us and they determined to watch by turns. Mr. P—— began; he had a double-barreled gun, pistol and sword, and walked round and round for two hours, and then awoke Mr. H——, but we could not help laughing, for Mr. H—— was so sleepy he told him he did not think there was any necessity for watching up there. I shall never forget the night; the moon and stars were so brilliant overhead, looking so peaceful in contrast to the scene below. I fixed up an umbrella over my head to keep off the ill effects of the moon; every hour the sentinels were calling to one another and answering, "All's well!" It was certainly more a scene from romance than real life. Sir Henry slept out, like the others, between two guns.

Mrs R. C. Germon, *A Diary Kept by Mrs R. C. Germon at Lucknow*

JUNE

1st – Death of the Prince Imperial

The Prince is carefully and calmly examining his bit and bridle, and, it is surmised, had not sufficiently tightened his girths. His grey horse is a fidgety, troublesome animal to mount, and now appears to be nervous and anxious to break away. Meanwhile all the escort stand to their horses and await the word, which the Prince now gives, "Prepare to mount." But this was the death-signal, for hardly had the order escaped the lips that gave it, and that spoke no other word on earth, than the fearful traditional "Usulu! Usulu!" awoke the echoes of the valley, and a tremendous volley was poured in from the favouring cover of the grass and mealies. All the horses swerved instinctively with terror, and some broke away. The Prince's tall grey, half mad with fright, became impossible to mount. Not a carbine was loaded, not a sentry placed. Surprise, the most unsoldierlike crime, was allowed, and white with fear each trooper galloped away to save himself, nor drew bridle-rein till miles of country placed safety in his path. Meanwhile, the gallant and unfortunate Prince is losing every chance of escape which the slightest attempt at succour would have given.

And then—oh, shame and humiliation!—this young lad, schooled to arms with English soldiers' sons, wearing an English uniform, and escorted by British soldiers to a bloody grave, was left alone to be speared to death, without a sword being drawn or a shot fired, even from a distance, in his defence.

The Zulus, seeing only one man unable to mount, burst at length from their treacherous cover, and with fiendish yells rush upon the Prince, who, holding the stirrup-leather with one hand and the holster-flap with the other, must have made one final and desperate attempt to spring into the saddle. But all is in vain, the untrustworthy leather gives way in his hand; his feet slip from under him; he falls beneath the horse, which treads upon his body and gallops away! The last that was seen of the Empress's beloved son was, that he was alone and on foot, with some dozen Zulus poising their assegais within a few feet from him, and his body was afterwards found pierced in front with some eighteen or twenty thrusts, and stripped of all but his mother's amulet.

Waller Asche & E. V. Wyatt-Edgell, *Story of the Zulu Campaign*

Napoleon Eugene Louis Jean Joseph Bonaparte (1856–79) was the son of the Emperor Napoleon III of France. He escaped to England after his father's defeat by the Prussians in 1870 and, following his father's death in 1873, he joined the British army. When the Zulu war began in 1879, the prince put pressure on the British government to let him serve, although there were objections from French political interests. He was sent to South Africa with his regiment. On 1 June he went out with a scouting party in an area thought to be safe, but the group was attacked by a party of Zulus, and the prince was killed.

2nd – Poetic Lamentation on the Insufficiency of Steam Locomotion in the Lake District

> Bright Summer spreads his various hue
> O'er nestling vales and mountains steep,
> Glad birds are singing in the blue,
> In joyous chorus bleat the sheep.
> But men are walking to and fro,
> Are riding, driving far and near,
> And nobody as yet can go
> By train to Buttermere.
>
> The sunny lake, the mountain track,
> The leafy groves are little gain,
> While Rydal's pleasant pathways lack
> The rattle of the passing train.
> But oh! what poet would not sing

That heaven-kissing rocky cone,
On whose steep side the railway king
Shall set his smoky throne?

Helvellyn in those happy days
With tunnelled base and grimy peak
Will mark the lamp's approaching rays,
Will hear the whistle's warning shriek:
Will note the coming of the mails,
And watch with unremitting stare
The dusky grove of iron rails
Which leads to Euston-square.

Wake, England, wake! 'tis now the hour
To sweep away this black disgrace –
The want of locomotive power
In so enjoyable a place.
Nature has done her part, and why
Is mightier man in his to fail?
I want to hear the porters cry;
'Change here for Ennerdale!'

Man! nature must be sought and found
In lonely pools, on verdant banks;
Go, fight her on her chosen ground,
Turn shapely Thirlmere into tanks:
Pursue her to her last retreats,
And if perchance a garden plot
Is found among the London streets,
Smoke, steam and spare it not.

Presumptuous nature! do not rate
Unduly high thy humble lot,
Nor vainly strive to emulate
The fame of Stephenson and Watt.
The beauties which thy lavish pride
Has scattered through the smiling land
Are little worth till sanctified
By man's completing hand.

                              J. K. Stephen

James Kenneth Stephen (1859–92) published several books of poetry. He was a cousin of Virginia Woolf, and tutor to Albert Victor, the Duke of Clarence and eldest son of the Prince of Wales. He died aged thirty-two as the combined result of a head injury, which had exacerbated a mental condition from which he suffered, and the news that his former pupil had succumbed to flu.

3rd – Teasing a Frenchman

Some years ago a famous and witty French critic was in London, with whom I walked the streets. I am ashamed to say that I informed him (being in hopes that he was about to write some papers regarding the manners and customs of this country) that all the statues he saw represented the Duke of Wellington. That on the arch opposite Apsley House? the Duke in a cloak, and a cocked-hat on horseback. That behind Apsley House in an airy fig-leaf costume? the Duke again. That in Cockspur Street? the Duke with a pig-tail—and so on. I showed him an army of Dukes.

W. M. Thackeray, *Roundabout Papers*

4th – The Prince's Derby Winner

In superabundant gratification at this right Royal triumph all conventionality was thrown to the winds. Hats rose in the air, sticks and umbrellas were cast away as mere bagatelles; and, with a marvellous decision of instinct, the huge throng broke in on the course, turned with one smiling, happy, radiant face towards the Royal box, and delivered such volleys of cheers as have never before, and probably never will again, be heard. There was no class distinction in this great demonstration. The aristocratic patrons of the Club enclosure were not differently constituted to the common clay. They cheered and cheered again, while the greater outside public waxed positively wild in raptures of enthusiasm ... Persimmon won magnificently; and the victory will go down to posterity with a halo of triumph. Henry V revelled in the memory of Crispian's Day; but who will say that an equal meed of glory will not attach to the day of St. Simon's gallant descendant?

Daily Telegraph, 4 June 1896

5th – On Musical Analysis

There probably are not many people in the world who are so utterly without any sort of musical sense and feeling as not to appreciate a good tune; but it must be confessed that there seem to be very few who really care for anything that is much more artistic or complicated than a simple song or a piece of dance music. Symphonies and sonatas and such larger forms of art are simply a bore to more than three-quarters of that portion of the human race which lies in the countries that are commonly described as civilised; and some people evidently have a suspicion that they are altogether a sham and delusion, got up to give conceited people a chance of pretending to be cleverer than they really are. As a matter of fact the same powers of mind which enable such people to enjoy a tune would also enable them to enjoy a great work of art like an orchestral symphony, if they cared to cultivate their powers, and took a little more respectful view of the art of music in general.

It seems strange indeed that people should make such a poor use of their capacities; and having the power to enjoy so many forms of art, should stop helplessly at the same level of dullness all their lives. The one musical object of most people is to get fresh impressions by constantly changing their favourite tunes; while they might be improving their intelligence up to the point of enjoying works of greater artistic value, which do not require to be frequently changed, because the more people hear them the more they find to enjoy in them. Of course there is no getting over people's dispositions. Even the highest capacities are more or less wasted in beings whose minds and moods are guided by the baleful spirit of frivolity. For them great composers and great poets lived and worked in vain. But for those whose views of life and art are more worthy of the dignity of a human being there are ways and means of rising from moderate powers of appreciation, such as may be met with among the least cultivated braches of society to the enjoyment of those great works of art which are among the greatest treasures of the world and the greatest triumphs of human powers.

Hubert Parry, published in the magazine *Atalanta*

Sir Charles Hubert Hastings Parry (1848–1918) was a celebrated composer. He became a professor at the Royal College of Music when it first opened and was its director from 1894. He is probably most famous for his setting of William Blake's poem 'Jerusalem'. Parry was particularly important for helping to revive English music; he influenced Sir Edward Elgar, Gustav Holst and Ralph Vaughan Williams amongst others.

6th – Mining 'Ladjword' (Lapis Lazuli)

The shaft by which you descent to the gallery is about ten feet square, and is not so perpendicular as to prevent your walking down. The gallery is eighty paces long, with a gentle descent; but it terminates abruptly in a hole twenty feet in diameter and as many deep.... No precaution has been taken to support by means of pillars the top of the mine, which formed of detached rocks wedged together, requires on a little more lateral expansion to drop into the cavity...

The method of extracting the lapis-lazuli is sufficiently simple. Under the spot to be quarried a fire is kindled, and its flame, fed by dry furze, is made to flicker over the surface. When he rock has become sufficiently soft, or, to use the workmen's expression, *nurím*, it is beaten with hammers, and flake after flake knocked off until the stone of which they are in search is discovered. Deep grooves are then picked out round the lapis-lazuli, into which crow-bars are inserted, and the stone and part of its matrix are detached.

The workmen enumerate three descriptions of ladjword. These are the Neeli, or indigo colour the Asmani, or light blue; and the Suvsi, or green. Their relative value is in the order in which I have mentioned them. The richest colours are found in the darkest rock, and the nearer the river the greater is said to be the purity of the stone. The search for ladjword is only prosecuted during winter, probably because labour in the mine being compulsory, the inhabitants are less injured by giving it in a season of comparative idleness than when the fields require their attention. Perhaps, also, during the cold of winter the rock may be more susceptible to the act of heat, and thus be more easily reduced, than we the temperature is higher.

Captain John Wood, *A Journey to the Source of the River Oxus*

7th – The Subject-Class

We must consider, too, that the possessors of the power have facilities in this case, greater than in any other, to prevent any uprising against it. Every one of the subjects lives under the very eye, and almost, it may be said, in the hands, of one of the masters in closer intimacy with him than with any of her fellow-subjects; with no means of combining against him, no power of even locally over mastering him, and, on the other hand, with the strongest motives for seeking his favour and avoiding to give him offence. In struggles for political emancipation, everybody knows how often its champions are bought off by bribes, or daunted by terrors. In the case of women, each individual of the subject-class is in a chronic state of bribery and intimidation combined. In setting up the standard of resistance, a large number of the leaders, and still more of the followers, must make an almost complete sacrifice of the pleasures or the alleviations of their own individual lot. If ever any system of privilege and enforced subjection had its yoke tightly riveted on those who are kept down by it, this has. I have not yet shown that it is a wrong system: but everyone who is capable of thinking on the subject must see that even if it is, it was certain to outlast all other forms of unjust authority. And when some of the grossest of the other forms still exist in many civilised countries, and have only recently been got rid of in others, it would be strange if that which is so much the deepest rooted had yet been perceptibly shaken anywhere. There is more reason to wonder that the protests and testimonies against it should have been so numerous and so weighty as they are.

John Stuart Mill, *On the Subjection of Women*

8th – Masters and Mistresses

It has been said that good masters and mistresses make good servants, and this to a great extent is true. There are certainly some men and women in the wide field of servitude whom it would be impossible to train into good servants, but the conduct of both master and mistress is seldom without its effect upon these dependents.

They are not mere machines, and no one has a right to consider them in that light. The sensible master and the kind mistress know, that if servants depend on them for their means of living, in their turn they are dependent on their servants for very many of the comforts of life; and that, with a proper amount of care in choosing servants, and treating them like reasonable beings, and making slight excuses for the shortcomings of human nature, they will, save in some exceptional case, be tolerably well served, and, in most instances, surround themselves with attached domestics.

Mrs Isabella Beeton, Mrs Beeton's Book of Household Management

9th – The Three Fishers

Three fishers went sailing away to the West,
Away to the West as the sun went down;
Each thought on the woman who loved him the best;
And the children stood watching them out of the town;
For men must work, and women must weep,
And there's little to earn, and many to keep,
Though the harbour bar be moaning.
Three wives sat up in the lighthouse tower.

And they trimmed the lamps as the sun went down;
They looked at the squall, and they looked at the shower,
And the night-rack came rolling up ragged and brown.
But men must work, and women must weep,
Though storms be sudden, and waters deep,
And the harbour bar be moaning.

Three corpses lay out on the shining sands
In the morning gleam as the tide went down,
And the women are weeping and wringing their hands
For those who will never come home to the town;
For men must work, and women must weep,
And the sooner it's over, the sooner to sleep;
And good-bye to the bar and its moaning.

Charles Kingsley

10th – Holidaying in Brighton

It is a Piccadilly crowd by the sea – exactly the same style of people you meet in Piccadilly, but freer in dress, and particularly in hats. All fashionable Brighton parades the King's Road twice a day, morning and afternoon, always on the side of the shops. The route is up and down the King's Road as far as Preston Street, back again and up East Street. Riding and driving Brighton extends its Rotten Row sometimes to Third Avenue, Hove. These well-dressed and leading people never look at the sea. Watching by the gold-plate shop you will not observe a single glance in the direction of the sea, beautiful as it is, gleaming under the sunlight. They do not take the slightest interest in sea, or sun, or sky, or the fresh breeze calling white horses from the deep. Their pursuits are purely "social," and neither ladies nor gentlemen ever go on the beach or lie where the surge comes to the feet. The beach is ignored; it is almost, perhaps quite vulgar; or rather it is entirely outside the pale. No one rows, very few sail; the sea is not "the thing" in Brighton, which is the least nautical of seaside places. There is more talk of horses.

Richard Jefferies, 'Sunny Brighton', *The Book of the Open Air*

11th – Watching Rooks

June, 1884:—I am very well, and greatly amused at this present by the rooks who are having a half holiday. Even rooks must relax from their sterner occupations sometimes. One of them has been sitting on the extreme point of a telephone pole, on the house opposite my window. The others came up and tried to push him off. He swore at them, and they retorted: at last they have succeeded in getting him off, but another one has taken his place and is swearing at being hustled. One solemn creature has been sitting on a revolving chimney pot, and going round and round as if he were at a Fair; another is balancing himself on the telephone wire, and one miscreant, perched on the wire close to its attachment, is trying to unpick it from the fastening. I wish they could feel a shock—not enough to hurt them, but just enough to surprise them—I should like to hear their exclamations. The noises they are making now are quite different from their usual discourse in trees.

Eliza Savage, *Letters between Samuel Butler and Miss E. M. A. Savage, 1871–1885*

12th – The Baccarat Scandal

Among us has arisen a second George IV, in the heir to the Throne of this vast Empire. He has been convicted of being concerned— and the people know him to have been concerned—in an infamous abomination; and the awful spectacle is presented of the heir to the Throne publicly acknowledging complicity in gambling transactions.

> The Reverend Dr Douglas, address delivered to the Wesleyan Methodist Conference, 12 June 1891

In September 1890 the Prince of Wales – later Edward VII – was one of a party of guests staying at Tranby Croft in Yorkshire, the guest of Arthur Wilson, a rich ship-owner. One of the other guests, Sir William Gordon-Cumming, a lieutenant-colonel in the Scots Guards, was accused of cheating while playing baccarat. He was asked to sign a paper promising never to play cards again; in return no one would mention the matter. The story got out, Gordon-Cummins sued Wilson for slander and lost. The court case, in which the Prince of Wales had to appear as a witness, shocked many people deeply. Not only was royalty involved, but also the prince had been gambling at a time when playing cards for money was illegal. For a time he was very unpopular.

13th – Dining with Gladstone

We dined with the Gladstones and I sat next to Gladstone. I thought him quite charming, so very agreeable and pleasant; he talked about monuments not being much use to commemorate people, and that those who were worth being remembered were so without monuments. He said he was trying to learn to sleep in the H. of C. but found it very difficult indeed and that he was annoyed by people behind putting their feet on the bench which shook it.

> Kate Stanley, *The Amberley Papers*

Kate Stanley (1844–74) married Lord Amberley, and was Bertrand Russell's mother. She came from a family of achievers; her mother had promoted women's education, being a founder of Girton College, Cambridge, the Girls Public Day School Trust and the Medical College for Women. Her sister Rosalind, Lady Carlisle, was a suffragist and supported the temperance movement. Lady Amberley demanded not only the right to vote but equal pay, equal education, equal access to professions and equality for wives. She died of diphtheria, aged thirty.

14th – Selling Girls

I have seen girls bought and sold just as young girls were at the time of the slave trade. Are you aware that there are gentlemen among the higher classes who pay so much per girl? When a gentleman sends to a professional brothel for a girl he pays for her. Is that not buying? By such a system the path of evil is made more easy for our sons and for the whole of the youth of this country. In as much as the moral restraint is withdrawn, the moment the government recognises and provides convenience for the practice of a vice which it declares necessary and venial.

Josephine Butler

Josephine Butler (1828–1906) was a feminist and social reformer. She was very concerned about prostitution; as an evangelical Christian, she condemned the sin but thought the women involved were exploited by men and that there were double standards of morality. The Contagious Diseases Act had been passed to try and control prostitution and the spread of venereal diseases in the army, but it involved a humiliating examination of any woman accused by the police. Infected women were locked up in hospital for three months; any woman refusing examination was imprisoned. She campaigned tirelessly for the abolition of the act. A further campaign highlighted the extent of child prostitution, particularly in London.

15th – A Taste to be Prayed For

If I were to pray for a taste which should stand me in stead under every variety of circumstances, and be a source of happiness and cheerfulness to me through life, and a shield against its ills, however things might go amiss, and the world frown upon me, it would be a taste for reading. I speak of it of course only as a worldly advantage, and not in the slightest degree as superseding or derogating from the higher office and surer and stronger panoply of religious principles—but as a taste, an instrument and a mode of pleasurable gratification. Give a man this taste, and the means of gratifying it, and you can hardly fail of making a happy man, unless, indeed, you put into his hands a most perverse selection of books. You place him in contact with the best society in every period of history—with the wisest, the wittiest—with the tenderest, the bravest, and the purest characters who have adorned humanity. You make him a denizen of all nations—a contemporary of all ages. The world has been created for him.

Sir J. Herschel, *Address to the Subscribers to the Windsor Public Library*

Sir John Herschel (1792–1871) was the son of the astronomer William Herschel. He was a scientist – mathematician, astronomer, chemist, inventor and photographer. For six years he served as Master of the Mint, but he turned down the presidency of the Royal Society.

16th – Wreck of the Drummond Castle

DRUMMOND CASTLE: Castle Line. Captain Pierce. Built by Elder & Co., Glasgow, 1881
Shortly before midnight on June 16th, 1896, homeward bound from Delagoa Bay and Capetown, she struck a group of rocks called the 'Pierres Vertes' near Molene, off Ushant, and sank in three minutes with the loss of all her passengers and crew save three persons. Details were provided by the survivors, Charles Wood, Quartermaster, J. Godbolt, seaman and Mr. Marquardt, passenger. Sailed from Capetown on May 28th, 1896 with 104 officers and crew and 143 passengers. After a stop of a few hours at Las Palmas on June 12th, she continued her voyage at full speed until, on June 16th, in a dense fog and a smooth sea, she struck rocks at 23:00. Captain Pierce immediately ordered all boats to be lowered but the sea swept in so fast that the boats were swamped before they could be got out.

Quartermaster Wood was in the act of loosing the cutter when he was dragged down by the sinking ship but resurfaced to cling onto some floating debris where he found Godbolt. They were picked up the next morning, June 17th, by some fishermen and landed on the island of Molene. Marquardt was rescued by another fishing boat.

Many corpses were washed up on the island and they were laid out in the houses of the village. The following day the corpses were buried, without coffins, in a number of graves. Wood was scarce on the island. Other bodies were washed up over the surrounding area. It was surmised that Captain Pierce steered for a safe distance off Ushant light so that the keepers could report his passage. With this object in view, she was carried out of her proper course by tidal currents. The survivors attested that no lights had been sighted when the vessel struck. Subscriptions were opened in London and Capetown for the relief of the families who would suffer financial distress, the Fund being headed by handsome contributions from the Castle Line and Sir Donald Currie.

Newspaper report dated 27 June 1896

The inhabitants of the islands of Ouessant and La Molène off the coast of western Brittany were extremely poor, but they did what they could for the victims of the *Drummond Castle* shipwreck. Queen Victoria was so impressed with the care and generosity of the islanders that she asked what she could do for them. They asked for a clock – she sent the man who had been responsible for Big Ben to install one – and a water tank so they could catch the winter rain for summer use. She presented every woman with a medal; these are rarely seen today as the women valued them so much they asked to be buried with them.

17th – Pugin's Publishing Problem

The success attending on the publication of the 'Contrasts' induced Pugin very soon afterwards, in 1841, to prepare another work, entitled 'True Principles of Gothic Architecture.' This volume was published by Mr. Weale, the architectural bookseller. It has been already noticed that Pugin's former work, 'The Contrasts', was published by himself at St. Marie's Grange. He was compelled to take this course in consequence of his failing to find a publisher who would incur the responsibility of giving to the world a work so strongly seasoned with personal abuse.

Benjamin Ferrey, Recollections of A. N. Welby Pugin and
His Father

18th – Bees in Mourning

I think one of the most curious notions is that connected with the manner of dealing with the bees when a death occurs in the household they belong to, and especially when the death in question is that of the master or head of the household. I remember when I was a schoolboy in Essex, my father being then curate of a country parish not far from Colchester, the news came that the rector was dead, which of course implied the consequent removal, after a space of weeks or months, of the curate. But that did not affect me or fix itself on my attention as did the proceedings taken in connection with the bees, of which a large stock belonged to the rectory. I cannot remember who the person acting on behalf of the rectorial family was, or by what authority the said person acted; but I do remember the key of the main door of the house being taken, together with sundry strips of some black material, and a kind of procession organised for a formal visit to the bee-stand. And when it was reached the bearer of the key proceeded to bind a black strip round each hive—this was called "putting the bees into mourning"— and as each strip was knotted, three taps with the key were given, and each hive severally informed that the master was dead. There was a sort of weird solemnity about the whole proceeding which produced a lasting impression on my young mind.

J. C. Atkinson, *Forty Years in a Moorland Parish*

19th – Cleopatra's Needle Arrives in London

After a very favourable voyage, the Needle ship arrived at Gravesend to-day, about 11 o'clock, and was towed to Blackwall. Great enthusiasm was manifested by a large number of persons who witnessed the passage of the vessel up the Thames. Mr. Dixon received a message from the Queen expressing the gratification of her Majesty at hearing of the safe arrival of the Needle. The Princess of Wales has also conveyed to Dr. Erasmus Wilson her appreciation of the liberality and public spirit which he has shown in defraying the cost of transporting the Needle from Egypt to England.

Annual Register, June 1879

20th – Victoria Becomes Queen

Welcome now, Victoria!
Welcome to the throne!
May all the trades begin to stir,
Now you are Queen of England;
For your most gracious Majesty,
May see what wretched poverty,
Is to be found on England's ground,
Now you are Queen of England.

While o'er the country you preside,
Providence will be your guide,
The people then will never chide
Victoria, Queen of England.
She doth declare it her intent
To extend reform in Parliament,
On doing good she's firmly bent,
While she is Queen of England.

Says she, I'll try my utmost skill,
That the poor may have their fill;
Forsake them! – no, I never will,
When I am Queen of England.
For oft my mother said to me,
Let this your study always be,
To see the people blest and free,
Should you be Queen of England.

And now, my daughter, you do reign,
Much opposition to sustain,
You'll surely have, before you gain
The blessings of Old England.
O yes, dear mother, that is true,
I know my sorrows won't be few,
Poor people shall have work to do,
When I am Queen of England.

I will encourage every trade,
For their labour must be paid,

In this free country then she said,
Victoria, Queen of England;
The poor-law bill, with many more,
Shall be trampled on the floor –
The rich must keep the helpless poor,
While I am Queen of England.

The Royal Queen of Britain's isle
Soon will make the people smile,
Her heart none can the least defile,
Victoria, Queen of England.
Although she is of early years,
She is possess'd of tender cares,
To wipe away the orphan's tears,
While she is Queen of England.

With joy each Briton doth exclaim,
Both far and near across the main,
Victoria we now proclaim
The Royal Queen of England;
Long may she live, and happy be,
Adorn'd with robes of Royalty,
With blessings from her subjects free,
While she is Queen of England.

In every town and village gay,
The bells shall ring, and music play,
Upon her Coronation-day,
Victoria, Queen of England.
While her affections we do win,
And every day fresh blessings bring,
Ladies, help me for to sing,
Victoria, Queen of England.

                                              Anonymous

21st – The Service for the Golden Jubilee

I sat *alone* (oh! without my beloved husband, for whom this would
have been such a proud day!) where I sat forty-nine years ago

and received the homage of the Princes and Peers, but in the old Coronation Chair of Edward III, with the old stone brought from Scotland, on which the old Kings of Scotland used to be crowned. My robes were beautifully draped on the chair. The service was very well done and arranged. The *Te Deum*, by my darling Albert, sounded beautiful, and the anthem, by Dr. Bridge, was fine, especially the way in which the National Anthem and dear Albert's Chorale were worked in. Dr. Stainer's beautiful *Amen* at the end of the service was most impressive. When the service was concluded, each of my sons, sons-in-law, grandsons (including little Alfred) and grandsons-in-law, stepped forward, bowed, and in succession kissed my hand, I kissing each; and the same with the daughters, daughters-in-law (poor dear Helen being nearly upset and for whom I felt so deeply), granddaughters, and granddaughter-in-law. They curtsied as they came up and I embraced them warmly. It was a very moving moment, and tears were in some of their eyes.

Queen Victoria, Journal entry, *Letters of Queen Victoria*

22nd – A Shropshire Lad

From Clee to heaven the beacon burns,
  The shires have seen it plain,
From north and south the sign returns
  And beacons burn again.

Look left, look right, the hills are bright,
  The dales are light between,
Because 'tis fifty years to-night
  That God has saved the Queen.

Now, when the flame they watch not towers
  About the soil they trod,
Lads, we'll remember friends of ours
  Who shared the work with God.

To skies that knit their heartstrings right,
  To fields that bred them brave,
The saviours come not home to-night:
  Themselves they could not save.

It dawns in Asia, tombstones show
    And Shropshire names are read;
And the Nile spills his overflow
    Beside the Severn's dead.

We pledge in peace by farm and town
    The Queen they served in war,
And fire the beacons up and down
    The land they perished for.

'God save the Queen' we living sing,
    From height to height 'tis heard;
And with the rest your voices ring,
    Lads of the Fifty-third.

Oh, God will save her, fear you not:
    Be you the men you've been,
Get you the sons your fathers got,
    And God will save the Queen.

                A. E. Houseman, 1887

Alfred Edward Housman (1859–1936) was a poet and scholar. He worked at the Patent Office in London, then became a professor of Latin: first at London University, then at Cambridge. His collection of poems *A Shropshire Lad*, based on a part of the country he had never visited, was very popular during the First World War, two decades after it was published in 1896. Their simplicity and lyricism made them popular with contemporary composers, who set them as songs.

23rd– A Birthday and an Accident

Last Saturday it was Geofs birthday he was ten years old, he got several presents, and we all had tea in the hay—On Friday poor Papa had a very bad accident at the Brewery, he was in one of the cellars when an immense safe or chest fell onto him & hurt his leg very much, and made a hole in it, he could not walk but they carried him up into his office and sent for Mama directly; it might have been a very bad accident, and he said he never was so near being killed in his life, for the safe was so big and heavy that five men could hardly lift it, but another safe prevented its falling on him & only let it hurt his leg—he slept in the brewery that night & in the morning I went up in the carriage to see him & he most unexpectedly was able to go home with Mama, he could not walk or stand but Uncle Charles & Uncle Barclay each held him, & so he managed to get downstairs & into the carriage, somehow I don't know how, the two Uncles had come to see him with Aunt Barclay—he got to Leytonstone very comfortably & then he was helped into the drawing-room, and lay on the sofa the rest of the day.

Tuesday—Papa I am glad to say is getting on very nicely, of course he will not be able to walk for several days, for his leg is stiff & bad, but it does not pain him when he keeps it quite still.

Ellen Buxton, *Journal*

24th – Andrew Lang Rescues a Cat

All beasts were his friends, just because they *were* beasts, unless they had been very badly brought up. He never could resist a cat, and cats, like beggars, tell each other these things and profit by them. A cat knew quite well that it had only to go on sitting for a few days outside the window where the man was writing, and that if it began to snow or even to rain, the window would be pushed up and the cat would spend the rest of its days stretched in front of the fire, with a saucer of milk beside it, and fish for every meal.

But life with cats was not all peace, and once a terrible thing happened when Dickon-draw-the-blade was the Puss in Possession. His master was passing through London on the way to take a journey to some beautiful old walled towns in the south of France where the English fought in the Hundred Years War, and he meant to spend a few weeks in the country along the Loire which is bound up with the memory of Joan of Arc. Unluckily, the night after he arrived from Scotland Dickon went out for a walk on the high trellis behind the house, and once there did not know how to get down again. Of course it was quite easy, and there were ropes of Virginia creeper to help, but Dickon lost his presence of mind, and instead of doing anything sensible only stood and shrieked, while his master got ladders and steps and clambered about in the dark and in the cold, till he put Dickon on the ground again. Then

Dickon's master went to bed, but woke up so ill that he was obliged to do without the old towns, and go when he was better to a horrid place called Cannes, all dust and tea-parties.

Mrs Andrew Lang, from her Preface to *Strange Stories*

25th – Family Trip to the Great Exhibition

This morning, Papa, Mama, Emmie, Johnney and I all went to the Exhibition, and had a charming day there, we went principally to the English oil colour painting, which I think are much more beautiful than any of the foreign ones, there are a great many of Gainsborough's and Reynold's there, and a lovely picture of the Prince and Princess of Prussia and their two children, and one of the Queen & the Prince Consort—We also went into the French Court which was most lovely, there were such exquisite pieces of spar made up into different things, and Papa bought a lovely little vase made of it, set in gold—Then there were most beautiful laces, and Babys robes &c they were lovely, and a hood we saw was made entirely of the lace plant. When we had seen heaps of other lovely things that I cannot describe, we had an ice and then went to the International Bazaar.

Ellen Buxton, *Journal*

26th – Dickens Invites a Friend to Stay with Him in Brighton

Tune – 'Lesbia hath a beaming eye'

1.
Lemon is a little hipped,
And this is Lemon's true position;
He is not pale, he's not white-lipped,
Yet wants a little fresh condition.
Sweeter 'tis to gaze upon
Old ocean's rising, falling billows,
Than on the houses every one,
That form the street called Saint Anne's Willers.
Oh, my Lemon, round and fat,

1. Queen Victoria *c.* 1843. The monarch who lends her name to a time of great change and discovery, Victoria ascended the throne at just eighteen, and her sixty-four-year reign was the longest for any monarch in British history, until she was recently surpassed by Elizabeth II in September 2015. (Courtesy of the National Gallery of Art)

Left: 2. '*La Saison*'. Keeping up with fashion was as important in the Victorian period as at any time in history. Clear instructions were also given for dressing in black or similar demure shades during the mourning period. Mourners who couldn't afford to purchase an entirely new wardrobe would have their original clothes dyed black. (Courtesy of the Rijksmuseum)

Right: 3. These ladies, by turning to view the locomotive in the background, give us a full view of their elaborate fashions, bonnets and hairstyles. (Courtesy of the Rijksmuseum)

Opposite top: 4. Florence Nightingale (1820–1910). The 'Lady with the Lamp' was the founder of modern nursing during the Victorian era, and she is most famously known for her treatments during the Crimean War (1853–6). In this colour lithograph by J. A. Vinter she is seen, along with others she has trained, tending to the wounded. (Courtesy of the Wellcome Library, London)

Opposite bottom: 5. Charge of the Light Brigade. Despite the fact that it ended in retreat and a large number of casualties, the Charge of the Light Brigade was immortalised in the famous poem by Alfred Lord Tennyson. (Courtesy of the Library of Congress)

6. *Keelmen Heaving in Coals by Midnight*, J. M. W. Turner. Turner's works encompassed watercolours, oils, and engravings, and became known as the 'painter of light'. Turner manages to capture the laborious reality that kept the Industrial Revolution turning, while romanticising the landscape that provides the background to their toil. (Courtesy of the National Gallery of Art)

7. The first transatlantic telegraph cable connected the old world with the new in 1858, using a cable nearly 2,000 miles long, laid at a depth of about 2 miles on the ocean floor. Sadly it broke down after only three weeks, but its potential value was so great two more substantial cables were laid soon after, using Brunel's ship the SS *Great Eastern*. (Courtesy of the Library of Congress)

8. London Fog combined river mist, soot from millions of coal fires, and sulphur dioxide. Nicknamed 'pea-souper' because of its yellow colour, it could be lethal. Pea-soupers are particularly associated with Victorian London, though they had been known for centuries. They required carriages to light torches during the day and allowed pickpockets to thieve unnoticed. (Courtesy of the Wellcome Library, London)

9. Raising Cleopatra's Needle. The obelisk was brought to London to commemorate the victory over Napoleon in 1815, and erected in 1878. The obelisk, although not from Cleopatra's time, is so named because it came over from her royal city, Alexandria. (Courtesy of the Wellcome Library, London)

Left: 10. This cartoon, titled 'British Benevolence' and published 19 July 1882, provides an American perspective on the British Empire and British expansion. The British lion uses its fists (labelled Army and Navy) to batter its way across the African continent. Below the cartoon is a quote from Earl Granville: 'It is painful to be obliged to use force against the weak'. (Courtesy of the Library of Congress)

Right: 11. Jumbo (1860–85), seen here carrying a group of children on a music cover illustration, was the first African elephant to be seen alive in Europe. He lived in London for sixteen years and gave rides to visitors. (Courtesy of the Library of Congress)

Opposite: 12. *Mrs Beeton's Guide to Household Management*, frontispiece. Originally serialised in *The Englishwoman's Domestic Magazine*, Mrs Isabella Beeton provided a guide for all aspects of running a household. Originally published in 1861, it has never been out of print. (Courtesy of the Wellcome Library, London)

BEETON'S

Book of

HOUSEHOLD

MANAGEMENT

EDITED

BY

MRS ISABELLA BEETON

S. O. BEETON

248 STRAND — LONDON. W.C.

13. Queen Victoria's First Council. The eighteen-year-old queen is said to have acted with 'perfect calmness and self-possession', according to Charles Grenville. This etching by F. Fraenkel, after a portrait by Sir David Wilkie, shows Grenville seated at the far right. (Courtesy of the British Library Flickr)

14. The Aftermath of Lucknow. Skulls and ribcages litter the courtyard after the siege of Lucknow in British India after the mutiny of 1857. The Residency (similar to an embassy) was evacuated and then abandoned. (Courtesy of the Wellcome Library, London)

Above: 15. The Great Exhibition opened in 1851 and was the first international exposition of manufactured products. Countries came to show off their designs but the British exhibits were deemed superior. (Courtesy of the Yale Center for British Art, Paul Mellon Collection)

Right: 16. The Crystal Palace interior. The Great Exhibition building itself was designed by Joseph Paxton, who had built the Duke of Devonshire's greenhouses. It had 300,000 vast panes of glass and over twenty-four miles of guttering. (Courtesy of the Rijksmuseum)

OLIVER ASKING FOR MORE.

Left: 17. Mary Kingsley made three trips to Africa in total between 1893 and 1900. She collected specimens and wrote about her experiences. She lived among the native populations and learnt from their experiences, writing two books about her travels. (Courtesy of the Wellcome Library, London)

Right: 18. 'Please sir!' Charles Dicken's *Oliver Twist* provides a social commentary on the workhouses, and explores themes such as London's criminal activity, the Poor Laws and how children were treated. (Courtesy of the British Library Flickr)

Opposite top: 19. *Donkey Rides on the Beach*, Isaac Israel. Donkey rides have their origins in Victorian pastimes. (Courtesy of the Rijksmuseum).

Opposite bottom: 20. This anonymous photograph, taken between 1878 and 1890, shows Victorian holidaymakers enjoying the growing tourism industry on the beach at Brighton. (Courtesy of the Rijksmuseum)

21. SER No. 136 *Folkstone*, at the Great Exhibition 1851. The photo shows a Crampton locomotive, the type that Robert Stephenson and Company built for the South Eastern Railway. (Courtesy of the Rijksmuseum)

22. *William Massey-Stanley Driving His Cabriolet in Hyde Park*. The Victorian age designed the public park as being for the working masses, with a focus on ration and ordered recreation. (Yale Center for British Art, Paul Mellon Collection)

23. This Torbay Express train, shown here on its modern journey between Plymouth and Bristol, steams along the South Devon Railway. Built by Brunel, the South Devon line runs along the coast before streaking inland and provides some of the best railway scenery. (Courtesy of Stewart Black on Flickr)

24. Horse-drawn omnibuses provided some of the first affordable public transport. This example, photographed in 1864, was operated by Thomas Tilling. They ran to timetables and passengers did not need to book in advance. (Courtesy of rv1864 on Flickr)

Left: 25. Charles Darwin (1809–82). Fascinated by nature, Darwin published the *Origin of Species* in 1859. Aside from this, he published books on coral atolls, emotional expression and earthworms. (Courtesy of the British Library Flickr)

Below: 26 & 27. William Ewart Gladstone (1809–98), shown here on the left, was a Liberal peer and served as prime minister four times, more than any other. Benjamin Disraeli, Lord Beaconsfield (1804–81), shown here on the right, was a Conservative peer and twice prime minister. Disraeli and Gladstone hated each other. (Courtesy of the British Library Flickr)

28. Colonel Robert Baden-Powell is best known for founding the Scouting movement, but he became a national hero after the siege of Mafeking, during which he was the garrison commander. Here he is seen inspecting the horses at Mafeking. (Courtesy of the Wellcome Library, London)

29. Lady Sarah Wilson (1865–1929) was the aunt of Winston Churchill and the first female war correspondent. She sent reports of the siege of Mafeking to London during the Second Boer War. In the original caption to this image she is described as 'having the finest siege residence in Mafeking'. (Courtesy of the Wellcome Library, London)

30. Zulu warriors, armed with spears and shields. The Anglo-Zulu War resulted in British annexation of the previously independent Zulu kingdom; it became part of the colony of Natal, and later part of South Africa. (Courtesy of the Library of Congress)

31. A memorial to the Prince Imperial, the exiled heir to the French throne, is located in Chislehurst, in south-east London. When the prince's body was recovered, it was brought back to Britain and was buried in Chislehurst before being moved to the Imperial Crypt in Hampshire. (Courtesy of James Brewins on Flickr)

Oh, my bright, my right, my tight 'un,
Think a little what you're at—
Don't stay at home, but come to Brighton!

2.
Lemon has a coat of frieze,
But all so seldom Lemon wears it,
That it is a prey to fleas,
And ev'ry moth that's hungry tears it.
Oh, that coat's the coat for me,
That braves the railway sparks and breezes,
Leaving every engine free
To smoke it, till its owner sneezes!
Then my Lemon, round and fat,
L., my bright, my right, my tight 'un,
Think a little what you're at—
On Tuesday first, come down to Brighton!

T. Sparkler
Charles Dickens, *Letters*

27th – My Aims

If I may speak of the objects I have had more or less definitely in view since I began to ascent of my hillock, they are briefly these: To promote the increase of natural knowledge and to forward the application of scientific methods of investigation of all the problems of life to the best of my ability, in the conviction which has grown with my growth and strengthened with my strength that there is no alleviation for the sufferings of mankind except veracity of thought and of action, and the resolute facing of the world as it is when the garment of make-believe by which pious hands have hidden its uglier features is stripped off.

It is with this intent that I have subordinated any reasonable, or unreasonable, ambition for scientific fame which I may have permitted myself to entertain to other ends; to the popularisation of science; to the development and organisation of scientific education; to the endless series of battles and skirmishes over evolution; and to untiring opposition to that ecclesiastical spirit, that clericalism, which in England, as everywhere else, and to whatever denomination it may belong, is the deadly enemy of science.

T. H. Huxley, 'Autobiography', from *Collected Essays*

Thomas Henry Huxley (1825–95) trained as a doctor before sailing as an assistant surgeon on HMS *Rattlesnake* to the Great Barrier Reef. Here he studied and collected marine organisms; the work he did and his subsequent publications supported Darwin's evolutionary theories. Highly esteemed as a scientist, Huxley eventually became president of the Royal Society. He was also interested in education, and was instrumental in setting up the first biological laboratory in Britain. He is credited with introducing the word 'agnostic', which he argued as describing his philosophical viewpoint.

28th – Prince Albert Lays a Foundation Stone

This afternoon at four o'clock we rode to see Prince Albert laying the foundation stone of a new "Merchant Seaman's Orphan Asylum": Papa went to see the stone laid, with Uncle Barclay. So at four Johnny Geoff Taffy and I got onto our ponies and rode to Aunt Barclay's where we found Edith, Hugh, Ada and Alice going to ride with us, so we went directly to the Whipps Cross corner and there on the grass we drew up our ponies all in line and so waited for about a quarter of an hour, then at five minutes to five we saw all the people's heads turn towards London and Aunt Barclay called out to us that Prince Consort was coming first came two people on horseback then a carriage with four bay horses and postilions in which was Prince Albert, with two gentlemen beside him, so when he saw all us eight children drawn up in a line on our ponies, and the boys took off their hats, he took off his hat to us, and Aunt Barclay heard and saw him say—"Oh how pretty"—, then he passed on and another carriage came with four grey horses with some more gentlemen in, then when they had all passed, we galloped as hard as we could home to Aunt Barclay's, and rode into the hay field and jumped over the long lines of hay and then went to one end of the field and galloped as hard as we could go to the other ...

Ellen Buxton, *Journal*

29th – The Coronation

June 29th, 1838

The Coronation (which, thank God, is over) went off very well. The day was fine, without heat or rain—the innumerable multitude which thronged the streets orderly and satisfied. The appearance of the Abbey was beautiful, particularly the benches of the Peeresses, who were blazing with diamonds. The entry of Soult was striking. He was saluted with a murmur of curiosity and applause as he passed through the nave, and nearly the same, as he advanced along the choir. His appearance is that of a veteran warrior, and he walked alone, with his numerous suite following at a respectful distance, preceded by heralds and ushers, who received him with marked attention, more certainly than any of the other Ambassadors. The Queen looked very diminutive, and the effect of the procession itself was spoilt by being too crowded; there was not interval enough between the Queen and the Lords and others going before her. The Bishop of London (Blomfield) preached a very good sermon. The different actors in the ceremonial were very imperfect in their parts, and had neglected to rehearse them. Lord John Thynne, who officiated for the Dean of Westminster, told me that nobody knew what was to be done except the Archbishop and himself (who had rehearsed), Lord Willoughby (who is experienced in these matters), and the Duke of Wellington, and consequently there was a continual difficulty and embarrassment, and the Queen never knew what she was to do next. They made her leave her chair and enter into St. Edward's Chapel before the prayers were concluded, much to the discomfiture of the Archbishop. She said to John Thynne, 'Pray tell me what I am to do, for they don't know;' and at the end, when the orb was put into her hand, she said to him, 'What am I to do with it?' 'Your Majesty is to carry it, if you please, in your hand.' 'Am I?' she said; 'it is very heavy.' The ruby ring was made for her little finger instead of the fourth, on which the rubric prescribes that it should be put. When the Archbishop was to put it on, she extended the former, but he said it must be on the latter. She said it was too small, and she could not get it on. He said it was right to put it there, and, as he insisted, she yielded, but had first to take off her other rings, and then this was forced on, but it hurt her very much, and as soon as the ceremony was over she was obliged to bathe her finger in iced water in order to get it off. The noise and confusion were very great when the medals were thrown about by Lord Surrey, everybody scrambling with all their might and main to get them, and none more vigorously than the Maids of Honour. There was a great demonstration of applause when the Duke of Wellington did homage. Lord Rolle, who is between eighty and ninety, fell down as he was getting up the steps of the throne. Her first impulse was to rise, and when afterwards he came again to do homage she said, 'May I not get up and meet him?' and then rose from the throne and advanced down one or two of the steps to prevent his coming up, an act of graciousness and kindness which made a great sensation. It is, in fact, the remarkable union of *naïveté*, kindness, nature, good nature, with propriety and dignity, which makes her so admirable and so endearing to those about her, as she certainly is. I have been repeatedly told that they are all warmly attached to her, but that all feel the impossibility of for a moment losing sight of the respect which they owe her. She never ceases to be a Queen, but is always the most charming, cheerful, obliging, unaffected Queen in the world.

Charles Greville, Diary

30th – Dealing with a Leopard

Every now and then I cautiously took a look at him with one eye round a rock-edge, and he remained in the same position. My feelings tell me he remained there twelve months, but my calmer judgment puts the time down at twenty minutes; and at last, on taking another cautious peep, I saw he was gone. At the time I wished I knew exactly where, but I do not care about that detail now, for I saw no more of him. He had moved off in one of those weird lulls which you get in a tornado, when for a few seconds the wild herd of hurrying winds seem to have lost themselves, and wander round crying and wailing like lost souls, until their common rage seizes them again and they rush back to their work of destruction. It was an immense pleasure to have seen the great creature like that. He was so evidently enraged and baffled by the uproar and dazzled by the floods of lightning that swept down into the deepest recesses of the forest, showing at one second every detail of twig, leaf, branch, and stone round you, and then leaving you in a sort of swirling dark until the next flash came; this, and the great conglomerate roar of the wind, rain and thunder, was enough to bewilder any living thing.

I have never hurt a leopard intentionally; I am habitually kind to animals, and besides I do not think it is ladylike to go shooting things with a gun. Twice, however, I have been in collision with them. On one occasion a big leopard had attacked a dog, who, with her family, was occupying a broken-down hut next to mine. The dog was a half-bred boarhound, and a savage brute on her own account. I, being roused by the uproar, rushed out into the feeble moonlight, thinking she was having one of her habitual turns-up with other dogs, and I saw a whirling mass of animal matter within a yard of me. I fired two mushroom-shaped native stools in rapid succession into the brown of it, and the meeting broke up into a leopard and a dog. The leopard crouched, I think to spring on me. I can see its great, beautiful, lambent eyes still and I seized an earthen water-cooler and flung it straight at them. It was a noble shot; it burst on the leopard's head like a shell and the leopard went for bush one time. Twenty minutes after people began to drop in cautiously and inquire if anything was the matter, and I civilly asked them to go and ask the leopard in the bush, but they firmly refused. We found the dog had got her shoulder slit open as if by a blow from a cutlass, and the leopard had evidently seized the dog by the scruff of her neck, but owing to the loose folds of skin no bones were broken and she got round all right after much ointment from me, which she paid me for with several bites. Do not mistake this for a sporting adventure. I no more thought it was a leopard than that it was a lotus when I joined the fight. My other leopard was also after a dog. Leopards always come after dogs, because once upon a time the leopard and the dog were great friends, and the leopard went out one day and left her whelps in charge of the dog, and the dog went out flirting, and a snake came and killed the whelps, so there is ill-feeling to this day between the two. For the benefit of sporting readers whose interest may have been excited by the mention of big game, I may remark that the largest leopard skin I ever measured myself was, tail included, 9 feet 7 inches. It was a dried skin, and every man who saw it said, 'It was the largest skin he had ever seen, except one that he had seen somewhere else.'

Mary Kingsley, *Travels in West Africa,* 1897

JULY

1st – A Whaling Incident: Barque 'Flying Childers'

I was cruising off the south-west cape of Tasmania, in company with several other vessels; at daylight we were among sperm whales. All the ships lowered their boats, and were in continual chase the whole day. About two P.M., the chief mate, being close to the vessel, went on board; I and the second mate being some miles to windward. The mate had only been on board a short time, when a whale came close to the vessel; he immediately lowered and struck.

The whale took to running before the wind and sea. In hauling up to kill him, the whale made a sudden stop, the boat ran on top of him and was upset; one man had his shoulder dislocated, and another lost his hold of the boat and was drowned. The whale was still towing the boat with him, and it was with difficulty that, after some time, the men were enabled to cut the line and to get clear.

The mate and remaining men lashed the oars across the boat to float it. The ship, being to windward, ran down and picked them up. They got the wounded man on board, bailed the water out of the boat, took two other men from the ship, again fastened to the whale, and killed it without any boat near them. On my return on board, I found a whale alongside, and this was the first I knew of the unfortunate accident that had occurred.

E. L., published in *The Albatross*, newsletter of
SS *Great Britain*

2nd – The Albert Memorial

Here, beneath a somewhat flimsy imitation of a Gothic shrine of the thirteenth century, the seated statue of the Prince is barely distinguishable through the dazzlement of a gilded glitter. The pedestal, whose classic forms so strangely contrast with the Gothic statue above, is decorated with a vast number of statuettes in high relief, representing different painters, sculptors, and musicians, from Hiram and Belzaleel, Cheops and Sennacherib, to Pugin and Barry and Cockerell.

Augustus Hare, *Walks in London*

Queen Victoria's husband, Prince Albert, died of typhoid fever in 1861, aged forty-two. The queen was devastated, withdrawing from public view for many years. However, she was keen that there should be a memorial for Albert, and a committee was formed to supervise. The queen chose the design submitted by the architect George Gilbert Scott, and a site in Kensington was selected, near the museums Albert had helped to found. The neo-Gothic design includes a statue of Albert, and many references to his interests and achievements.

3rd – Death of Sir Robert Peel

Sir Robert Peel is no more. After three days of excessive suffering, at a few minutes past eleven last night, the greatest statesman of his time quitted the scene in which he had performed so conspicuous a part. Even the anxiety and the rumours which have penetrated every household since the first alarming intelligence will have failed to prepare the country for the deplorable result. Except, indeed, in the field of battle, never was the transition from a life to death so marked and so touching. On Friday the House of Commons, which for more than forty years has witnessed the triumphs and reverses of the great Conservative chief, was filled with an extraordinary assemblage anxious for the result of a great political crisis. Sir Robert addressed them with an ability and a spirit which recalled his more youthful efforts, and more powerful days. It was the first occasion for four years that elicited any serious or direct opposition to the policy of Her Majesty's present advisers, and, not to reopen a debate full of mistakes and crosspurposes, it must be allowed that the speech was at least an admirable defence of the principles on which Sir Robert and his colleagues had ever proceeded. He sat down, as our report says, amid "loud and long-continued cheering." Within a few hours the statesman who had commanded the applause of that listening senate was a wreck of life and strength, shattered, feeble, restless, and agonized. The feverish interval is past. That heart has ceased to beat; that tongue is ever still. That ardent spirit and capacious intellect are now in another and an unknown world.

The Times, 3 July 1850

4th – Doing Without Servants

When we awoke we found all the servants had deserted excepting my Kitmagar and Mrs. B—'s, and one or two Ayahs. The F—'s had not one servant left, so we were obliged to get up and act as servants ourselves, and do everything, excepting the cooking, even to washing plates and dishes; and perhaps it was a good thing, for it kept us from dwelling on our misery. Dear Charlie came to see me in the afternoon, and brought a jug of milk for the poor children. I was glad to hear he had had a good luncheon, for the day before when he came he said he had had nothing for some days but dal (peas) and rice; we happened to be at dinner, and I gave him a piece of meat, but he seemed too much done up to eat it, and actually carried it away in a piece of paper to some other gentleman who could get none. No arrangements have been made for messing at present, and no one can tell where to get anything.

Mrs R. C. Germon, *A Diary Kept by Mrs R. C. Germon at Lucknow*

5th – Darwin's Letter

Down
July 5, 1844

My Dear Emma

... I have just finished my sketch of my species theory. If, as I believe, my theory in time be accepted even by one competent judge, it will be a considerable step in science.

I therefore write this in case of my sudden death, as my most solemn and last request, which I am sure you will consider the same as if legally entered in my will, that you will devote £400 to its publication, and further will yourself, or through Hensleigh, take trouble in promoting it. I wish that my sketch be given to some competent person, with this sum to induce him to take trouble in its improvement and enlargement. I give to him all my books on Natural History, which are either scored or have references at the end to the pages, begging him carefully to look over and consider such passages as actually bearing, or by possibility bearing, on this subject. I wish you to make a list of all such books as some temptation to an editor. I also request that you will hand over to him all those scraps roughly divided into eight or ten brown paper portfolios. The scraps, with copied quotations from various works, are those which may aid my editor. I also request that you, or some amanuensis, will aid in deciphering any of the scraps which the editor may think possibly of use. I leave to the editor's judgment whether to interpolate these facts in the text, or as notes, or under appendices. As the looking over the references and scraps will be a long labour, and as the *correcting* and enlarging and altering my sketch will also take considerable time, I leave this sum of £400 as some remuneration, and any profits from the work. I consider that for this the editor is bound to get the sketch published either at a publisher's or his own risk. Many of the scraps in the portfolios contain mere rude suggestions and early views, now useless, and many of the facts will probably turn out as having no bearing on my theory.

With respect to editors, Mr Lyell would be the best if he would undertake it; I believe he would find the work pleasant, and he would learn some facts new to him. As the editor must be a geologist as well as a naturalist, the next best editor would be Professor Forbes of London. The next best (and quite best in many respects) would be Professor Henslow. Dr Hooker would be *very* good. The next, Mr Strickland. If none of these would undertake it, I would request you to consult with Mr Lyell, or some other capable man, for some editor, a geologist and naturalist. Should one other hundred pounds make the difference of procuring a good editor, I request earnestly that you will raise £500.

My remaining collections in Natural History may be given to any one or any museum where they would be accepted.

Charles Darwin to Mrs Darwin

Part of letter from *Foundations of the Origin of Species: Two Essays by Charles Darwin*

6th – The Bellows-Menders Dinner

There was a gentleman near us—a very lean old Bellows-Mender indeed—who had three platefuls. His old hands trembled, and his plate quivered with excitement, as he asked again and again. That old man is not destined to eat much more of the green fat of this life. As he took it he shook all over like the jelly in the dish opposite to him. He gasped out a quick laugh once or twice to his neighbour, when his two or three old tusks showed, still standing up in those jaws which had swallowed such a deal of calipash. He winked at the waiters, knowing them from former banquets.

This banquet, which I am describing at Christmas, took place at the end of May. At that time the vegetables called peas were exceedingly scarce, and cost six-and-twenty shillings a quart.

'There are two hundred quarts of peas,' said the old fellow, winking with blood-shot eyes, and a laugh that was perfectly frightful. They were consumed with the fragrant ducks, by those who were inclined: or with the venison, which now came in.

That was a great sight. On a centre table in the hall, on which already stood a cold Baron of Beef—a grotesque piece of meat—a dish as big as a dish in a pantomime, with a little Standard of England stuck into the top of it, as if it were round this we were to rally—on this centre table, six men placed as many huge dishes under covers; and at a given signal the master cook and five assistants in white caps and jackets marched rapidly up to the dish-covers, which being withdrawn, discovered to our sight six haunches, on which the six carvers, taking out six sharp knives from their girdles, began operating ...

Conversation, rapid and befitting the place and occasion, went on all round. 'Waiter, where's the turtle-fins?'—Gobble, gobble. 'Hice Punch or My deary, sir?' 'Smelts or salmon, Jowler my boy?' 'Always take cold beef after turtle.'—Hobble-gobble. 'These year peas have no taste.' Hobble-gobble-obble. 'Jones, a glass of 'Ock with you? Smith, jine us? Waiter, three 'Ocks. S., mind your manners! There's Mrs. S. a-looking at you from the gallery.'—Hobble-obbl-gobble-gob-gob-gob. A steam of meats, a flare of candles, a rushing to and fro of waiters, a ceaseless clinking of glass and steel, a dizzy mist of gluttony, out of which I see my old friend of the turtle soup making terrific play among the peas, his knife darting down his throat.

W. M. Thackeray, *Sketches and Travels in London*, 1847

7th – Escape to the Country from the Stench of London

The blessed woods and fields have done me a world of good, and I am quite myself again. The children are all as happy as children can be. My eldest daughter, Mary, keeps house, with a state and gravity becoming that high position; wherein she is assisted by her sister Katie, and by her aunt Georgina, who is, and always has been, like another sister. Two big dogs, a bloodhound and a St. Bernard, direct from a convent of that name, where I think you once were, are their principal attendants in the green lanes. These latter instantly untie the neckerchiefs of all tramps and prowlers who approach their presence, so that they wander about without any escort, and drive big horses in basket-phaetons through murderous bye-ways, and never come to grief. They are very curious about your daughters, and send all kinds of loves to them and to Mrs. Cerjat, in which I heartily join.

You will have read in the papers that the Thames in London is most horrible. I have to cross Waterloo or London Bridge to get to the railroad when I come down here, and I can certify that the offensive smells, even in that short whiff, have been of a most head-and-stomach-distending nature. Nobody knows what is to be done; at least everybody knows a plan, and everybody else knows it won't do; in the meantime cartloads of chloride of lime are shot into the filthy stream, and do something I hope. ... the weather has been exceptionally hot, but is now quite cool. On the top of this hill it has been cold, actually cold at night, for more than a week past.

Charles Dickens, from letter to M. de Cerjat, 7 July 1858

8th – Comments on the Crystal Palace

It is two miles in circumference and has three stories of prodigious height; it would easily hold five or six buildings like our Palace of Industry, and it is of glass; it consists first of an immense rectangular structure rising towards the centre in a semicircle like a hot-house, and flanked by two Chinese towers; then, on either side, long buildings descend at right angles, enclosing the garden with its fountains, statues, summerhouses, strips of turf, groups of large trees, exotic plants, and beds of flowers. The acres of glass sparkle in the sunlight; at the horizon an undulating line of green eminences is bathed in the luminous vapour which softens all colours and spreads an expression of tender beauty over an entire landscape. Always the same English method of decoration—on the one side a park and natural embellishments, which it must be granted are beautiful and adapted to the climate; on the other the building, which is a monstrous jumble, wanting in style, and bearing witness not to taste but to English power. The interior consists of a museum of antiquities, composed of plaster facsimiles of all the Grecian and Roman statues scattered over Europe; of a museum of the Middle Ages; of a Revival museum; of an Egyptian museum; of a Nineveh museum; of an Indian museum; of a reproduction of a Pompeian house; of a reproduction of the Alhambra. The ornaments of the Alhambra have been moulded, and these moulds are preserved in an adjoining room as proofs of authenticity. In order to omit nothing, copies have been made of the most notable Italian paintings, and these are daubs worthy of a country fair. There is a huge tropical hot-house, wherein are fountains, swimming turtles, large aquatic plants in flower, the Sphinx and Egyptian statues sixty feet high, specimens of colossal or rare trees, among others the bark of a Sequoia California 450 feet in height and measuring 116 feet in circumference. The bark is arranged and fastened to an inner framework in such a manner as to give an idea of the tree itself. There is a circular concert room, with tiers of benches as in a Coliseum. Lastly, in the gardens are to be seen life-size reproductions of antediluvian monsters, megatheriums, deinotheriums, and others. In these gardens Blondin does his tricks at the height of a hundred feet. I pass over half the things; but does not this conglomeration of odds and ends carry back one's thoughts to the Rome of Caesar and the Antonines? At that period, also, pleasure-palaces were erected for the sovereign people; circuses, theatres, baths wherein were collected statues, paintings, animals, musicians, acrobats, all the treasures and all the oddities of the world; pantheons of opulence and curiosity; genuine bazaars where the liking for what was novel, heterogeneous, and fantastic ousted the feeling of appreciation for simple beauty. In truth, Rome enriched herself with these things by conquest, England by industry. Thus it is that at Rome the paintings, the statues, were stolen originals, and the monsters, whether rhinoceroses or lions, were perfectly alive and tore human beings to pieces; whereas here the statues are made of plaster and the monsters of goldbeater's skin. The spectacle is one of the second class, but of the same kind. A Greek would not have regarded it with satisfaction; he would have considered it appropriate to powerful barbarians who, trying to become refined, had utterly failed.

Hippolyte Taine, *Notes on England*

Hippolyte Taine (1828–93) was a philosopher and historian. In 1864 he was appointed as professor of aesthetics and history of art at the Ecole des Beaux Arts in Paris, where he lectured for 20 years. His long visit to England in 1858 resulted in *Notes sur l'Angleterre*, published in 1872. His work influenced writers such as Emile Zola and Guy de Maupassant.

9th – A Servant's Wages

The following table of the average yearly wages paid to domestics, with the various members of the household placed in the order in which they are usually ranked, will serve as a guide to regulate the expenditure of an establishment:—

	When not found in Livery	When found in Livery
The House Steward	From £10 to £80	—
The Valet	” 25 to 50	From £20 to £30
The Butler	” 25 to 50	—
The Cook	” 20 to 40	—
The Gardener	” 20 to 40	—
The Footman	” 20 to 40	” 15 to 25
The Under Butler	” 15 to 30	” 15 to 25
The Coachman	—	” 20 to 35
The Groom	” 15 to 30	” 12 to 20
The Under Footman	—	” 12 to 20
The Page or Footboy	” 8 to 18	” 6 to 14
The Stableboy	” 6 to 12	—

	When no extra allowance is made for Tea, Sugar and Beer	When an extra allowance is made for Tea, Sugar, and Beer
The Housekeeper	From £20 to £15	From £18 to £40

The Lady's-maid	" 12 to 25	"10 to 20
The Head Nurse	" 15 to 30	" 13 to 26
The Cook	" 11 to 30	" 12 to 26
The Upper Housemaid	" 12 to 20	" 10 to 17
The Upper Laundry-maid	" 12 to 18	" 10 to 15
The Maid-of-all-work	" 9 to 14	" 7-1/2 to 11
The Under Housemaid	" 8 to 12	" 6-1/2 to 10
The Still-room Maid	" 9 to 14	" 8 to 13
The Nursemaid	" 8 to 12	" 5 to 10
The Under Laundry-maid	" 9 to 11	" 8 to 12
The Kitchen-maid	" 9 to 14	" 8 to 12
The Scullery-maid	" 5 to 9	" 4 to 8

These quotations of wages are those usually given in or near the metropolis; but, of course, there are many circumstances connected with locality, and also having reference to the long service on the one hand, or the inexperience on the other, of domestics, which may render the wages still higher or lower than those named above. All the domestics mentioned in the above table would enter into the establishment of a wealthy nobleman. The number of servants, of course, would become smaller in proportion to the lesser size of the establishment; and we may here enumerate a scale of servants suited to various incomes, commencing with—

About £1,000 a year—A cook, upper housemaid, nursemaid, under housemaid, and a man servant.
About £750 a year—A cook, housemaid, nursemaid, and footboy.
About £500 a year—A cook, housemaid, and nursemaid.
About £300 a year—A maid-of-all-work and nursemaid.
About £200 or £150 a year—A maid-of-all-work (and girl occasionally).

Mrs Isabella Beeton, *Mrs Beeton's Book of Household Management*

10th – Lay of the Trilobite

A mountain's giddy height I sought,
Because I could not find
Sufficient vague and mighty thought
To fill my mighty mind;
And as I wandered ill at ease,
There chanced upon my sight
A native of Silurian seas,
An ancient Trilobite.

So calm, so peacefully he lay,
I watched him even with tears:
I thought of Monads far away
In the forgotten years.
How wonderful it seemed and right,
The providential plan,
That he should be a Trilobite,
And I should be a Man!

And then, quite natural and free
Out of his rocky bed,
That Trilobite he spoke to me
And this is what he said:
'I don't know how the thing was done,
Although I cannot doubt it;
But Huxley – he if anyone
Can tell you all about it;

'How all your faiths are ghosts and dreams,
How in the silent sea
Your ancestors were Monotremes –
Whatever these may be;
How you evolved your shining lights
Of wisdom and perfection
From Jelly-fish and Trilobites
By Natural Selection.

'You've Kant to make your brains go round,
Hegel you have to clear them,

You've Mr. Browning to confound,
And Mr. Punch to cheer them!
The native of an alien land
You call a man and brother,
And greet with hymn-book in one hand
And pistol in the other!

'You've Politics to make you fight
As if you were possessed:
You've cannon and you've dynamite
To give the nations rest:
The side that makes the loudest din
Is surest to be right,
And oh, a pretty fix you're in!'
Remarked the Trilobite.

But gentle, stupid, free from woe
I lived among my nation,
I didn't care – I didn't know
That I was a Crustacean.*
I didn't grumble, didn't steal,
I *never* took to rhyme:
Salt water was my frugal meal,
And carbonate of lime.'

Reluctantly I turned away,
No other word he said;
An ancient Trilobite, he lay
Within his rocky bed.
I did not answer him, for that
Would have annoyed my pride:
I merely bowed, and raised my hat,
But in my heart I cried: –

'I wish our brains were not so good,
I wish our skulls were thicker,
I wish that Evolution could
Have stopped a little quicker;
For oh, it was a happy plight,
Of liberty and ease,

To be a simple Trilobite
In the Silurian seas!'

May Kendall

* He was not a Crustacean. He has since discovered that he was
  an Arachnid, or something similar. But he says it does not
  matter. He says they told him wrong once, and they may again.
  [Kendall's note]

May Kendall (1861–1943) was a poet, novelist and satirist. She was
also interested in social reforms, working with the Rowntrees in York.
Her most famous poem, 'The Lay of the Trilobite', was published first
in *Punch* in 1885, then in her collection *Dreams to Sell*, which came out
in 1887. It is a send-up of people's response to Darwin's theory of
evolution. May Kendall died in poverty in York.

11th – Grave Robbing

Don't go to weep upon my grave,
And think that there I be.
They haven't left an atom there
Of my anatomie.

Thomas Hood

Thomas Hood (1799–1845) originally started training to be an engraver,
but illness turned him to writing. He produced short stories, novels
and a travel book, but he is best known for his poems, many of which
are funny. He was particularly good at using puns in his verse. He also
wrote about the working conditions of the poor: 'The Song of the Shirt'
deals with the exploitation of labour. It first appeared in Punch, but
was reprinted at once by several newspapers and translated into four
languages, as well as becoming a popular song.

12th – A Visit to Conway Castle

It is altogether impossible to describe Conway Castle. Nothing ever
can have been so perfect in its own style, and for its own purposes,
when it was first built; and now nothing else can be so perfect as a

picture of ivy-grown, peaceful ruin. The banqueting-hall, all open to the sky and with thick curtains of ivy tapestrying the walls, and grass and weeds growing on the arches that overpass it, is indescribably beautiful. The hearthstones of the great old fireplaces, all about the castle, seem to be favorite spots for weeds to grow. There are eight large round towers, and out of four of them, I think, rise smaller towers, ascending to a much greater height, and once containing winding staircases, all of which are now broken, and inaccessible from below, though, in at least one of the towers, the stairs seemed perfect, high aloft. It must have been the rudest violence that broke down these stairs; for each step was a thick and heavy slab of stone, built into the wall of the tower. There is no such thing as a roof in any part; towers, hall, kitchen, all are open to the sky. One round tower, directly overhanging the railway, is so shattered by the falling away of the lower part, that you can look quite up into it and through it, while sitting in the cars; and yet it has stood thus, without falling into complete ruin, for more than two hundred years. I think that it was in this tower that we found the castle oven, an immense cavern, big enough to bake bread for an army. The railway passes exactly at the base of the high rock, on which this part of the castle is situated, and goes into the town through a great arch that has been opened in the castle wall.

Nathaniel Hawthorne, *English Note-books*

13th – Reaching the Top of the Matterhorn

We went back to the northern end of the ridge. Croz now took the tent-pole and planted it in the highest snow. "Yes," we said, "there is the flagstaff, but where is the flag?" "Here it is," he answered, pulling off his blouse and fixing it to the stick. It made a poor flag, and there was no wind to float it out, yet it was seen all around. They saw it at Zermatt, at the Riffel, in the Val Tournanche ...
We returned to the southern end of the ridge to build a cairn, and then paid homage to the view. The day was one of those superlatively calm and clear ones which usually precede bad weather. The atmosphere was perfectly still and free from all clouds or vapors. Mountains fifty—nay, a hundred—miles off looked sharp and near. All their details—ridge and crag, snow and glacier—stood out with faultless definition. Pleasant thoughts of happy days in bygone years

came up unbidden as we recognized the old, familiar forms. All were revealed—not one of the principal peaks of the Alps was hidden.

Edward Whymper, *Scrambles Amongst the Alps*

Edward Whymper (1840–1911) was a mountaineer who led the first ascent of the Matterhorn. He also climbed mountains in South America, Canada and elsewhere – often for the first time – and explored Greenland. He made contributions to the study of altitude sickness, and designed a tent, which was manufactured for a century. He illustrated many of his books himself, as he was a wood-engraver by training.

14th – Disaster on the Matterhorn

A few minutes afterward I tied myself to young Peter, ran down after the others, and caught them just as they were commencing the descent of the difficult part. Great care was being taken. Only one man was moving at a time: when he was firmly planted, the next advanced, and so on. They had not, however, attached the additional rope to rocks, and nothing was said about it. The suggestion was not made for my own sake, and I am not sure that it even occurred to me again. For some little distance we two followed the others, detached from them, and should have continued so had not Lord F. Douglas asked me, about 3 p.m. to tie on to old Peter, as he feared, he said, that Taugwalder would not be able to hold his ground if a slip occurred. ...

Michel Croz had laid aside his axe, and in order to give Mr. Hadow greater security was absolutely taking hold of his legs and putting his feet, one by one, into their proper positions. As far as I know, no one was actually descending. I cannot speak with certainty, because the two leading men were partially hidden from my sight by an intervening mass of rock, but it is my belief, from the movements of their shoulders, that Croz, having done as I have said, was in the act of turning round to go down a step or two himself: at this moment Mr. Hadow slipped, fell against him and knocked him over. I heard one startled exclamation from Croz, then saw him and Mr. Hadow flying downward: in another moment Hudson was dragged from his steps, and Lord F. Douglas immediately after him. All this was the work of a moment. Immediately we heard Croz's exclamation, old Peter and I planted ourselves as firmly as the rocks would permit: the rope was taut between us, and the jerk came on us both as on one man. We held, but the rope broke midway between Taugwalder and Lord Francis Douglas. For a few seconds we saw our unfortunate companions sliding downward on their backs, and spreading out their hands, endeavoring to save themselves. They passed from our sight uninjured, disappeared one by one, and fell from precipice to precipice on to the Matterhorngletscher below, a distance of nearly four thousand feet in height. From the moment the rope broke it was impossible to help them.

So perished our comrades! For the space of half an hour we remained on the spot without moving a single step. The two men, paralyzed by terror, cried like infants, and trembled in such a manner as to threaten us with the fate of the others. Old Peter rent the air with exclamations of "Chamounix!—oh, what will Chamounix say?" He meant, Who would believe that Croz could fall?

Edward Whymper, *Scrambles Amongst the Alps*

15th – The Railroad

I took a flight, awhile agoo,
Along the raïls, a stage or two,
An' while the heavy wheels did spin
An' rottle, wi' a deafnèn din,
In clouds o' steam, the zweepèn traïn
Did shoot along the hill-bound plaïn,
As sheädes o' birds in flight, do pass
Below em on the zunny grass.
An' as I zot, an' look'd abrode
On leänen land an' windèn road,
The ground a-spread along our flight
Did vlee behind us out o' zight;
The while the zun, our heav'nly guide,
Did ride on wi' us, zide by zide.
An' zoo, while time, vrom stage to stage,
Do car us on vrom youth to age,
The e'thly pleasures we do vind
Be soon a-met, an' left behind;
But God, beholdèn vrom above
Our lowly road, wi' yearnèn love,

Do keep bezide us, stage by stage,
Vrom be'th to youth, vrom youth to age.
William Barnes, *Poems of Rural Life in the Dorset Dialect*

William Barnes (1801–86) was a schoolmaster and a clergyman, with a keen interest in philology. He proposed ridding English of foreign words, going back to a pure Anglo-Saxon form of the language. A Dorset man, he thought the local dialect was the nearest to Anglo-Saxon English then available, and he wrote poems in that dialect. Three collections were published – they showed that he was a good poet too.

16th – Meeting the Author

Some little time after the publication of "Alice's Adventures" we went for our summer holiday to Whitby. We were visiting friends, and my brother and sister went to the hotel. They soon after asked us to dine with them there at the *table d'hôte*. I had on one side of me a gentleman whom I did not know, but as I had spent a good deal of time travelling in foreign countries, I always, at once, speak to any one I am placed next. I found on this occasion I had a very agreeable neighbour, and we seemed to be much interested in the same books, and politics also were touched on. After dinner my sister and brother rather took me to task for talking so much to a complete stranger. I said. "But it was quite a treat to talk to him and to hear him talk. Of one thing I am quite sure, he is a genius." My brother and sister, who had not heard him speak, again laughed at me, and said, "You are far too easily pleased." I, however, maintained my point, and said what great delight his conversation had given me, and how remarkably clever it had been. Next morning nurse took out our two little twin daughters in front of the sea. I went out a short time afterwards, looked for them, and found them seated with my friend of the *table d'hôte* between them, and they were listening to him, open-mouthed, and in the greatest state of enjoyment, with his knee covered with minute toys. I, seeing their great delight, motioned to him to go on; this he did for some time. A most charming story he told them about sea-urchins and Ammonites. When it was over, I said, "You must be the author of 'Alice's Adventures.'" He laughed, but looked astonished, and said, "My dear Madam, my name is Dodgson, and 'Alice's Adventures' was written by Lewis Carroll." I replied, "Then you must have borrowed the name, for only he could have told a story as you have just done." After a little sparring he admitted the fact, and I went home and proudly told my sister and brother how my genius had turned out a greater one than I expected. They assured me I must be mistaken, and that, as I had suggested it to him, he had taken advantage of the idea, and said he was what I wanted him to be. A few days after some friends came to Whitby who knew his aunts, and confirmed the truth of his statement, and thus I made the acquaintance of one whose friendship has been the source of great pleasure for nearly thirty years. He has most generously sent us all his books, with kind inscriptions, to "Minnie and Doe," whom he photographed, but would not take Canon Bennie or me; he said he never took portraits of people of more than seventeen years of age until they were seventy. He visited us, and we often met him at Eastbourne, and his death was indeed a great loss after so many happy years of friendship with one we so greatly admired and loved.

Mrs Bennie, wife of the Rector of Glenfield, near Leicester

17th – Dinners and Dishes

A man can live for three days without bread, but no man can live for one day without poetry, was an aphorism of Baudelaire. You can live without pictures and music but you cannot live without eating, says the author of *Dinners and Dishes*; and this latter view is, no doubt, the more popular. Who, indeed, in these degenerate days would hesitate between an ode and an omelette, a sonnet and a salmis? Yet the position is not entirely Philistine; cookery is an art; are not its principles the subject of South Kensington lectures, and does not the Royal Academy give a banquet once a year? Besides, as the coming democracy will, no doubt, insist on feeding us all on penny dinners, it is well that the laws of cookery should be explained: for were the national meal burned, or badly seasoned, or served up with the wrong sauce a dreadful revolution might follow.

Under these circumstances we strongly recommend *Dinners and Dishes* to every one: it is brief and concise and makes no attempt at eloquence, which is extremely fortunate. For even on ortolans who could endure oratory? It also has the advantage of not being illustrated. The subject of a work of art has, of course, nothing to do with its beauty, but still there is always something depressing about the coloured lithograph of a leg of mutton.

Oscar Wilde, *Pall Mall Gazette*, March 1885 (reprinted in *A Critic in Pall Mall*)

18th – The Clifton Suspension Bridge

Mr. Brunel ultimately determined to adopt the Egyptian style of architecture. His brother-in-law, Mr. John Callcott Horsley, R. A., gives the following account of the proposed designs for the towers:—

'His conception of the towers or gateways at either end of the bridge was peculiarly grand and effective, as may be seen from his sketches still existing. They were to be purely Egyptian; and, in his design, he had caught the true spirit of the great remains at Philæ and Thebes. He intended to case the towers with cast iron, and, as in perfect accordance with the Egyptian character of his design, to decorate them with a series of figure subjects, illustrating the whole work of constructing the bridge, with the manufacture of the materials—beginning with quarrying the iron ore, and making the iron, and ending with a design representing the last piece of construction necessary for the bridge itself. The subjects would have been arranged in tiers (divided by simple lines) from top to bottom of the towers, and in the exact proportion of those found upon Egyptian buildings. He made very clever sketches for some of these proposed figure subjects, just to show what he intended by them. I remember a group of men carrying one of the links of the chainwork, which was excellent in character. He proposed that I should design the figure subjects, and he asked me to go down with him to Merthyr Tydvil, and make sketches of the iron processes. We accomplished our journey, and all the requisite drawings for the intended designs were made.'

The works were commenced with the Leigh abutment, which was completed in 1840, great delay having been caused by the failure of the contractors. This misfortune led to a large excess of expenditure over the original estimates. In 1843 the whole of the funds raised (amounting to 45,000*l.*) were exhausted, and there still remained to be executed the ornamental additions to the piers (the cost of which was estimated at about 4,000*l.*), half of the iron work, the suspension of the chains and rods, the construction of the flooring, and the completion of the approaches, &c., the estimate for the execution of which was 30,000*l.*

Unfortunately, all efforts to raise further subscriptions were unsuccessful; and in July 1853, when the time limited for the completion of the bridge had expired, the works were closed in, and the undertaking abandoned.

Several proposals for completing the bridge were made in Mr. Brunel's lifetime, and he took every opportunity of furthering this object, which he had very much at heart. It was not, however, till about a year after his death that the superstructure of the bridge was actually commenced.

Isambard Brunel, *The Life of Isambard Kingdom Brunel,*
Civil Engineer

19th – Changes in Education for Girls

The middle of this century saw the beginning of a wonderful change, a change which was at first brought about so gradually, that few were aware of its importance. Up to the year 1847, few girls had opportunities for obtaining anything that can be called systematic and thorough education. True, there were women like Mrs. Somerville, and Harriet Martineau, and Caroline Cornwallis, who took a high place in the intellectual world. There were charming writers, poets and novelists whom we still hold in honour, but only women of exceptional character could break through the various barriers which fenced them off from the intellectual fields in which their brothers roamed.

Mr. Llewellyn Davies has rightly called the opening of Queen's College, in 1848 (that year of revolution), an era in the history of women's education. Up to that time, girls of the middle classes were usually educated at home, under private governesses assisted by masters, or they were sent to small boarding schools; day schools were not the fashion. In most of these small boarding schools, much time was spent in learning by rote what the Schools' Inquiry Commissioners call "miserable catechisms," "lamentable catechisms," "the noxious brood of catechisms," or epitomes of miscellaneous knowledge, as "Mangnall's Questions," etc., books which taught facts, " such facts as the number of houses burnt in the Fire of London," knowledge "fragmentary, multifarious, disconnected; taught not scientifically as a subject, but merely as so much information, and hence, like a wall of stones without mortar, it readily fell to pieces." Mr. Fitch wrote, "I have seen girls learning by heart the terminology of the Linnean system, to whom the very elements of vegetable physiology were unknown; learning from a catechism the meaning of such words as divisibility, inertia, who knew nothing of the physical facts of which these words are the representatives."

Dorothea Beale, *History of Cheltenham Ladies' College*

20th – Action in the Sudan

On arrival off Aden the battalion was detained, and received orders to proceed to Suakim on the coast of Nubia, to join an expeditionary force organized under command of Sir Gerald Graham V.C., K.C.B., to operate against fanatical Arabs in the Soudan, led by Osman Digna a lieutenant of the Mahdi's. The "Jumna" arrived there on the 19th of February; on the 23rd February the battalion proceeded round the coast to Trinkitat, disembarked and formed a part of the 1st Brigade under command of Sir Redvers Buller, V.C., K.C.M.G., and advanced a few days afterwards to Fort Baker, which they occupied until sufficient supplies were collected for a general advance. On the morning of the 29th February, the whole division being then concentrated, an advance towards Tokar was ordered, the object being to relieve the town which was supposed to be in the hands of the arabs. On arriving at El Teb about 4 miles distant from Fort Baker the arabs were discovered to be strongly entrenched, and had several guns in position which they had previously taken from Baker Pasha's Egyptian force, and whose troops they had totally defeated. The division advanced in a hollow square, guns manned by sailors from the fleet placed at each angle, the 2nd battalion Royal Irish Fusiliers forming the right face of the square. The division moved steadily on by the left flank of the enemy at a distance of about 600 yards, General Graham intending to attack them on their reverse flank. During this movement the square was subjected to a smart rifle fire, but no casualties occurred in the Fusiliers at this time. On reaching the reverse flank of the enemy's position, the square moved to its left, the Fusiliers thus became its rear face. The attack then became general and lasted for four hours, the enemy were finally driven from their position, their guns taken, besides suffering a very heavy loss of killed and wounded, estimated at about 2000. In this action the Regiment was peculiarly fortunate, only one officer and seven rank and file being wounded. During the ensuing night the battalion bivouacked in the enemy's entrenchments sending "A" company under Captain Gordon on outlying picquet.

The division continued its march towards Tokar the following morning at 8 o'clock, and reached the town about 4 o'clock in the afternoon, after a dreary and tedious march of 12 miles, through the desert in the same formation as the day before with the exception of the Fusiliers being placed in the front face of the square. The town offered no resistance; on the march the men suffered much from want of water, and also the excessive heat. A banner of the Mahdi's was captured, and sent as a trophy home to Her Majesty the Queen. The division returned to Trinkitat on the 4th March, after a long and toilsome march of seventeen miles over sand and brushwood.

1884

THE SOUDAN

The 89th (Princess Victoria's) Regiment, *Regimental History*

21st – For a Cat Losing Its Coat

Give the cat access to grass and have the following made up at a chemists and rub into the skin daily. Sulphuric acid 1 oz oxide of zinc 1/2 oz; balsam of Peru 1/2 oz; paraffin 1 dram.

Sarah Caroline Gildea, *Recipe Book*

22nd – Eye-Glassed Damsels

The very latest fashion among the "smart" young ladies of the present day is the wearing of a single eye-glass, fixed in the eye, after the manner of our male dandies. These eye-glassed damsels are to be met everywhere—at the theatres, at the picture-galleries, and in the Row. But truly it is a painful sight to witness. The new innovation is simply hideous and the efforts to keep the glass in position are utterly absurd. How can pretty women so disfigure their charming faces by adopting so ridiculous a custom?

At the Literary Ladies' Dinner, which took place at the Criterion on the 25th ult, there was quite a large gathering of lady journalists and authoresses ... The menu was excellent, and the champagne was appropriately sweet. A box of cigarettes was sent by a well-known publisher, but only three ladies availed themselves of the privilege to indulge in the soothing weed.

The Lady, July 1891

23rd – Ill, not Mad

In another room, a kind of purgatory or place of transition, six or eight noisy madwomen were gathered together, under the superintendence of one sane attendant. Among them was a girl of two or three and twenty, very prettily dressed, of most respectable appearance and good manners, who had been brought in from the house where she had lived as domestic servant (having, I suppose, no friends), on account of being subject to epileptic fits, and requiring to be removed under the influence of a very bad one. She was by no means of the same stuff, or the same breeding, or the same experience, or in the same state of mind, as those by whom she was surrounded; and she pathetically complained that the daily association and the nightly noise made her worse, and was driving her mad—which was perfectly evident. The case was noted for inquiry and redress, but she said she had already been there for some weeks.

If this girl had stolen her mistress's watch, I do not hesitate to say she would have been infinitely better off. We have come to this absurd, this dangerous, this monstrous pass, that the dishonest felon is, in respect of cleanliness, order, diet, and accommodation, better provided for, and taken care of, than the honest pauper.

Charles Dickens, 'A Walk in a Workhouse', from
Reprinted Pieces

24th – Burying Five Ducks

Today the boys and I began to build a "church", and enclosed it with a wall as a burial ground and in it we buried five little ducks, and one little chicken, that had died, the church we built of bricks; and plaistered them together with mold and water, the steeple was about four feet high, and the church was about 2 feet; there were four windows on each side of the church and a door at the end, then we cut a very long tombstone to put all along the graves of the little ducks for they were all in a row, the tombstone was made of deal wood, first we white-washed it and then wrote "5 LITTLE DUCKS ONE CHICKEN" on it with Indian Ink.

Ellen Buxton, *Journal*

25th – Country Boys

I plead guilty to a strong partiality towards that unpopular class of beings, country boys: I have a large acquaintance amongst them, and I can almost say, that I know good of many and harm of none. In general they are an open, spirited, good-humoured race, with a proneness to embrace the pleasures and eschew the evils of their condition, a capacity for happiness, quite unmatched in man, or woman, or a girl. They are patient, too, and bear their fate as scape-goats (for all sins whatsoever are laid as matters of course to their door), whether at home or abroad, with amazing resignation and, considering the many lies of which they are the objects, they tell wonderfully few in return. The worst that can be said of them is, that they seldom, when grown to man's estate, keep the promise of their boyhood; but that is a fault to come—a fault that may not come, and ought not to be anticipated. It is astonishing how sensible they are to notice from their betters, or those whom they think such. I do not speak of money, or gifts, or praise, or the more coarse and common briberies—they are more delicate courtiers; a word, a nod, a smile, or the mere calling of them by their names, is enough to ensure their hearts and their services.

Mary Russell Mitford, *Our Village*

26th – Loafing

Few places are better loafing-ground than a pier, with its tranquil "lucid interval" between steamers, the ever recurrent throb of paddle-wheel, the rush and foam of beaten water among the piles, splash of ropes and rumble of gangways, and all the attendant hurry and scurry of the human race. Here, *tanquam in speculo*, the Loafer as he lounges may, by attorney as it were, touch gently every stop in the great organ of the emotions of mortality. Rapture of meeting, departing woe, love at first sight, disdain, laughter, indifference — he may experience them all, but attenuated and as if he saw them in a dream; as if, indeed, he were Heine's god in dream on a mountain-side. Let the drowsy deity awake and all these puppets, emanations of his dream, will vanish into the nothing whence they came. And these emotions may be renewed each morning; if a fair one sail to-day, be sure that one as fair will land to-morrow. The supply is inexhaustible.

Kenneth Grahame, *Pagan Papers*

27th – Cecil Rhodes

A tall, burly gentleman in a homely costume of flannels and a slouch hat emerged from the unfinished room, where he would seem to have been directing the workmen, and we were introduced to Cecil John Rhodes, the Prime Minister of Cape Colony.

I looked at the man, of whom I had heard so much, with a great deal of curiosity. Shy and diffident with strangers, his manner even somewhat abrupt, one could not fail to be impressed with the expression of power, resolution, and kindness, on the rugged countenance, and with the keen, piercing glance of the blue eyes, which seemed to read one through in an instant. He greeted us, as he did every newcomer, most warmly, and under his guidance we passed into the completed portion of the house, the rooms of which were not only most comfortable, but also perfect in every detail as regards the model he wished to copy—viz., a Dutch house of 200 years ago, even down to the massive door aforementioned, which he had just purchased for £200 from a colonial family mansion, and which seemed to afford him immense pleasure. As a first fleeting memory of the interior of Groot Schuur, I call to mind Dutch armoires, all incontestably old and of lovely designs, Dutch chests, inlaid high-backed chairs, costly Oriental rugs, and everywhere teak panelling—the whole producing a vision of perfect taste and old-world repose. It was then Mr. Rhodes's intention to have no electric light, or even lamps, and burn nothing but tallow candles, so as to keep up the illusion of antiquity; but whether he would have adhered to this determination it is impossible to say, as the house we saw was burnt to the ground later on, and is now rebuilt on exactly the same lines, but with electric light, every modern comfort, and lovely old red tiles to replace the quaint thatched roof.

Lady Sarah Wilson, *Book of South African Memories*

28th – For Exmoor

For Exmoor, where the red deer run, my weary heart doth cry;
She that will a rover wed, far her feet shall hie.
Narrow, narrow, shows the street, dull the narrow sky,
  –Buy my cherries, whiteheart cherries, good my masters, buy!

O he left me, left alone, aye to think and sign–
'Lambs feed down yon sunny coombe, hind and yearling shy
Mid the shrouding vapours walk now like ghosts on high.'
  –Buy my cherries, blackheart cherries, lads and lasses, buy!

Dear my dear, why did ye so? Evil day have I:
Mark no more the antler'd stag, hear the curlew cry,
Milking at my father's gate while he leans anigh.
  –Buy my cherries, whiteheart, blackheart, golden girls, O buy!

Jean Ingelow

Jean Ingelow (1820–97) is best known for her children's stories and her poetry, though she wrote novels as well. Born in Lincolnshire, she eventually moved to London, living there for the rest of her life. Although she had travelled regularly on the Continent (she said she had visited every cathedral in France) she had never been to the theatre. Her books were popular in her day, and she gave 'copyright dinners', entertaining poorer people with the proceeds of her work. She was a friend of Tennyson's, who admired her work, and at one point Queen Victoria was petitioned to make her Poet Laureate.

29th – A Goat in Church

On one occasion at church in Tipperary, I noticed a rather satanic goat come pattering up the church and occupy an empty pew, where he lay down with perfect self-complacency and remained quiescent, chewing the cud, while we knelt; but each time the congregation stood up, up jumped the goat, his pale eyes and enormous horns just appearing over the high front of the pew. Then as we knelt again he would subside also, till he was startled to his feet once more by the rustle of the people rising, and then his wild head was again visible over the top of the pew, staring about him. Not a single person took any notice of the weird creature or seemed to think him out of place or at all funny. And so he continued to rise and fall with the rest to the end.

Elizabeth Butler, from *Sketch-book and Diary*

Elizabeth Thompson, Lady Butler (1846–1933) was a painter, best known for her large historical canvasses showing battle scenes. She had studied in Italy and France, as well as in London, and her work was highly esteemed. Queen Victoria bought *The Roll-Call* (a picture of the Crimean War), and other paintings show scenes from a variety of military campaigns, including the Battle of Waterloo, the retreat from Kabul, Rorke's Drift, and later the First World War. She married Lieutenant General Sir William Butler, and with him travelled to different parts of the Empire. Butler, an Irishman, had doubts about whether colonial imperialism was the best thing for native peoples of the countries involved, but she still painted war scenes.

30th – A Fire-Engine in Action

Those who have never seen a London fire-engine go to a fire have no conception of what it is—much less have they any conception of what it is to ride on the engine! To those accustomed to it, no doubt, it may be tame enough—I cannot tell; but to those who mount an engine for the first time and dash through the crowded thoroughfares at a wild tearing gallop, it is probably the most exciting drive conceivable. It beats steeplechasing! It feels like driving to destruction—so desperate and reckless is it. And yet, it is not reckless in the strict sense of that word; for there is a stern need-be in the case. Every moment, (not to mention minutes or hours), is of the utmost importance in the progress of a fire, for when it gets the mastery and bursts into flames it flashes to its work, and completes it quickly. At such times one moment wasted may involve the loss of thousands of pounds, ay, and of human lives also. This is well-known to those whose profession it is to fight the flames. Hence the union of apparent mad desperation, with cool, quiet self-possession in their proceedings. When firemen can work in silence they do so. No unnecessary word is uttered, no voice is needlessly raised; but, when occasion requires it, their course is a tumultuous rush, amid a storm of shouting and gesticulation!

R. M. Ballantine, *Personal Reminiscences in Book Making*

31st – Daddy Wouldn't Buy Me a Bow Wow

I love my little cat, I do
Its coat is oh so warm
It comes with me each day to school
And sits upon the form
When teacher says "why do you bring
That little pet of yours?"
I tell her that I bring my cat
Along with me because

Daddy wouldn't buy me a bow-wow! bow wow!
Daddy wouldn't buy me a bow-wow! bow wow!
I've got a little cat
And I'm very fond of that
But I'd rather have a bow-wow
Wow, wow, wow, wow

We used to have two tiny dogs
Such pretty little dears
But daddy sold 'em 'cause they used
To bite each other's ears
I cried all day, at eight each night
Papa sent me to bed
When Ma came home and wiped my eyes
I cried again and said

Daddy wouldn't buy me a bow-wow! bow wow!
Daddy wouldn't buy me a bow-wow! bow wow!
I've got a little cat
And I'm very fond of that
But I'd rather have a bow-wow
Wow, wow, wow, wow

I'll be so glad when I get old
To do just as I "likes"
I'll keep a parrot and at least
A half a dozen tykes
And when I've got a tiny pet
I'll kiss the little thing
Then put it in its little cot
And on to it I'll sing

Daddy wouldn't buy me a bow-wow! bow wow!
Daddy wouldn't buy me a bow-wow! bow wow!
I've got a little cat
And I'm very fond of that
But I'd rather have a bow-wow
Wow, wow, wow, wow

Joseph Tabrar, 1892

Joseph Tabrar (1857–1931) was born into a theatrical family, and started singing in a church choir. He became one of the most famous writers of songs for the Victorian music hall, in a career lasting sixty years.

AUGUST

1st – Bee Lore

I happened to receive a long letter from the then rector of Sessay, in which, among a variety of other matters, all more or less illustrated by classical quotations, he gave me an account of a recent experience of his when he had been called upon to bury one of his elder parishioners, and had accordingly been "bidden" to the house where the deceased man was lying, some hours before the "body was to be lifted" and taken to the churchyard. He told me he had partaken of the accustomed hospitality, and had retired to the garden to smoke his pipe in quiet, and had seated himself accordingly in a sort of arbour or summer-house. Presently his attention was aroused by the passage of a woman, the wife of the eldest son of the deceased man. She was carrying a tray, on which he saw there were piled a variety of eatable and drinkable matters, She went straight to the beehives, and he heard her address the bees themselves. Naming the late owner, she said, "John G—is dead, and his son is now master. He has sent you something out of every dish and jug on the table, and we hope you will be content to take him as the new master."

J. C. Atkinson, *Forty Years in a Moorland Parish*

2nd – The Hard Summer

For my part, I really like this wet season. It keeps us within, to be sure, rather more than is quite agreeable; but then we are at least awake and alive there, and the world out of doors is so much the pleasanter when we can get abroad. Everything does well, except those fastidious bipeds, men and women; corn ripens, grass grows, fruit is plentiful; there is no lack of birds to eat it, and there has not been such a wasp-season these dozen years. My garden wants no watering, and is more beautiful than ever, beating my old rival in that primitive art, the pretty wife of the little mason, out and out. Measured with mine, her flowers are naught. Look at those hollyhocks, like pyramids of roses; those garlands of the convolvulus major of all colours, hanging around that tall pole, like the wreathy hop-bine; those magnificent dusky cloves, breathing of the Spice Islands; those flaunting double dahlias; those splendid scarlet geraniums, and those fierce and warlike flowers the tiger-lilies. Oh, how beautiful they are! Besides, the weather clears sometimes—it has cleared this evening; and here are we, after a merry walk up the hill, almost as quick as in the winter, bounding lightly along the bright green turf of the pleasant common, enticed by the gay shouts of a dozen clear young voices, to linger awhile, and see the boys play at cricket.

Mary Russell Mitford, *Our Village*

3rd – To Make an Amblongus Pie

Take 4 pounds (say 4½ pounds) of fresh Amblongusses, and put them in a small pipkin.

Cover them with water and boil them for 8 hours incessantly, after which add 2 pints of new milk, and proceed to boil for 4 hours more.

When you have ascertained that the Amblongusses are quite soft, take them out and place them in a wide pan, taking care to shake them well previously.

Grate some nutmeg over the surface, and cover them carefully with powdered gingerbread, curry powder, and a sufficient quantity of cayenne pepper.

Remove the pan into the next room, and place it on the floor. Bring it back again, and let it simmer for three-quarters of an hour. Shake the pan violently till all the Amblongusses have become a pale purple colour.

Then, having prepared the paste, insert the whole carefully, adding at the same time a small pigeon, 2 slices of beef, 4 cauliflowers, and any number of oysters.

Watch patiently till the crust begins to rise, and add a pinch of salt from time to time.

Serve up in a clean dish, and throw the whole out of the window as fast as possible.

Edward Lear, *Nonsense Songs, Stories, Botany and Alphabets*

Edward Lear (1812–88) was originally known as an artist – he taught Queen Victoria. He also travelled extensively, and wrote a number of travel books, which he also illustrated. It was while working for Lord Derby, who wanted pictures of the animals in his menagerie, that Edward Lear started writing nonsense verses – they were for Lord Derby's children. Later he drew nonsense pictures to go with them. His funny poems and limericks have subsequently been enjoyed by children and adults alike.

4th – The Beauty of a Snow-Drift

In the range of inorganic nature I doubt if any object can be found more perfectly beautiful, than a fresh, deep snow-drift, seen under warm light. Its curves are of inconceivable perfection and changefulness; its surface and transparency alike exquisite; its light and shade of inexhaustible variety and inimitable finish,—the shadows sharp, pale, and of heavenly colour, the reflected lights intense and multitudinous, and mingled with the sweet occurrences of transmitted light.

John Ruskin, *Modern Painters*

John Ruskin (1819–1900) had admired the paintings of Turner since his teens, and his first book, *Modern Painters*, started out as a defence of Turner – though it grew into something much bigger. The book brought him to public attention, and he followed it with works of architectural and artistic criticism. As well as a major involvement with art, he was also interested in geology and botany, and as he grew older he became concerned with the social and economic problems of his time. He published essays on these topics, as well as continuing to write about every aspect of art.

5th – Rough Living in the Crimea

The oldest soldiers never witnessed nor heard of a campaign in which general officers were obliged to live out in tents on she open field, for the want of a roof to cover them, and generals who passed their youth in the Peninsular War, and who had witnessed a good deal of fighting since that time in various parts of the world, were unanimous in declaring that they never knew or read of war in which officers were exposed to such hardships. They landed without anything but what they could carry, and they marched beside their men, slept by them, fought by them, and died by them, undistinguished from them in any respect, except by the deadly epaulet and swordbelt, which have cost so many lives to this country. The survivors were often unable to get their things from on board ship. They laid down at night in the clothes which they wore during the day; many delicately nurtured youths never changed shirt and shoes for weeks together, and they were deprived of the use of water for ablution, except to a very limited extent.

W. H. Russell, *The British Expedition to the Crimea*

William Howard Russell (1820–1907) was an Irishman who wrote his first articles for *The Times* while teaching maths at Kensington Grammar School. The editor liked his work, and soon he was employed full-time as a journalist. Sent to the Crimea in 1854, his vivid, exciting reports brought home to readers of *The Times* the frightful conditions endured by the soldiers. The establishment was outraged – Prince Albert called him 'a miserable scribbler', but public feeling was such that the government had to take action. One result was the despatch of Florence Nightingale to improve the care of the wounded. William Russell was regarded as one of the first modern war correspondents: after the Crimean War he covered other actions including the Indian Mutiny, the American Civil War, and the Franco-Prussian War.

6th – Nine Rules for Letter-Writing

1st Rule. *Write legibly.*
2nd Rule. Don't fill *more* than a page and a half with apologies for not having written sooner! The best subject, to *begin* with, is your friend's last letter.

3rd Rule. *Don't repeat yourself.*

4th Rule. When you have written a letter that you feel may possibly irritate your friend, however necessary you may have felt it to so express yourself, *put it aside till the next day*. Then read it over again, and fancy it addressed to yourself.

5th Rule. If your friend makes a severe remark, either leave it unnoticed, or make your reply distinctly *less* severe: and if he makes a friendly remark, tending towards "making up" the little difference that has arisen between you, let your reply be distinctly *more* friendly.

6th Rule. *Don't try to have the last word!*

7th Rule. If it should ever occur to you to write, jestingly, in *dispraise* of your friend, be sure you exaggerate enough to make the jesting *obvious*: a word spoken in *jest*, but taken as earnest, may lead to very serious consequences.

8th Rule. When you say, in your letter, "I enclose cheque for £5," or "I enclose John's letter for you to see," leave off writing for a moment—go and get the document referred to—and *put it into the envelope*. Otherwise, you are pretty certain to find it lying about, *after the Post has gone!*

9th Rule. When you get to the end of a notesheet, and find you have more to say, take another piece of paper—a whole sheet, or a scrap, as the case may demand: but whatever you do, *don't cross!*

Remember the old proverb: *Cross-writing makes cross reading.*

Lewis Carroll, from *Eight or Nine Wise Words about Letter-Writing*

7th – Turner's Landscapes

In conclusion of our present sketch of the course of landscape art, it may be generally stated that Turner is the only painter, so far as I know, who has ever drawn the sky, (not the clear sky, which we before saw belonged exclusively to the religious schools, but the various forms and phenomena of the cloudy heavens,) all previous artists having only represented it typically or partially; but he absolutely and universally: he is the only painter who has ever drawn a mountain, or a stone; no other man ever having learned their organization, or possessed himself of their spirit, except in part and obscurely, (the one or two stones noted of Tintoret's, are perhaps hardly enough on which to found an exception in his favor). He is the only painter who ever drew the stem of a tree, Titian having come the nearest before him, and excelling him in the muscular development of the larger trunks, (though sometimes losing the woody strength in a serpent-like flaccidity,) but missing the grace and character of the ramifications. He is the only painter who has ever represented the surface of calm, or the force of agitated water; who has represented the effects of space on distant objects, or who has rendered the abstract beauty of natural color. These assertions I make deliberately, after careful weighing and consideration, in no spirit of dispute, or momentary zeal; but from strong and convinced feeling, and with the consciousness of being able to prove them.

John Ruskin, Modern Painters

8th – A Boat Trip on the Mersey

Day before yesterday I escorted my family to Rock Ferry, two miles either up or down the Mersey (and I really don't know which) by steamer, which runs every half-hour. There are steamers going continually to Birkenhead and other landings, and almost always a great many passengers on the transit. At this time the boat was crowded so as to afford scanty standing-room; it being Saturday, and therefore a kind of gala-day. I think I have never seen a populace before coming to England; but this crowd afforded a specimen of one, both male and female. The women were the most remarkable; though they seemed not disreputable, there was in them a coarseness, a freedom, and—I don't know what, that was purely English. In fact, men and women here do things that would at least make them ridiculous in America. They are not afraid to enjoy themselves in their own way, and have no pseudo-gentility to support. Some girls danced upon the crowded deck, to the miserable music of a little fragment of a band which goes up and down the river on each trip of the boat. Just before the termination of the voyage a man goes round with a bugle turned upwards to receive the eleemosynary pence and half-pence of the passengers. I gave one of them, the other day, a silver fourpence, which fell into the vitals of the instrument, and compelled the man to take it to pieces.

Nathaniel Hawthorne, English Note-books

9th – Inquisitive Americans

August 9th [1853]. Left Richmond at 7 a.m., and after about five hours in the train, reached a place they call Aquia Creek, where we embarked on a steamer, the Baltimore, which conveyed us up the river Potomac to Washington, a pleasant little voyage; the banks of the river green and pretty, though tame. In this part of the United States there is much resemblance to our counties of Kent and Surrey. Green fields, orchards, and a kitchen-gardeny look about the country, added to red brick houses in the towns, still further increases the likeness. The people, however, are different in almost every respect. Nothing strikes me more, as an Englishwoman, than the interest, or as some call it, the curiosity, displayed by the people here about the affairs of strangers. They guess, reckon, or calculate upon all your actions, and even your motives. Nevertheless, I am never inclined either to think or treat this inquisitiveness as an impertinence, and, moreover, I do not think they mean it themselves as such; I believe it arises from their desire to compare themselves, their sayings and doings, with every stranger they come across, and in their anxiety to do this, they occasionally lose sight of the bounds of good breeding. On the other hand we English go into an opposite extreme. The indifference with which we view everybody we do not know, the fright we are in lest we *should* know some one who is not as high up as ourselves in the social scale. And as to asking questions! I suspect if we could, Asmodeus-like, look into the minds of nineteen out of twenty travellers who meet each other at home, their reflexions would run somewhat as follows: 'I don't care where you live or what you are, where you come from or where you are going to, and I only hope you are not going to speak to me.'

Mrs Bromley, *A Woman's Wanderings in the Western World*

10th – The First Detective Story

Mr. R. Henderson to the Secretary of the — Life Assurance Association.
Private Enquiry Office, Clement's Inn,
GENTLEMEN,
  In laying before you the extraordinary revelations arising from

my examination into the case of the late Madame R—, I have to apologise for the delay in carrying out your instructions of November last. It has been occasioned, not by any neglect on my part, but by the unexpected extent and intricacy of the enquiry into which I have been led. I confess that after this minute and laborious investigation I could still have wished a more satisfactory result, but a perusal of the accompanying documents, on the accuracy and completeness of which you may fully rely, will I doubt not satisfy you of the unusual difficulty of the case.

My enquiries have had reference to a policy of assurance for 5000*l.*, the maximum amount permitted by your rules, on the life of the late Madame R—, effected in your office by her husband, the Baron R—, and bearing date 1st November, 1855. Similar policies were held in the — of Manchester, the — of Liverpool, the — of Edinburgh, and the — of Dublin, the whole amounting to 25,000*l.*; the dates, 23rd December, 1855, 10th January, 25th January, and 15th February, 1856, respectively, being in effect almost identical. These companies joined in the instructions under which I have been acting; and, from the voluminous nature of this letter and its enclosures, I shall be obliged by your considering my present reply as addressed to them conjointly with yourselves.

Before entering upon the subject of my investigations, it may be as well to recapitulate the circumstances under which they were originated. Of these the first was the coincidence of dates, above noticed; and an apparent desire on the part of the assurer to conceal from each of the various offices the fact of similar policies having been elsewhere simultaneously effected. On examining further into the matter your Board was also struck with the peculiar conditions under which the marriage appeared to have taken place, and the relation in which Madame R— had formerly stood to the Baron. To these points, therefore, my attention was especially directed, and the facts thus elicited form a very important link in the singular chain of evidence I have been enabled to put together.

The chief element of suspicion, however, was to be found in the very unusual circumstances attendant on the death of Madame R—, especially following so speedily as it did on the assurance for so large an aggregate amount.

Charles Felix (Charles Warren Adams), *The Notting Hill Mystery*

Charles Felix was the pen-name of Charles Warren Adams (1833–1903), a lawyer who is believed to be the author of the first full-length detective story written in English. *The Notting Hill Mystery* was first brought out as a serial in the magazine *Once A Week*, with illustrations by George du Maurier, then in book form by the publishers Saunders, Otley & Co., a firm Adams was advising in his legal capacity. The author's true identity was not discovered until fifty years after he died. On another note, he was also the secretary of the Anti-Vivisection Society.

11th – A Farewell Letter

To SIR ROBERT PEEL
Devonshire Lodge, New Finchley Road, [1845].
Dear Sir,
We are not to meet in the flesh. Given over by my physicians and by myself, I am only kept alive by frequent instalments of mulled port wine. In this extremity I feel a comfort, for which I cannot refrain from again thanking you, with all the sincerity of a dying man,— and, at the same time, bidding you a respectful farewell.

Thank God my mind is composed and my reason undisturbed, but my race as an author is run. My physical debility finds no tonic virtue in a steel pen, otherwise I would have written one more paper—a forewarning one—against an evil, or the danger of it, arising from a literary movement in which I have had some share, a one-sided humanity, opposite to that Catholic Shakespearian sympathy, which felt with King as well as Peasant, and duly estimated the mortal temptations of both stations. Certain classes at the poles of Society are already too far asunder; it should be the duty of our writers to draw them nearer by kindly attraction, not to aggravate the existing repulsion, and place a wider moral gulf between Rich and Poor, with Hate on the one side and Fear on the other. But I am too weak for this task, the last I had set myself; it is death that stops my pen, you see, and not the pension.
God bless you, Sir, and prosper all your measures for the benefit of my beloved country

Thomas Hood

M. Duckitt & H. Wragg, *Selected English Letters (XV–XIX Centuries)*

12th – The Calico Printer's Clerk

In Manchester that city, of cotton, twist and twills
Lived the subject of my ditty, and the cause of all my ills
She was handsome, young and twenty, her eyes are azure blue
Admirers she had plenty and her name was Dorothy Drew.

Chorus
She was very fond of dancing,
But allow me to remark,
That one fine day she danced away
With a calico printer's clerk.

At a private ball I met her in eighteen sixty-three
I never can forget her, though she was unkind to me
I was dressed in the pink of fashion, my lavender gloves were new
I danced the Valse Circassian with the charming Dorothy Drew.

Chorus

We Schottisched and we Polka'd to the strains the band did play
We valsed and we Mazurka'd, til she valsed my heart away
I whispered in this manner as around the room we flew
Doing Varsovianna, "How I love you, Dorothy Drew."

Chorus

For months and months attention unto her I did pay,
'Til with her condescension, she led me quite astray;
The money I expended, I'm ashamed to tell to you
I'll inform you how it ended with myself and Dorothy Drew.

Chorus

I received an intimation she a visit meant to pay
Unto a near relation, who lived some miles away
In a month she'd be returning, I must take a short adieu
But her love for me was burning, deceitful Dorothy Drew!

Chorus

At nine o'clock next morning, to breakfast I sat down
The smile my face adorning was soon changed to a frown
For in the morning paper, a paragraph met my view
That Jones, a calico printer's clerk, had married Miss Dorothy
    Drew.

Chorus
Repeat first verse

Harry Clifton

This is an early music hall song, written, composed and performed by Harry Clifton (1832–72). He was responsible for several popular songs, including 'The Weepin' Willer', 'The Watercress Girl', and, perhaps the best known, 'Pretty Polly Perkins of Paddington Green'.

13th – Fishing

The fishing-boats and the fishing, the nets, and all the fishing work are a great ornament to Brighton. They are real; there is something about them that forms a link with the facts of the sea, with the forces of the tides and winds, and the sunlight gleaming on the white crests of the waves. They speak to thoughts lurking in the mind; they float between life and death as with a billow on either hand; their anchors go down to the roots of existence. This is real work, real labour of man, to draw forth food from the deep as the plough draws it from the earth. It is in utter contrast to the artificial work—the feathers, the jewellery, the writing at desks of the town. The writings of a thousand clerks, the busy factory work, the trimmings and feathers, and counter attendance do not touch the real. They are all artificial. For food you must still go to the earth and to the sea, as in primeval days. Where would your thousand clerks, your trimmers, and counter-salesmen be without a loaf of bread, without meat, without fish? The old brown sails and the nets, the anchors and tarry ropes, go straight to nature. You do not care for nature now? Well! all I can say is, you will have to go to nature one day—when you die: you will find nature very real then. I urge you to recognise the sunlight and the sea, the flowers and woods *now*.

    Richard Jefferies 'Sunny Brighton', *The Book of the Open Air*

14th – The Launch of the Baroda

The large and beautiful iron ship Baroda is the first vessel launched from the yard of the Millwall Iron Works and Ship-building Company, who have in hand the Northumberland frigate and other extensive commissions for the Government. The Baroda, a vessel of 2,091 tons and 400-horse power, is one of those two we have mentioned as being intended for the Peninsular and Oriental Company's service.

Today we have all been to Millwall to see the launch of the "Baroda". When we arrived at Millwall we went first to see the largest piece of iron in the world wrought. When it came out of the huge furnace we could not go near it was tremendously hot and so brilliant I could scarcely look at it. It was a very dangerous place to be in I think for there were large pieces of red hot iron lying all about, and great sparks flew from the furnaces in all directions. About 1.30, the owner of the ship and iron works took us all to the ship, he asked Aunt Buxton to christen her, she would not, but said that Emmie would. They were very much pleased to have her do it and we all had to get up into a sort of raised platform under the bow of the ship higher than all the other people, which was meant for the ladies and gentlemen. About 2 o'clock when everything was ready the master gave the word of command, she threw the bottle at the ship, it broke, and the instant after the ship went away at a great pace, it was grand to see it go, so quickly but perfectly upright, then directly she got into the water she heaved right over onto her side. Everybody was really frightened, they thought she had gone right over so that the whole crowd ceased cheering, but then again she righted herself, and turned up the river, but so much did go over that three men were thrown into the water. She looked beautiful in the river and they directly began to tow her back again opposite the yard to put in her engines &c.

Ellen Buxton, *Journal*

15th – The Great Eastern and the Transatlantic Cable

The history of the laying of the Atlantic cable is well known. The 'Great Eastern' started from Valentia on June 23, 1865, under the command of Captain (now Sir James) Anderson, and the cable was laid more than half way across the Atlantic; but, on hauling in to recover a fault, it was broken, and dropped to the bottom of the sea.

The grappling tackle was not sufficiently strong. The cable was three times partially raised, and each time lost; and the expedition returned to England defeated, but with the knowledge that ultimate success was certain.

The engineers and scientific men on board the 'Great Eastern' drew up a memorandum as to the results of this expedition, and, among other things, stated—'That the steam-ship "Great Eastern," from her size and constant steadiness, and from the control over her afforded by the joint use of paddles and screw, renders it safe to lay an Atlantic cable in any weather.'

Sufficient additional cable was made to lay a second one and to finish the old cable when it should be recovered. The ship started again on July 13, 1866, and laid the cable across the Atlantic without the slightest mishap. She then returned, and after three weeks of hard work, the end of the cable which had been lost the year before was picked up, and completed to Newfoundland.

Isambard Brunel, *The Life of Isambard Kingdom Brunel,*
Civil Engineer

16th – The First Transatlantic Telegraph Message

Glory to God in the highest; on earth, peace and good will toward men.

Sent from Valentia Island, Ireland, on 16 August 1858

17th – Advantages of Railway-Tunnels

We cannot help repeating a narrative which we heard on one occasion, told with infinite gravity by a clergyman whose name we at once inquired about, and of whom we shall only say, that he is one of the worthiest and best sons of the kirk, and knows when to be serious as well as when to jest. "Don't tell me," said he to a simple-looking Highland brother, who had apparently made his first trial of railway travelling in coming up to the Assembly— "don't tell me that tunnels on railways are an unmitigated evil:

they serve high moral and aesthetical purposes. Only the other day I got into a railway carriage, and I had hardly taken my seat, when the train started. On looking up, I saw sitting opposite to me two of the most rabid dissenters in Scotland. I felt at once that there could be no pleasure for me in that journey, and with gloomy heart and countenance I leaned back in my corner. But all at once we plunged into a deep tunnel, black as night, and when we emerged at the other end, my brow was clear and my ill-humour was entirely dissipated. Shall I tell you how this came to be? All the way through the tunnel I was shaking my fists in the dissenters' faces, and making horrible mouths at them, and *that* relieved me, and set me all right. Don't speak against tunnels again, my dear friend."

Anon, *Fraser's Magazine, Railway Adventures and Anecdotes*

18th – Veils on Horseback

Never wear a veil on horseback, except it be a black one, and nothing with a border looks well. A plain band of spotted net, just reaching below the nostrils, and gathered away into a neat knot behind, is the most *distingué*. Do not wear anything sufficiently long to cover the mouth, or it will cause you inconvenience on wet and frosty days. For dusty roads a black gauze veil will be found useful, but avoid, as you would poison, every temptation to wear even the faintest scrap of colour on horseback. All such atrocities as blue and green veils have happily long since vanished, but, even still, a red bow, a gaudy flower stuck in the button-hole, and, oh, horror of horrors! a pocket handkerchief appearing at an opening in the bosom, looking like a miniature fomentation—these still occasionally shock the eyes of sensitive persons, and cause us to marvel at the wearer's bad taste.

Nannie Lambert, *Ladies on Horseback*

19th – Cats and Dogs in London

The number of dogs in London is supposed to be about two hundred thousand; no doubt it is really greater, since many dogs escape the tax. Cats in London are very much more numerous than dogs. Thus, in the streets I know best, in the part of London where I live, there are about eight cats to every dog; in some streets there are ten or twelve, in others not more than six. If a census could be taken it would probably show that the entire cat population does not fall short of three-quarters of a million; but I may be wide of the mark in this estimate, and should prefer at present to say that there are certainly not less than half a million cats in London. Even this may seem an astonishing number, since it is not usual for any house to have more than one, and in a good many houses not one is kept. On the other hand there is a vast population of ownerless cats. These cannot well be called homeless since they all attach themselves to some house, which they make their home, and to which they return as regularly as any wild beast to its den or lair. Judging solely from my own observation, I do not think that there can be less than from eighty thousand to one hundred thousand of these ownerless cats in the metropolis. Let me take the case of the house I live in. No cat is kept, yet from year's end to year's end there are seldom less than three cats to make use of it, or to make it their home. At all hours of the day they are to be seen in the area, or on the doorsteps, or somewhere near; and at odd times they go into the basement rooms—they get in at the windows, or at any door that happens to be left open, and if not discovered spend the night in the house. There are scores of houses in my immediate neighbourhood which have no smell of valerian about them and are favoured in the same way.

W. H. Hudson, *Birds in London*

20th – A Lifeboat in Action

At another time, however, I had an opportunity of seeing the Lifeboat in action. It was when I was spending a couple of weeks on board of the "Gull" Lightship, which lies between Ramsgate and the Goodwins.

A "dirty" day had culminated in a tempestuous night. The watch on deck, clad in drenched oil-skins, was tramping overhead, rendering my repose fitful. Suddenly he opened the skylight, and shouted that the Southsand Head Lightship was firing, and sending up rockets. As this meant a wreck on the sands we all rushed on deck, and saw the flare of a tar-barrel in the far distance. Already our watch was loading, and firing our signal-gun, and sending up rockets for the purpose of calling off the Ramsgate Lifeboat. It chanced that the Broadstairs boat observed the signals first, and, not long after, she flew past us under sail, making for the wreck.

A little later we saw the signal-light of the Ramsgate tug, looming through the mist like the great eye of the storm-fiend. She ranged close up, in order to ask whereaway the wreck was. Being answered, she sheared off, and as she did so, the Lifeboat, towing astern, came full into view. It seemed as if she had no crew, save only one man—doubtless my friend Jarman—holding the steering lines; but, on closer inspection, we could see the men crouching down, like a mass of oilskin coats and sou'westers. In a few minutes they were out of sight, and we saw them no more, but afterwards heard that the wrecked crew had been rescued and landed at Deal.

R. M. Ballantine, *Personal Reminiscences in Book Making*

21st – Felix Randal

Felix Randal the farrier, O he is dead then? my duty all ended,
Who have watched his mould of man, big-boned and
   hardy-handsome
Pining, pining, till time when reason rambled in it and some
Fatal four disorders, fleshed there, all contended?

Sickness broke him. Impatient he cursed at first, but mended
Being anointed and all; though a heavenlier heart began some
Months earlier, since I had our sweet reprieve and ransom
Tendered to him. Ah well, God rest him all road ever he offended!

This seeing the sick endears them to us, us too it endears.
My tongue had taught thee comfort, touch had quenched thy
   tears,
Thy tears that touched my heart, child, Felix, poor Felix Randal;

How far from then forethought of, all thy more boisterous years,
When thou at the random grim forge, powerful amidst peers,
Didst fettle for the great grey drayhorse his bright and battering
   sandal!

Gerard Manley Hopkins

Gerard Manley Hopkins (1844–89) wrote poetry from his childhood. In his early twenties he converted to Catholicism, becoming a member of the Jesuit order. After ordination in 1877 he worked in various parishes in England and Scotland, before going to Stoneyhurst School as a teacher of Greek and Latin. From there he went to University College Dublin, as Professor of Classics, and he died there of typhoid fever. When he became a Jesuit, Gerard Manley Hopkins thought he should not write any more poetry but one of the clergy he knew encouraged him to write about five nuns who drowned when the *Deutschland* sank, and after that he wrote regularly. His work was not published in his lifetime (one editor said he dared not print it) because his use of language was very idiosyncratic, and also he did not want the publicity.

22nd – The Indian Mutiny

In the month of July, the rebels having advanced after many defeats, from Gwalior, to threaten Rajpootana, and attempt to raise the numerous independent states in that region; several columns were put in motion, either in pursuit or to cover important points which the rebels might have attempted to seize. The principle column left Nusseerabad, under Major General Roberts. Being foiled in an advance on Jeypoor by this column, the rebels turned in a south-westerly direction, and after much delay had been experienced on both sides from the rainy season being at its height, they entered Oodeypore State, apparently with the desperate resolve to seize that city (Oodeypore), the capital of Meywar, and then to push on to Guzerat. They were closely followed by General Roberts and Colonel Holmes. From the Oodeypore State, passes intersect the Aravulli Mountains, opening into Marwar or Jondpore; one, the Chutterbooj Pass, is narrow and difficult, but through it the rebels might have gained the Jondpore States, or might have turned southwards through Seerohee into Guzerat. To counteract this possible move on the part of the enemy, a small field force was quickly despatched from Deesa, towards Nusseerabad, leaving the former place on the 13th August. It comprised (including a company from Mount Aboo, which joined at Anadra), 200 of the 89th, under Captain Selby, half a battery of Artillery, a detachment 31st Native Infantry, and some Guzerat Horse, with other irregular Cavalry, the whole under command of Major Boyle, 89th.

These field detachments marched to Erinpoora, but before their arrival, the Chutterbooj Pass, had with others been secured, and Major-General Roberts, had inflicted two signal defeats on the rebels, causing them to leave Oodypore, and turn eastwards to re-cross the Chumbul. He thereafter dispensed with the further services of the field detachments, which accordingly returned to Deesa, except the company from Mount Aboo, which returned to the latter place and not to Deesa, until three weeks later, *i.e.*, about the 25th September.

In consequence of the above mentioned advance of the rebels into Rajpootana, the field force of Major Grimes which had remained near Edur, was moved on early in August to Oodeypore. It was found necessary, to avert disturbances among the Hill Tribes near Edur, to detach fresh troops from Ahmedabad to that district. A company of the 89th left Ahmedabad under Captain Conyers (with Lieutenant Browning), who was shortly after relieved by Captain Heycock, on whom the command of field detachments amounting to several hundred men, and comprising the three arms of the service devolved. The malcontents continuing troublesome, and resisting the reasonable demands made upon them, it was found necessary to attack the strongly situated and fortified village of Mondetti, which was in a short time carried. A few days after this vindication of the British Power, the greater part of the force returned to Ahmedabad.

Indian Mutiny, the 89th (Princess Victoria's) Regiment in
Oodeypore, 1858

23rd – A Visit to London

On my way back through London I went to my first evening party. It was at Lambeth Palace. Well do I remember my Aunt Kitty (Mrs. Stanley) looking me over before we set out, and then saying slowly, "Yes, you will *do*." At Lambeth I first heard on this occasion the beautiful singing of Mrs. Wilson, one of the three daughters of the Archbishop (Sumner). His other daughters, Miss Sumner and Mrs. Thomas and her children lived with him, and the household of united families dwelling harmoniously together was like that of Sir Thomas More. Another evening during this visit in London I made the acquaintance of the well-known Miss Marsh, and went with her to visit a refuge for reclaimed thieves in Westminster. As we were going over one of the rooms where they were at work, she began to speak to them, and warmed with her subject into a regular address, during which her bonnet fell off upon her shoulders, and, with her sparkling eyes and rippled hair, she looked quite inspired. It was on the same day—in the morning—that, under the auspices of Lea, who was a friend of the steward, I first saw Apsley House, where the sitting-room of the great Duke was then preserved just as he left it the year before, the pen lying by the dusty inkstand, and the litter of papers remaining as he had scattered them.

Augustus Hare, *The Story of My Life*

24th – The Bough-Houses of Horncastle

A curious custom which formerly prevailed in the town at the time of the great fairs, and which continued to later than the middle of the 19th century, was the opening of what were termed "Bough-houses," for the entertainment of visitors. Horncastle has still an unusually large number of licensed public-houses, and not many years ago had nearly twice the number, many of them with extensive stabling, for the accommodation of man and beast, at the fairs for which it is famous; but, beyond these, it was a custom, from time immemorial, that any private house could sell beer without a licence, if a bough, or bush, was hung out at the door. This, no doubt, gave rise to the old saying, "good wine needs no bush," *i.e.*, the quarters where it was sold would need no bough or bush hung out to advertise its merits, as they would be a matter of common bruit. This, as was to be expected, was a privilege liable to be abused, and, only to give one instance, a couple living in the town and owning a name not unknown at Woodhall Spa, are said to have ordered for themselves a goodly barrel of beer to be ready for the fair, but, the barrel having been delivered two or three days before the fair commenced, they had themselves tried its merits so frequently, that when the day arrived there was none left to sell, and the barrel was unpaid for, with no means received to pay for it, while they themselves were no better for the transaction.

J. Conway Walter, *Records of Woodhall Spa and Neighbourhood*

25th – Taming a Robin

One summer, many years ago, we occupied an old-fashioned house in the country, where, in perfect quietude, one could make acquaintance with birds and study their habits and manners without interruption. From the veranda of a large, low-ceilinged sitting-room one looked out upon a garden of the olden type, full of moss-grown apple-trees, golden daffodils, lupines and sweet herbs, that pleasant mixture of the kitchen and flower garden which always seems so enjoyable. It was an ideal home for birds, no cat was ever visible, and from the numbers of the feathered folk one could believe that countless generations had been reared in these apple-trees and lived out their little lives in perfect happiness. I soon found a friend amongst the robins; one in particular began to pay me frequent visits as I sat at work indoors. At first he ventured in rather timidly, took a furtive glance and then flew away, but finding that crumbs were scattered for him, and while he picked them up a kindly voice encouraged his advances, he soon became at ease, made his way into the room and seemed to examine by turns, with birdish curiosity, all the pieces of furniture and the various ornaments on the mantelpiece and tables. Much to my pleasure he began to sing to me, and very pretty he looked, sitting amongst the flowers in a tall vase, warbling his charming little ditty, keeping his large black eyes fixed upon me as if to see if I seemed impressed by his vocal efforts.

Once he stopped in the middle of his song, looked keenly at a corner of the ceiling, and after a swift flight there, he returned with a spider in his beak; one can well believe what good helpers the insect-eating birds must be to the gardener, by destroying countless hosts of minute caterpillars and grubs that would otherwise prey upon the garden produce. Bobbie continued his visits to me throughout the summer, remaining happy and content for hours at a time, pluming himself, singing, and at times investigating the contents of a little cupboard, where he sometimes discovered a cake which was much to his taste, on which he feasted without any leave asked, though truly it would have been readily given to such a pleasant little visitor. He soon showed such entire confidence in me that he would perch on the book I was reading, and alight on my lap for crumbs even when many people were in the room.

Eliza Brightwen, *Wild Nature Won by Kindness*

Eliza Brightwen (1830–1906) was Scottish, but spent most of her life in London and its suburbs. She had a lonely childhood and, after she married, health problems meant she mostly stayed at home. She loved nature, and studied it in the 170-acre gardens of her home. Her first book was written when she was sixty; she was to publish half a dozen titles. In her day she was a very popular naturalist.

26th – How a Fox Caught a Pheasant

A farmer saw a pheasant go to roost in a tree, standing alone in the field. Presently he saw a fox approach, go to the tree, and look up at the pheasant. After pausing for a moment, regarding the bird, he proceeded to run rapidly round the tree in a narrow circle. This he did for some time, continuing his circuit without intermission; when, to the farmer's astonishment, the pheasant fell from its roost, and before it reached the ground was seized by the fox, who went off with his prey to a neighbouring plantation. This would seem to have been a case of hypnotism, rather than neurasthenia. The bird was mesmerised, or made giddy, by the fox's circular motion, and literally fell into the operator's arms.

J. Conway Walter, *Records of Woodhall Spa and Neighbourhood*

27th – Gifts

Give a man a horse he can ride,
Give a man a boat he can sail;
And his rank and wealth, his strength and health,
On sea nor shore shall fail.

Give a man a pipe he can smoke,
Give a man a book he can read:
And his home is bright with a calm delight,
Though the room be poor indeed.

Give a man a girl he can love,
As I, O my love, love thee;

And his heart is great with the pulse of Fate,
At home, on land, on sea.

James Thomson

James Thomson (1834–82) was born in Scotland, but sent to an orphanage in London after his father had a stroke. He was trained as an army schoolmaster, and worked in that profession for some years, before becoming a solicitor's clerk. Working for a mining company took him to the western United States in 1872, and he worked as a journalist in Spain for the *New York World* in 1873. Throughout his life he wrote poetry, essays and criticism: his most famous work is a long and very gloomy, pessimistic poem entitled *The City of Dreadful Night*.

28th – A Cautionary Tale

Once upon a time, there lived two men who determined to try and reach the source of light. And one of them, A, obtained wings and by their aid soared aloft; and looking down saw the other man B poking about here and there among a heap of stones and rubbish, and thought how foolish he was to waste his time in grovelling.

The next time he looked, he saw that B was sorting out some of the stones, and was beginning to pile them one on another; but he could not waste his time any longer in looking down, so he went on soaring heavenwards.

But B still went on piling up stones, and his building rose higher and higher; and onlookers were divided in their opinions as to which was the more likely to succeed, and some among them thought that neither would actually reach the goal. At first, everyone thought that A would get the higher, but after a time their opinion changed, for when he had risen a certain distance, some laws of nature, which he might have discovered had he paid a little more attention to earthly things—those relating to gravity, for instance—prevented him from rising any higher, and he was wafted hither and thither by every wind—now rising as a higher wave of air passed, and then sinking into the trough of the wave as a depression came by.

And still B went on with his building, till in time it grew to be an exceedingly high tower. And all the while, A kept on beating the air with his pinions in the vain endeavour to rise higher. But at last he grew very weary, and was fain to rest a while on the summit of B's tower. And thence he took a fresh flight upwards and was for a time able to keep himself aloft, but he soon sank again to his former level. Still it never entered his thoughts that B had adopted the better plan, and must in the long run leave him far behind.

And some people say that the real name of A was "Philosopher," and that of B "Scientist."

Dorothea Beale, *Philosophy Versus Science*

29th – Dartmoor and the Drought

During the abnormally dry summers of 1893 and 1897 Dartmoor proved of incalculable advantage not to the County of Devon only, but far further afield. When grass was burnt up everywhere, and water failed, then the moor was green, and was twinkling with dancing streams. From every quarter the starving cattle were driven there in thousands and tens of thousands. Drovers came from so far east as Kent, there to obtain food and drink unobtainable elsewhere. Thousands and tens of thousands more might have been sustained there but for the enclosures that have been suffered to be made— nay, have been encouraged.

Sabine Baring-Gould, *A Book of the West*

30th – Liberty

The object of this essay is to assert one very simple principle, as entitled to govern absolutely the dealings of society with the individual in the way of compulsion and control, whether the means used be physical force in the form of legal penalties, or the moral coercion of public opinion. That principle is, that the sole end for which mankind are warranted, individually or collectively, in interfering with the liberty of action of any of their number, is self-protection. That the only purpose for which power can be rightfully exercised over any member of a civilized community, against his will, is to prevent harm to others. His own good, either physical or moral, is not a sufficient warrant. He cannot rightfully be compelled to do or forbear because it will be better for him to do so, because it will make him happier, because, in the opinions of others, to do so would be wise, or even right. These are good reasons for remonstrating with him, or reasoning with him, or persuading him or entreating him, but not for compelling him, or visiting him with any evil, in case he do otherwise. To justify that, the conduct from which it is desired to deter him must be calculated to produce evil to some one else. The only part of the conduct of any one, for which he is amenable to society, is that which concerns others. In the part which merely concerns himself, his independence is, of right, absolute. Over himself, over his own body and mind, the individual is sovereign.

John Stuart Mill, *On Liberty*

31st – How to Clean Shoes

We need hardly dwell on the boot-cleaning process: three good brushes and good blacking must be provided; one of the brushes hard, to brush off the mud; the other soft, to lay on the blacking; the third of a medium hardness, for polishing; and each should be kept for its particular use. The blacking should be kept corked up, except when in use, and applied to the brush with a sponge tied to a stick, which, when put away, rests in a notch cut in the cork. When boots come in very muddy, it is a good practice to wash off the mud, and wipe them dry with a sponge; then leave them to dry very gradually on their sides, taking care they are not placed near the fire, or scorched. Much delicacy of treatment is required in cleaning ladies' boots, so as to make the leather look well-polished, and the upper part retain a fresh appearance, with the lining free from hand-marks, which are very offensive to a lady of refined tastes.

Patent leather boots require to be wiped with a wet sponge, and afterwards with a soft dry cloth, and occasionally with a soft cloth and sweet oil, blacking and polishing the edge of the soles in the usual way, but so as not to cover the patent polish with blacking. A little milk may also be used with very good effect for patent leather boots.

Top boots are still occasionally worn by gentlemen. While cleaning the lower part in the usual manner, protect the tops, by inserting a cloth or brown paper under the edges and bringing it over them. In cleaning the tops, let the covering fall down over the boot; wash the tops clean with soap and flannel, and rub out any spots with pumice-stone. If the tops are to be whiter, dissolve an ounce of oxalic acid and half an ounce of pumice-stone in a pint of soft water; if a brown colour is intended, mix an ounce of muriatic acid, half an ounce of alum, half an ounce of gum Arabic, and half an ounce of spirit of lavender, in a pint and a half of skimmed milk "turned." These mixtures apply by means of a sponge, and polish, when dry, with a rubber made of soft flannel.

Mrs Isabella Beeton, *Mrs Beeton's Book of Household Management*

SEPTEMBER

1st – A First Aid Course

FIRST LECTURE.
A. Preliminary remarks, object of Instruction, &c.
B. A general outline of the Structure and Functions of the Human Body, including a brief description of the Bones, Muscles, Arteries, and Veins. The Functions of the Circulation, Respiration, and of the Nervous System.
C. The triangular and roller bandages; their application.

SECOND LECTURE.
A. The general direction of the Main Arteries indicating the points where the circulation may be arrested by digital pressure, or by the application of a tourniquet.
B. The difference between Arterial, Venous, and Capillary Bleeding, and the various extemporary means of arresting it.
C. The triangular and roller bandages.

THIRD LECTURE.
A. The signs of Fracture, and first aid to be rendered in such accidents. The application of splints, or other restraining apparatus.
B. The triangular and roller bandages.

FOURTH LECTURE.
A. First aid to those suffering collapse from injury, to those stunned, to the apoplectic, inebriated, epileptic, fainting, and to those bitten by rabid animals.

B. The immediate treatment of the apparently drowned, or otherwise suffocated.

C. Burns, scalds, and poisons.

FIFTH LECTURE FOR *FEMALES* ONLY.

A. Hints on nursing, warming and ventilating the sick chamber. The use of the thermometer.

B. Tending and observing the sick, dressing wounds, making poultices, changing sheets, lifting helpless patients, feeding the sick.

C. Improvised methods of carrying helpless patients.

FIFTH LECTURE FOR *MALES* ONLY.

A. The improvised method of lifting and carrying the sick or injured.

B. Methods of lifting and carrying the sick or injured on stretchers.

C. The conveyance of such by rail, or in country carts.

Note I.

The subject of poisons should be treated in a general manner. The common poisons classified, and only their general symptoms and effects taught.

With regard to the treatment, the first indication, viz., how to get rid of the poison, is the only one which can be safely practiced by non-professional persons. The administration of antidotes is the medical man's duty.

Note II.

The last half-hour of each lecture should be devoted to practical work, such as the application of bandages and splints, lifting wounded, and carrying on stretchers. All female pupils will have to satisfy the Examiner as to their knowledge of the application of both the roller and triangular bandages. Male pupils will also receive instruction in both, but will have to pass in the latter only.

Note III.

There should be an interval of a week between each lecture. A candidate for examination must attend at least four out of the five lectures.

Syllabus from the Order of St John/St John's Ambulance

2nd – Salaries of the Liberal Professions

PRIVATE FORTUNES

My English friends confirm what I had guessed about the large number and the vastness of the private fortunes. "Take a cab from Sydenham; for five miles you will pass houses which indicate an annual outlay of £1,500 and upwards." According to the official statistics of 1841, there are one million of servants to sixteen millions of inhabitants. The liberal professions are much better remunerated than on the Continent. I know a musician at Leipzig of first-class talent; he receives 3s. a lesson at the Academy of Leipzig, 6s. in the city, and one guinea in London. The visit of a doctor who is not celebrated costs 4s. or 9s. in Paris, and a guinea here. With us a professor at the College of France receives £300, at the Sorbonne £480, at the School of Medicine £400. A professor at Oxford, a head of a house, has often from £1,000 to £3,000. Tennyson, who writes little, is said to make £5,000 a year. The Head Master of Eton has a salary of £6,080, of Harrow £6,280, of Rugby £2,960; many of the masters in these establishments have salaries from £1,200 to £1,240—one of them at Harrow has £2,220. The Bishop of London has £10,000 a year, the Archbishop of York has £15,000. An article is paid for at the rate of £8 the sheet in the *Revue des Deux Mondes*, and £20 in the English Quarterlies. The *Times* has paid £100 for a certain article. Thackeray, the novelist, has made £160 in twenty-four hours through the medium of two lectures, the one being delivered in Brighton, the other in London; from the magazine to which he contributed his novels he received £2,000 a year, and £10 a page in addition; this magazine had 100,000 subscribers; he estimated his own yearly earnings at £4,800.

Hippolyte Taine, *Notes on England*

3rd – A Train Journey through the Slums

Over the pest-stricken regions of East London, sweltering in sunshine which served only to reveal the intimacies of abomination; across miles of a city of the damned, such as thought never conceived before this age of ours; above streets swarming with a nameless populace, cruelly exposed by the unwonted light of heaven; stopping at stations which it crushes the heart to think should be the destination of any mortal, the train made its way at length beyond the utmost limits of dread, and entered upon a land of level meadows, of hedges and trees, of crops and cattle.

George Gissing, *The Nether World*, 1889

George Gissing (1858–1903) was a brilliant student, but was expelled from Owens College, Manchester, for stealing, which meant he could not take up a place he had gained at London University. After a month in prison, he was sent to America, where he taught and wrote. On his return, he married the prostitute for whom he had stolen money. She was a drunk, and eventually he paid her to live apart from him. He wrote many novels, but it took time before he earned very much by writing. Conscious of his humble origins, he was also lonely, though he did make friends with H G Wells. Many of his books deal with slum conditions, and the problems caused by domestic, financial and social difficulties.

4th – The Inexplicable Unpopularity of Lord Palmerston

Osborne, 4th September 1858
The most remarkable feature of the last Session of Parliament has been the extraordinary unpopularity of Lord Palmerston, for which nothing can account; the only direct reproach which is made to him, is to have appointed Lord Clanricarde Privy Seal, and to have been overbearing in his manner. Yet a House of Commons, having been elected solely for the object, and on the ground of supporting Lord Palmerston personally (an instance in our Parliamentary history without parallel), holds him suddenly in such abhorrence, that not satisfied with having upset his Government, which had been successful in all its policy, and thrown him out, it will hardly listen to him when he speaks. He is frequently received with hooting, and throughout the last Session it sufficed that [he] took up any cause for the whole House voting against it, even if contrary to the principles which they had themselves advocated, merely to have the satisfaction of putting him into a minority. How can this be accounted for? The man who was without rhyme or reason stamped the only *English* statesman, the champion of liberty, the man of the people, etc., etc., now, without his having changed in

any one respect, having still the same virtues and the same faults that he always had, young and vigorous in his seventy-fifth year, and having succeeded in his policy, is now considered the head of a clique, the man of intrigue, past his work, etc., etc.—in fact hated! and this throughout the country. I cannot explain the enigma except by supposing that people had before joined in a cry which they thought was popular without themselves believing what they said and wrote, and that they now do the same; that the Radicals used his name to destroy other statesmen and politicians, and are destroying him now in his turn; that they hoped to govern through him, and that they see a better chance now of doing it through a weak and incapable Tory Government which has entered into a secret bargain for their support. Still the phenomenon remains most curious.

Lord Palmerston himself remains, outwardly at least, quite cheerful, and seems to care very little about his reverses; he speaks on all subjects, bids for the Liberal support as before, even at the expense of his better conviction (as he used to do), and keeps as much as possible before the public; he made an official tour in Ireland, and is gone to visit the Emperor Napoleon at Paris; his Chinese policy upon which the general Dissolution had taken place in 1867 has just been crowned by the most complete success by the advantageous treaty signed at Pekin by Lord Elgin; and yet even for this the public will not allow him any credit. Lady Palmerston, on the contrary, is said to be very unhappy and very much hurt.

Prince Albert, Memorandum

Albert of Saxe-Coburg, Prince Consort (1819–61), married Queen Victoria when they were both twenty. He had been well-educated; he was a linguist and loved history and the natural sciences, and was a gifted composer and organist. Victoria wanted him to be present at state occasions, but would not give him any share in her political duties, which he found frustrating. He worked hard on a project to make South Kensington a centre for education and arts, and reformed and modernised Cambridge University as its chancellor. His interest in arts, science and technology led to his organisation of the Great Exhibition of 1851.

5th – Jenny Lind

Was it in 1847 that I first saw Jenny Lind? It was as she ran in upon the stage at Her Majesty's Opera House in the 'Figlia del Reggimento',— a wild, fair-haired fawn of genius, all gold and goodness, from her native snow-clad hills, looking round with scared eyes, stepping rhythmically, and beating her little drum. No operatic sensation in my memory equals that. What a ravishment about Jenny Lind there was that season throughout London,— crammed houses every night to hear her and adore her in public; and the old Duke of Wellington hanging about her at private concerts like an enamoured grandfather, and forgetting Waterloo as he put her shawl round her after her songs!

David Masson, *Memories of London in the 'Forties*

Jenny Lind (1820–87) grew up in poverty in Stockholm. As a child, she would sing to herself or her cat. When she was nine, a ballet dancer's attendant heard her singing through a window. She got her mistress to come and listen, and she took the child to the director of the Swedish Royal Opera, who was amazed at Lind's voice. She gained many admirers in Sweden, then internationally, after studies in Paris and performances throughout Europe. Crowds flocked to see her and hear her sing. Many Americans were not familiar with opera, but a tour organised by P. T. Barnum was a huge success, musically and financially. His promotion of 'The Swedish Nightingale', on the back of her triumph in England, where she had made friends with Queen Victoria and Prince Albert, made Jenny Lind the first modern 'celebrity'.

6th – History

If the Past has been an obstacle and a burden, knowledge of the Past is the safest and the surest emancipation. And the earnest search for it is one of the signs that distinguish the four centuries of which I speak from those that went before. The Middle Ages, which possessed good writers of contemporary narrative, were careless and impatient of older fact. They became content to be deceived, to live in a twilight of fiction, under clouds of false witness, inventing according to convenience, and glad to welcome the forger and the cheat. As time went on, the atmosphere of accredited mendacity thickened, until, in the Renaissance, the art of exposing falsehood dawned upon keen Italian minds. It was then that History as we understand it began to be understood, and the illustrious dynasty of scholars arose to whom we still look both for method and material. Unlike the dreaming prehistoric world, ours knows the need and the duty to make itself master of the earlier times, and to forfeit nothing of their wisdom or their warnings, and has devoted its best energy and treasure to the sovereign purpose of detecting error and vindicating entrusted truth.

Lord Acton, *Lectures on Modern History*

John Acton (1834–1902) was a historian and writer. Brought up largely in Europe, he was a liberal Catholic, writing articles for Catholic magazines. Reporting on the Vatican Council of 1870–71, he was opposed to the doctrine of papal infallibility. He served as an MP, was Regius Professor of Modern History at Cambridge, and edited the multi-volume Cambridge Modern History. He was particularly interested in freedom, and the role of individuals in bringing about freedom and progress in church and state.

7th – Arrival at the New Castle at Balmoral

7 September 1855. At a quarter-past seven o'clock we arrived at dear *Balmoral*. Strange, very strange, it seemed to me to drive past, indeed *through*, the old house; the connecting part between it and the offices being broken through. The new house looks beautiful. The tower and the rooms in the connecting part are, however, only half finished, and the offices are still unbuilt: therefore the gentlemen (except the Minister*) live in the old house, and so do most of the servants; there is a long wooden passage which connects the new house with the offices. An old shoe was thrown after us into the house, for good luck, when we entered the hall. The house is charming; the rooms delightful; the furniture, papers, everything perfection.

A Cabinet Minister is always in attendance upon the Queen at Balmoral.

Queen Victoria, *Leaves from our Highland Journal*

8th – Harvest Festival at Burcombe

Dear Mother,

The Harvest Home is over and in the midst of getting rid of things, whilst I am waiting for a wagon, I will tell you a little about it, as I know you will be interested. I write shabbily for I am very tired but not too much done up. Annie is wonderful, she exerted herself more perhaps than was prudent (but <u>who</u> can help doing so on such an occasion?) but is not the worse, I am thankful to say.

It is like a dream – for it was not thought of till Sunday morning. I did not know whether it would be wished, after the deaths among the Farmers in the past year. But they were all agog for it. Farmers and labourers here now seem to think Harvest isn't over till we have had our Festival. Had we not had it yesterday we must have waited a fortnight and thus have been <u>after others</u>, which doesn't suit our book – so we determined to do it off hand.

Freeman and John Rogers worked like slaves and got up the skeleton of the Tent in a day and a half. It was put away, carefully marked and packed, so as to be easily fitted together. I went to Salisbury on Monday morning, ordered the Tent cover – Beer – Crockery etc. and above all, hearing that the Bishop of Brisbane was at the Palace and coming to a meeting at Barford on Wednesday evening, I went to see if I could catch him on the way. I was successful. Tuesday we were busy collecting tables and forms, no small trouble this year, as I did not ask for Lady Herbert's because I had come to the conclusion that I could not honestly ask her as usual. The Misses Shephard were very energetic in decorating the Church – to which we gave them but little help. On Tuesday evening the Tent cover was on and the tent posts etc. decorated with evergreens and flags much as last year.

We were all abroad early on Wednesday morning, so many things have to be done, and thought of, in a little place like this. No one knows the work of it unless they have done the kind of thing, as we have here <u>ourselves</u>. By 12 o'clock or 12.30, the tables were laid and looked very nice. This year I only hired the ½ pint cups for the party. The Labourers on each farm brought plates for themselves and party, marked to their respective farmhouses on the morning of Wednesday. They were brought to the table in a basket and at the end of dinner taken away in the same manner. It saved a little expense and much washing and packing. Dishes I borrowed in the village.

Mr. Mayo killed a sheep and sent the 2 legs roasted, also 1 shoulder ditto, and six large meat pies, six apple ditto, potatoes, milk for tea and bread and butter for the children. Mr. Shephard also killed a sheep and sent much as Mr. Mayo. Mr. Rogers provided 3 large joints of beef. Mr. Lash of Ugford one joint of beef, Mr. T. Pain a splendid joint of beef, Mr. M. Lash a leg of mutton. All sent flowers, fruit and tarts. Mr. Hutchings sent 5/- and Haines (the Publican) bread.

The pudding (about 100 lbs.) came up hot as last year just as they sat down to dinner. The potatoes were cooked partly in our copper and partly in Haines'. The children had tea and cake just <u>outside</u> the Tent, as the weather was superb, a delightful contrast to last year.

Church hour was 2.30. The Band preceded the people to church at 2.15, they were in such a hurry to begin their fete. Unfortunately the Bishop did not arrive til 2.45 so they had to wait some time in Church. I had asked only Messrs. Hinxman, Buchanan and Swainson. We four accompanied the Bishop to Church in surplices.

The Church looked lovely from its very simplicity. Round the capitals the wild clematis, which now has a <u>fluffy</u> appearance, with berries of the wild Alder (red). The candlesticks with wheat, oats and barley alternatively, the Standards wreathed with small ivy. The windows had springs of evergreen almost hidden with flowers, Dahlias, German Asters etc. Over the Communion Table Annie had made a lovely reredos of black and white grapes with vine leaves.

The Bishop gave us a short, simple and most strikingly appropriate sermon, which was listened to with breathless silence. I was charmed with it. We attempted nothing Choral for we had had no time to practise, but I liked the plain service best and don't think I shall ever try the other again. The Psalms and Lessons were very appropriate, the responses very congregational and the singing hearty. Though we had asked no foreigners the Church was more crowded than ever. All our children went to Church. Edward was obliged to be taken out at once. The Baby bore all but the sermon. The collection at the door (for Brisbane) was £4. 0. 5½d. This amongst our quite poor people. In the evening Mr. Mayo brought me £1 more for himself and wife, so pleased were they with Brisbane, and a dissenter brought over this morning 1 shilling, which made £5. 1. 5½d.

Church over we adjourned to dinner. The order of march was Band – School Children – Mayo's farm – Shephard's farm – Roger's farm. This all depends on the arrangement of the Tent, so that places may be taken in an orderly manner. All seated, I brought the Bishop, Mr Hinxman and Mr. Mayo (Church warden) to their places of honour at the head of the Tent. I welcomed the guests in a few opening words – the Bishop said Grace.

After Grace the Band played on the lawn, and the Tent was cleared of victuals etc. and prepared for the evening. The dancing was very energetic – and the singing at intervals good. We had the large can for Tea as last year, which was very popular. At 9.30 after a round of cheers and National Anthem I dismissed them – all sober and thoroughly happy. Everyone said it was the best Harvest Home we have had yet. There was no contre-temps, and the weather superb – so hot that the men took off their coats to dance. Though we did not ask strangers we were very full. For our own Parishioners, high and low, were there in force, with friends many of them.

To-day I have got rid of everything. The last waggon load is just gone – only the Tent skeleton and beer barrels remaining. We are tired of course but not over done. The children have enjoyed it all immensely.

Edward Fiennes Trotman, letter to his mother

9th – The Giant's Causeway

And now, by force of money, having got rid of the sea and land beggars ... and at last you are left tranquil to look at the strange scene with your own eyes, and enjoy your own thoughts at leisure.

It looks like the beginning of the world, somehow: the sea looks older than in other places, the hills and rocks strange, and formed differently from other rocks and hills – as those vast dubious monsters were formed who possessed the earth before man. The hill-tops are shattered into a thousand cragged fantastical shapes; the water comes swelling into scores of little strange creeks, or goes off with a leap, roaring into those mysterious caves yonder, which penetrate who knows how far into our common world?

The savage rock-sides are painted of a hundred colours. Does the sun ever shine here? When the world was moulded and fashioned out of formless chaos this must have been the *bit over* — a remnant of chaos? Think of that! — it is a tailor's simile. Well, I am a Cockney: I wish I were in Pall Mall! Yonder is a kelp-burner: a lurid smoke from his burning kelp rises up to the leaden sky, and he looks as naked and fierce as Cain. Bubbling up out of the rocks at the very brim of the sea rises a little crystal spring: how comes it there? and there is an old grey hag beside, who has been there for hundreds and hundreds of years and there sits and sells whiskey at the extremity of creation! How do you dare to sell whiskey there, old woman? Did you serve old Saturn with a glass when he lay along the Causeway here? In reply she says, she has no change for a shilling: she never has; but her whiskey is good.

This is not a description of the Giant's Causeway (as some clever critic will remark), but of a Londoner there who is by no means so interesting an object as the natural curiosity in question. That single hint is sufficient; I have not a word more to say. "If," says he, "you cannot describe the scene lying before us — if you cannot state from your personal observation that the number of basaltic pillars composing the Causeway has been computed at about forty thousand which vary in diameter, their surface presenting the appearance of a tesselated pavement of polygonal stones — that each pillar is formed of several distinct joints, the convex end of the one being accurately fitted in the concave of the next, and the length of the joints varying from five feet to four inches — that although the pillars are polygonal, there is but one of three sides in the whole forty thousand (think of that!), but three of nine sides and that it may be safely computed that ninety nine out of one hundred pillars have either five, six, or seven sides — if you cannot state something useful, you had much better, sir, retire and get your dinner."

Never was summons more gladly obeyed. The dinner must be ready by this time, so, remain you, and look on at the awful scene, and copy it down in words if you can. If at the end of the trial you are dissatisfied with your skill as a painter and find that the biggest of your words cannot render the hues and vastness of that tremendous swelling sea — of those lean solitary crags standing rigid along the shore, where they have been watching the ocean ever since it was made — of those grey towers of Dunluce standing upon a leaden rock and looking as if some old, old princess, of old, old fairy times, were dragon-guarded within — of yon flat stretches

of sand where the Scotch and Irish mermaids hold conference —
come away too, and prate no more afloat the scene! There is that
in nature, dear Jenkins, which passes even our powers.

William Makepeace Thackeray, *The Irish Sketchbook*

10th – Whistler Deals with a Critic

On Saturday evening Mr. Whistler, the painter and epigrammatist,
distinguished himself during an entr'acte at Drury Lane Theatre
by making a disturbance in the foyer. The following description of
this gentlemanly and creditable affair is, we believe, substantially
correct. A number of gentlemen had assembled in the lobby to
enjoy a peaceful cigarette. Among the well dressed crowd was Mr.
Augustus Moore, the editor of a society paper which had printed
some uncomplimentary things about his work. Disdaining a formal
cartel, Mr. Whistler took the law into his own hands, and brought
his walking-stick into repeated contact with the editor's person.
Thereupon, Mr. Whistler was knocked down. Honour or revenge
having thus been satisfied, the principals were led from the field by
their sorrowing friends.

St. James's Gazette, September 1890

11th – The Gad-Whip and the Lectern

The only quaint custom associated with the lectern is the one
connected with the use of the gad-whip at Caistor, Lincolnshire,
on Palm Sunday. This extraordinary usage is sufficiently described
in a petition presented to the House of Lords in 1836 by the lord
of the manor of Hundon, near Caistor (Sir Culling Eardley Smith),
begging for its suppression. In this document it is said "that the lord
of the manor of Broughton, near Brigg, yearly, on Palm Sunday,
employs a person to perform the following ceremony in the parish
church of Caistor; a cart-whip of the fashion of several centuries
since, called a gad-whip, with four pieces of wyche-elm bound
round the stock, and a leather purse attached to the extremity of
the stock, containing thirty pence, is, during divine service, cracked
in the church porch; and, while the second lesson is reading, is
brought into the church, and held over the reading-desk by the

person who carries it. It is afterwards deposited with the tenant of Hundon." It was traditionally asserted that this act was originally a penance for a murder, and that the lord of Hundon could exact some penalty from the lord of Broughton if it were omitted. Sir Culling, in his capacity as the former of these magnates, made every effort to stop so indecent an interruption to the service, offering to indemnify any one who should be a loser by its cessation; but for some time in vain. At last in 1846 the land was sold, which was supposed to be held by this objectionable tenure, and the practice was allowed to lapse*.

The last gad-whip used is in the possession of Mr. William Andrews, of Hull.

George Smith Tyack, *Lore and Legend of the English Church*

12th – The Houses of Parliament

After coming out of the Abbey, we looked at the two Houses of Parliament, directly across the way,—an immense structure, and certainly most splendid, built of a beautiful warm-coloured stone. The building has a very elaborate finish, and delighted me at first; but by-and-by I began to be sensible of a weariness in the effect, a lack of variety in the plan and ornament, a deficiency of invention; so that, instead of being more and more interested the longer one looks, as is the case with an old Gothic edifice, and continually reading deeper into it, one finds that one has seen all in seeing a little piece, and that the magnificent palace has nothing better to show one or to do for one. It is wonderful how the old weather-stained and smoke-blackened Abbey shames down this brand-newness; not that the Parliament houses are not fine objects to look at, too.

Nathaniel Hawthorne, The *English Note-Books*

13th – Meeting Stanley

It was a reception given to meet Henry Stanley, the African explorer, by Colonel Grant, the discoverer of the sources of the Nile—and it was *the* event of the moment ... Other houses were deserted that night—such houses as had the misfortune to have unwittingly fixed upon it for their own entertainments. These were by no means so multifarious as they are now, and there were really no counter-balancing attractions of any consequence to draw off the surplus of the crowd in Upper Grosvenor Street ...

Well, the moment came at last, and I still see it before me. But I really do not know what made it so great. Henry Stanley did undoubtedly succeed in a great undertaking, but he did not in any way impress one as a great man. A space had been cleared in the front drawing-room; and in the centre of it turned and twisted the little explorer, looking for all the world like "Frog-in-the-Middle." He was all smiles and bows and shakes of the hand—looking as he no doubt felt, exceedingly proud and gratified by such an ovation—but to my mind he had a hard, cruel, relentless face, and an uneasy eye.

I wondered. Did he feel by what an uncertain tenure he held the world's esteem? Would things come out presently that would change its gracious front to one of indignation and contempt? Would the upright, noble-hearted Grant who was so entirely effacing his own claims to notice in favour of his rival on that memorable evening, would he one day wince at the sound of Stanley's name?

L. B. Walford, *Memoirs of Victorian London*

Lucy Bethia Walford (1845–1915) was a Scottish romantic novelist. She made every effort to research her stories, as she liked to be as accurate as possible. As well as forty-five novels, she wrote some short biographies of English female authors, and two books of memoirs.

Sir Henry Morton Stanley (1841–1904) was born in a Welsh workhouse, but went to the United States, where he became a journalist. In 1871, the *New York Herald* sent him to Africa, where he found David Livingstone, of whom nothing had been heard for some time. Thereafter, he led several exploratory expeditions to Africa: the last one (1886–9) from the Congo area to the Upper Nile caused controversy because of his ruthless and arrogant behaviour.

14th – Ode on the Death of the Duke of Wellington

A Selection
Lo, the leader in these glorious wars

Now to glorious burial slowly borne,
Followed by the brave of other lands,
He, on whom from both her open hands
Lavish Honor showered all her stars,
And affluent Fortune emptied all her horn.
Yea, let all good things await
Him who cares not to be great,
But as he saves or serves the state.
Not once or twice in our rough island-story,
The path of duty was the way to glory:
He that walks it, only thirsting
For the right, and learns to deaden
Love of self, before his journey closes,
He shall find the stubborn thistle bursting
Into glossy purples, which outredden
All voluptuous garden roses.
Not once or twice in our fair island-story,
The path of duty was the way to glory:
He, that ever following her commands,
On with toil of heart and knees and hands,
Thro' the long gorge to the far light has won
His path upward, and prevailed,
Shall find the toppling crags of Duty scaled
Are close upon the shining table lands
To which our God himself is moon and sun,
Such was he: his work is done,
But while the races of mankind endure,
Let his great example stand
Colossal, seen of every land,
And keep the soldier firm, the statesman pure;
Till in all lands and thro' all human story
The path of duty be the way to glory:
And let the land whose hearths he saved from shame
For many and many an age proclaim
At civic revel and pomp and game,
And when the long-illumined cities flame,
Their ever loyal iron leader's fame,
With honor, honor, honor, honor to him,
Eternal honor to his name.

Alfred, Lord Tennyson

Alfred Tennyson (1809–92) won a prize for his poetry at Cambridge, but a book of verse published just after he left university was very badly reviewed. This put him off publishing for over ten years, but in 1842 he brought out two collections of poems, both of which were very successful. He was appointed Poet Laureate in 1850, a position he occupied until he died, and was the first writer to become a peer – Queen Victoria made him a baron in 1884 – as a result of his work. He became an esteemed theatre designer, working on plays by dramatists such as Wilde, Bernard Shaw and W. B. Yeats.

15th – A Paradise for Children

Several following years of early childhood were spent at Norwood, with the Crystal Palace as an entrancing playground. In the early seventies the place was rich with the scent of the beds for tropical vegetation, stale buns, and new paint; and in the more rapturous end—where the parrots were kept—came unmistakable gusts and shrieks from the monkey-house, entrancing to the infantile mind, but deemed unhealthy and too exciting by parents and governess alike. The Crystal Palace was at that time a paradise for children, and one of the most comprehensive art museums in the world (this I knew later); it was also the home of music in England of that decade, with daily concerts, a small local opera, crashing brass bands, a mammoth organ, great Saturday classical concerts, and huge Handel Festivals. The place was not only full of appeals to the imagination, from the toy stalls to great intimidating groups of statuary, it was a world full of sound. The loud strains of a symphony might burst from the closed concert-room, interrupting the musical whiz and purring of a top spun by a toy-stall assistant; simultaneously would come the scarlet cries of a cockatoo and the persistent cadences of a popular valse played by a mechanical piano, and, most delightful of all, the tinny sounds of clockwork toys, which moved if a penny were dropped into them by an indulgent elder. Thereupon glass waterfalls would trickle in landscapes of Virginian cork; whilst a train, with cotton-wool smoke, darted over a Lilliputian bridge, and small Swiss peasants valsed, all too briefly, to the sound of a tired musical box.

Charles Ricketts, *Self-Portrait*

The half-French Charles Ricketts (1866–1931) was an illustrator, book designer, typographer, printer, set designer and writer. With his great friend Charles Shannon, he founded the Vale Press. He was a friend of Oscar Wilde, and one of the two artists who illustrated Wilde's work.

16th – News of the Death of Wellington

Alt-na-Giuthasach, Thursday 16 September 1852
We were startled this morning, at seven o'clock, by a letter from Colonel Phipps, enclosing a telegraphic despatch with the report, from the sixth edition of the *Sun*, of the Duke of Wellington's death the day before yesterday, which report, however, we did not at all believe. Would to God that we had been right; and that this day had not been cruelly saddened in the afternoon, when Mackenzie returned, bringing letters: amongst them there was one from Lord Derby, which I tore open, and alas! it contained the confirmation of the fatal news: that *England's*, or rather *Britain's* pride, her glory, her hero, the greatest man she ever had produced, was no more! Sad day! Great and irreparable national loss!

Lord Derby enclosed a few lines from Lord Charles Wellesley, saying that his dear great father had died on Tuesday at three o'clock, after a few hours' illness and no suffering. God's will be done! The day must have come: the Duke was eighty-three. It is well for him that he has been taken when still in the possession of his great mind, and without a long illness,—but what a *loss*! One cannot think of this country without 'the Duke,'—our immortal hero!

In him centred almost every earthly honour a subject could possess. His position was the highest a subject ever had,—above party,—looked up to by all,—revered by the whole nation,—the friend of the Sovereign;—and *how* simply he carried these honours! With what singleness of purpose, what straightforwardness, what courage, were all the motives of his actions guided. The Crown never possessed,—and I fear never *will*—so *devoted*, loyal, and faithful a subject, so staunch a supporter! To *us* (who alas! have lost, now, so many of our valued and experienced friends,) his loss is *irreparable*, for his readiness to aid and advise, if it could be of use to us, and to overcome any and every difficulty, was unequalled. To Albert he showed the greatest kindness and the utmost confidence. His experience and his knowledge of the past were so great too;

he was a link which connected us with bygone times, with the last century. Not an eye will be dry in the whole country.

> Queen Victoria, from *Leaves from the Journal of our Life in the Highlands*

17th – Adulterated Tea

Chinese tea has frequently been adulterated in this country, by the admixture of the dried leaves of certain plants. The leaves of the sloe, white thorn, ash, elder, and some others, have been employed for this purpose; such as the leaves of the speedwell, wild germander, black currants, syringa, purple-spiked willow-herb, sweet-brier, and cherry-tree. Some of these are harmless, others are to a certain degree poisonous; as, for example, are the leaves of all the varieties of the plum and cherry tribe, to which the sloe belongs. Adulteration by means of these leaves is by no means a new species of fraud; and several acts of parliament, from the time of George II, have been passed, specifying severe penalties against those guilty of the offence, which, notwithstanding numerous convictions, continues to the present time.

> Mrs Isabella Beeton, *Mrs Beeton's Book of Household Management*

18th – Picking Apples and Pears

Ah! they are gathering in the orchard harvest. Look at that young rogue in the old mossy apple-tree—that great tree, bending with the weight of its golden-rennets—see how he pelts his little sister beneath with apples as red and as round as her own cheeks, while she, with her outstretched frock, is trying to catch them, and laughing and offering to pelt again as often as one bobs against her; and look at that still younger imp, who, as grave as a judge, is creeping on hands and knees under the tree, picking up the apples as they fall so deedily, and depositing them so honestly in the great basket on the grass, already fixed so firmly and opened so widely, and filled almost to overflowing by the brown rough fruitage of the golden-rennet's next neighbour the russeting; and see that smallest urchin of all, seated apart in infantine state on the turfy bank, with that toothsome piece of deformity a crumpling in each hand, now biting from one sweet, hard, juicy morsel and now from another—Is not that a pretty English picture? And then, farther up the orchard, that bold hardy lad, the eldest born, who has scaled (Heaven knows how) the tall, straight upper branch of that great pear-tree, and is sitting there as securely and as fearlessly, in as much real safety and apparent danger, as a sailor on the top-mast. Now he shakes the tree with a mighty swing that brings down a pelting shower of stony bergamots, which the father gathers rapidly up, whilst the mother can hardly assist for her motherly fear—a fear which only spurs the spirited boy to bolder ventures.

Mary Russell Mitford, *Our Village*

19th – Building the Bell Rock Lighthouse

One day, soon after the men had commenced work, it began to blow hard, and the crew of the boat belonging to the attending vessel, named the "Smeaton," fearing that her moorings might be insufficient, went off to examine them. This was wrong. The workmen on the rock were sufficiently numerous to completely fill three boats. For one of these to leave the rock was to run a great risk, as the event proved. Almost as soon as they reached the "Smeaton," her cables parted and she went adrift, carrying the boat with her away to leeward, and although sail was instantly made, they found it impossible to regain the rock against wind and tide. Mr Stevenson observed this with the deepest anxiety, but the men (busy as bees about the rock), were not aware of it at first.

The situation was terrible. There were thirty-two men left on a rock which would in a short time be overflowed to a depth of twelve or fifteen feet by a stormy sea, and only two boats in which to remove them. These two boats, if loaded to the gunwales, could have held only a few more than the half of them.

While the sound of the numerous hammers and the ring of the anvil were heard, the situation did not appear so hopeless; but soon the men at the lowest part of the foundation were driven from work by the rising tide; then the forge-fire was extinguished, and the men generally began to make towards their respective boats for their jackets and dry socks. When it was discovered that one of the three boats was gone not a word was uttered, but the men looked at each other in evident perplexity. They seemed to realise their position at once.

In a few minutes some of that band must inevitably be left to perish, for the absent boat and vessel were seen drifting farther and farther away to leeward. ...While they were thus gazing in silence at each other and at the distant vessel, their enterprising leader had been casting about in his mind as to the best method of at least attempting the deliverance of his men, and he finally turned round to propose, as a forlorn hope, that all hands should strip off their upper clothing, that every unnecessary article should be removed from the boats, that a specified number should get into each, and that the remainder should hang on by the gunwales, and thus be dragged through the water while they were rowed cautiously towards the "Smeaton"! ... He was about to speak when some one shouted "a boat! a boat!" and, sure enough, a large boat was seen through the haze making towards the rock. This timely visitor was James Spink, the Bell Rock pilot, who had come off express from Arbroath with letters. His visit was altogether an unusual one, and his truly providential appearance unquestionably prevented loss of life on that critical occasion. This is one specimen—selected from innumerable instances of danger and risk—which may give one some idea of what is encountered by those who build such lighthouses as the Bell Rock.

R. M. Ballantine, *Personal Reminiscences in Book Making*

20th – The Arrival of Bloomers

On Sunday last much amusement was occasioned the public in St. James's Park by the arrival among them of a complete batch of "Bloomers," consisting of five females and two males, evidently belonging to the upper classes of society. Two of the ladies were Frenchwomen. They were certainly most elegantly attired. The Frenchwomen wore blue trousers, while those of our own countrywomen were pink ... The novel style of dress did not appear to be agreeable to the mob, for the "Bloomers" had scarce made their appearance before they were assailed with an unlimited quantity of vulgar jokes from the bystanders, causing them to beat a hasty retreat.

Illustrated London News, 20 September 1851

21st – Baby Law

The railways generously permit a baby to be carried without charge; but not, it seems, without incurring responsibility. It has been lately decided, in "Austin *v.* the Great Western Railway Company," 16 L. T. Rep., N. S., 320, that where a child in arms, not paid for as a passenger, is injured by an accident caused by negligence, the company is liable in damages under Lord Campbell's Act. Three of the judges were clearly of opinion that the company had, by permitting the mother to take the child in her arms, contracted to carry safely both mother and child; and Blackburn, J., went still further, and was of opinion that, independently of any such contract, express or implied, the law cast upon the company a duty to use proper and reasonable care in carrying the child, though unpaid for. It may appear somewhat hard upon railway companies to incur liabilities through an act of liberality, but they have chosen to do so. The law is against them, that is clear; but they have the remedy in their own hands. There was some reason for exempting a child in arms, for it occupies no place in the carriage, and is but a trifling addition of weight. But now it is established that the company is responsible for the consequences of accident to that child, the company is clearly entitled to make such a charge as will secure them against the risk. The right course would be to have a tariff, say one-fifth or one-fourth of the full fare, for a child in arms; and if strict justice was done, this would be deducted from the fares of the passengers who have the ill-luck to face and flank the squaller.

Anon, *Law Times*, 1867, *Railway Adventures and Anecdotes*

22nd – The Enthronement of the Archbishop of York

I arrived at Bishopthorpe the day before the Archbishop's enthronement, and found a large party of relations assembling; but it would be difficult to crowd the house, as there are forty bedrooms and the dining-room is huge. The palace lies low, and out of the dining-room window you could very nearly fish in the Ouse, which often floods the cellars, the only part remaining of the original house of Walter de Gray. The rococo gateway is imposed by guidebooks upon the uninitiated as that of Wolsey's palace at

Cawood: perhaps a few of its ornaments came from thence. The ceremony in the Minster was very imposing, the more so as a military escort was given to the Archbishop, as having been an old soldier. Most moving was his address upon the responsibilities, and what he felt to be the duties, of his office. The ebb and flow of processional music was beautiful, as the long stream of choristers and clergy flowed in and out of the Minster. The Archbishop's brothers—one of them, Sir Douglas-Maclagan, being eighty—made a very remarkable group.

Augustus Hare, *My Life*

23rd – The Two Old Bachelors

Two old Bachelors were living in one house;
One caught a Muffin, the other caught a Mouse.
Said he who caught the Muffin to him who caught the Mouse,—
"This happens just in time! For we've nothing in the house,
Save a tiny slice of lemon and a teaspoonful of honey,
And what to do for dinner—since we haven't any money?
And what can we expect if we haven't any dinner,
But to lose our teeth and eyelashes and keep on growing
      thinner?"

Said he who caught the Mouse to him who caught the Muffin,—
"We might cook this little Mouse, if we only had some Stuffin'!
If we had but Sage and Onion we could do extremely well;
But how to get that Stuffin' it is difficult to tell!"

Those two old Bachelors ran quickly to the town
And asked for Sage and Onion as they wandered up and down;
They borrowed two large Onions, but no Sage was to be found
In the Shops, or in the Market, or in all the Gardens round.

But some one said, "A hill there is, a little to the north,
And to its purpledicular top a narrow way leads forth;
And there among the rugged rocks abides an ancient Sage,—
An earnest Man, who reads all day a most perplexing page.
Climb up, and seize him by the toes,—all studious as he sits,—
And pull him down, and chop him into endless little bits!

Then mix him with your Onion (cut up likewise into Scraps),—
When your Stuffin' will be ready, and very good—perhaps."

Those two old Bachelors without loss of time
The nearly purpledicular crags at once began to climb;
And at the top, among the rocks, all seated in a nook,
They saw that Sage a-reading of a most enormous book.
"You earnest Sage!" aloud they cried, "your book you've read
    enough in!
We wish to chop you into bits to mix you into Stuffin'!"
But that old Sage looked calmly up, and with his awful book,
At those two Bachelors' bald heads a certain aim he took;
And over Crag and precipice they rolled promiscuous down,—
At once they rolled, and never stopped in lane or field or town;
And when they reached their house, they found (besides their
    want of Stuffin'),
The Mouse had fled—and, previously, had eaten up the Muffin.

They left their home in silence by the once convivial door;
And from that hour those Bachelors were never heard of more.

Edward Lear

24th – The Tub of Holy Water

But the chapel! Shall I ever forget the tub of holy water, on my
first Sunday, placed before the rickety little altar on the mud
floor, where the people, on coming in, splashed the water up
into their faces? The old women had all brought big bottles from
their homes in far-away glens to fill at the tub, and nothing could
surpass the comicality of their attitudes as they stooped over their
pious business, all wearing the hooded cloak that made them look
as broad as they were long. One old lady, in her nice white cap,
monopolized the tub an unconscionably long time, for, catching
sight of her wind-tossed tresses in that looking-glass, she finished
her devout ablutions by smoothing her few grey hairs with her
moistened fingers into tidy bands, with alternate signs of the cross.
The windows were all broken, and the men and boys stuffed the
holes with their hats and caps to keep out the mountain blast.

  Last Sunday, a very hot day, the tub happened to be placed

outside the door, and it was well my horse was not tied up within reach, or a former catastrophe might have been repeated, and a 'blessed baist' have carried me home. The heat in the rickety little gallery, where the 'quality' have their seats, was such that I went out into the open air and followed the rest of the service with a rock for my hassock, and two rosy pigs toddling about me in that friendly way I notice as characteristic of all the animals in these parts. They seem to feel they are members of the family, and you see calves, goats, pigs, and donkeys sauntering in and out of the cabin doors in a free-and-easy harmony with the human beings which takes my fancy greatly. But the beasts are by far the happiest; their lives seem passed in perfect contentment and satisfaction, whereas the poor human animals have a hard struggle for existence in this stony and difficult land of Kerry.

Elizabeth Butler, *Sketch-book and Diary*

25th – The Archangelic Bird

Michaelmas is a season of sad associations. The quarter's rent is due, alas! The quarter's gas, alas! and, alas a hundred times! the half-yearly rates. Bank accounts dwindle; spirits sink; life seems but a blank and dreary desert.

Into the gloom, settling down thicker and more throttling than November's fog, there flutters and waddles a big white bird, a saviour of men. It is the noble goose, the goose, ridiculed and misunderstood, that comes chivalrously and fearlessly to the rescue; the goose that once saved Rome's Capitol, the goose still honoured as most alert of sentinels within Barcelona's cathedral precincts, the goose that, followed by a goose-girl, is the beloved of artists. Because of its nobility of character, its devotion, wherein it rivals benevolent mastiff and kindly terrier, its courage, its strength, St Michael, glorious and effulgent archangel, took it for his own bird of birds, to be so intimately connected with him that now to show respect to the Saint is to eat the goose. The Feast of Michaelmas, to the right-minded and the orthodox, means roast goose and apple sauce. Soulless authorities, burrowing in mouldy records, can find no better reason for this close relationship than that, at September's close, great is the number of geese cackling in homely barnyard, great their perfection. Numerous generations since England's fourth

Edward sat upon the throne (and who can say how many before his time?), have held the cooking of the goose for dinner as no less sacred a ceremony on the Angel's feast day than the morning's service in church. And this, would the pugnacious Michael have permitted for such gross material considerations? Never; let it be said once and for all: never. He knew the goose for the bird that lays the golden egg; he knew full well its dignity and might that make it still a terror to be met on lonely common by them who use its name as symbol of silliness; he knew that strong as well as faint hearted hesitate to say "Bo" discourteously to any goose, whether it be a wanderer in French pastures or one of the dust-raising flock, in the twilight, cackling homeward over Transylvanian highways. In a word, Michael knew his bird; and our duty it is to believe in it a dish for Michaelmas with the blind, unquestioning allegiance of perfect faith. Coarse its flesh may be in comparison with the dainty duck and tender chicken; commonplace in comparison with the glorious grouse and proud partridge. The modest, respectable *bourgeois* it may seem among poultry. And yet, if the Archangel has chosen it for his own, who shall say him nay? Study rather to disguise its native coarseness, to enliven its excellent dulness.

Elizabeth Robbins Pennell, *The Feasts of Autolycus*

Elizabeth Robbins Pennell (1855–1936) was an American writer. Raised as a Catholic, she scandalised her family and their society by marrying the English Quaker Joseph Pennell, an artist and illustrator (his family were deeply shocked as well). The young couple further scandalised people by tricycling together through France, the Alps and Italy. She wrote – and he illustrated – an account of their travels. The couple lived for some time in Europe, then returned to London. As there was no café society there, as there had been on the Continent, they started Thursday night salons, where artists, writers and publishers could meet and talk. Elizabeth Robbins Pennell wrote food columns for the *Pall Mall Gazette*, and made an important collection of cookery books, at one point owning over 1,000 rare texts. She also wrote a number of travel books and biographies.

26th – The Barley Harvest

Rose this morning about 5 o'clock. I thought I heard the pattering of the rain upon my garden groves. In drawing aside the blind to my utter dismay the water was standing in a pool on the carriage drive, which indicated a heavy fall of rain for several hours. This is the third drenching for my barley. It is a mercy that it had become tolerably dry yesterday, for under the hedgerows it had already begun to sprout. This is a morning of disappointment to us farmers. Yesterday we were vigorously retrieving matters, carrying in the morning and tying in the afternoon and the foreman and I were planning for managing most the binding today. But all our schemes are upset by Divine Providence for some wise end. Perhaps to drive us to prayer to more humble dependence upon His Almighty power and wisdom and love. He makes us behold His severity as well as goodness. How dark and gloomy the prospect! How thick and hazy the air! How leaden the skies! Yesterday I was pulling ketlocks out of the turnips, also neadles, redrobbin and scarlet poppies. It is a proverb that weeds grow apace. Experience brings home the truth. There is not a weed now growing in my turnip fields but will come to maturity and yield its thousandfold increase many months before the turnip itself. It forms part of the curse still lingering in the ground. What a tenacious hold they still have upon our soil. If we cease our vigilance they soon become predominant. A skilful and persevering hand is required to maintain empire over this department of natural laws and forces.

Cornelius Stovin, *Diaries*

27th – Celebrations for the Restoration of a Church

Never shall I forget the re-opening on September 27th, 1859. The procession of parishioners wending its way across the bridge from the village headed by the brass band which Burcombe then possessed, was witnessed by a company of visitors from the Parsonage garden. It was a very pretty sight. The saintly Bishop Hamilton officiated at the morning service, with the Rev I B Pearson, then Prior of St John's Hospital. Few indeed are now surviving who can remember the dinner under the elm trees which followed the morning service.

One little incident I must record. A few days before the opening, Mr Sidney Herbert had a shooting party. He most kindly sent 'the bag', which was on wheels, to me for the proposed entertainment of my friends and parishioners: it consisted of 60 brace of partridges and 13 hares. I had other presents of the same kind from Hurdcote, Compton and Dinton, with the result that on the plate of every adult resident in Burcombe, was a cold roast partridge. The children had tea on the lawn. There was a second service late in the afternoon, at which the Prior Pearson preached. I can truly say that never was a church restoration more needed, more appreciated at the time and followed by a more distinct improvement in church feeling and church conduct.

E. F. Trotman, vicar of St John the Baptist, Burcombe, 1858–69

28th – The Sleeping-Sack

It was already hard upon October before I was ready to set forth, and at the high altitudes over which my road lay there was no Indian summer to be looked for. I was determined, if not to camp out, at least to have the means of camping out in my possession; for there is nothing more harassing to an easy mind than the necessity of reaching shelter by dusk, and the hospitality of a village inn is not always to be reckoned sure by those who trudge on foot. A tent, above all for a solitary traveller, is troublesome to pitch, and troublesome to strike again; and even on the march it forms a conspicuous feature in your baggage. A sleeping-sack, on the other hand, is always ready—you have only to get into it; it serves a double purpose—a bed by night, a portmanteau by day; and it does not advertise your intention of camping out to every curious passer-by. This is a huge point. If a camp is not secret, it is but a troubled resting-place; you become a public character; the convivial rustic visits your bedside after an early supper; and you must sleep with one eye open, and be up before the day. I decided on a sleeping-sack; and after repeated visits to Le Puy, and a deal of high living for myself and my advisers, a sleeping-sack was designed, constructed, and triumphantly brought home.

This child of my invention was nearly six feet square, exclusive of two triangular flaps to serve as a pillow by night and as the top and bottom of the sack by day. I call it 'the sack,' but it was never a sack by more than courtesy: only a sort of long roll or sausage, green waterproof cart-cloth without and blue sheep's fur within. It was commodious as a valise, warm and dry for a bed. There was luxurious turning room for one; and at a pinch the thing might serve for two. I could bury myself in it up to the neck; for my head I trusted to a fur cap, with a hood to fold down over my ears and a band to pass under my nose like a respirator; and in case of heavy rain I proposed to make myself a little tent, or tentlet, with my waterproof coat, three stones, and a bent branch.

Robert Louis Stevenson, *Travels with a Donkey*

29th – Thank You, but No Thanks

Walmer Castle, Sept 29th.
I am much obliged to you for the offer of a Bible in large Print. That which I now have answers perfectly, and I will not deprive you of another.

The Duke of Wellington, *The Letters of The Duke of Wellington to Miss J. 1834–1851*

One of the problems of being very prominent is that it can attract the attention of stalkers or other obsessive people. Arthur Wellesley, 1st Duke of Wellington, found himself in this difficult position. 'Miss J' started to write to him when she was in her twenties – he was a government minister and an elder statesman. Miss J's sister had married an American and emigrated: she was alone, with a tendency to religious fervour, which developed into fanaticism. She wrote to him on the subject of 'the necessity of a new *birth* unto righteousness': this was the start of a flood of letters, which showed her getting more and more unstable. Wellington replied to most of them – he did ask her on several occasions to stop writing, as he was busy, but she paid no attention. He was surprisingly kind to her, only ignoring her in the last months of his life.

30th – A Dog's Dinner

"It was with pleasure," observes Mr. Taylor, in his "General Character of the Dog," "that I watched the motions of a grateful animal belonging to one of the workmen employed at Portsmouth dockyard. This man had a large cur dog, who regularly every day brought him his dinner upwards of a mile. When his wife had prepared the repast, she tied it up in a cloth, and put it in a hand-basket; then calling Trusty (for so he was properly named), desired him to be expeditious, and carry his master's dinner, and be sure not to stop by the way. The dog, who perfectly well understood his orders, immediately obeyed, by taking the handle of the basket in his mouth, and began his journey. It was laughable to observe that, when tired by the way, he would very cautiously set the basket on the ground; but by no means would suffer any person to come near it. When he had sufficiently rested himself, he again took up his load, and proceeded forward until he came to the dock gates. Here he was frequently obliged to stop, and wait with patience until the porter, or some other person, opened the door. His joy was then visible to every one. His pace increased; and with wagging tail, expressive of his pleasure, he ran to his master with the refreshment. The caresses were then mutual; and after receiving his morsel as a recompense for his fidelity, he was ordered home with the empty basket and plates, which he carried back with the greatest precision, to the high diversion of all spectators."

Edward Jesse, *Anecdotes of Dogs*

OCTOBER

1st – Secret Languages

SLANG

There is the 'Cadgers' (beggars') cant', as it is called—a style of language which is distinct from the slang of the thieves, being arranged on the principle of using words that are similar in sound to the ordinary expressions for the same idea. 'S'pose now, your honour,' said a 'shallow cove', who was giving us a lesson, in the St. Giles' classics, 'I wanted to ask a *codger* to come and have a *glass* of *rum* with me, and smoke a *pipe* of *baccer* over a game of *cards* with some *blokes* at *home*—I should say, *Splodger*, will you have a Jack-sur*pass* of finger-and-*thumb*, and blow your yard of *tripe* of nosey-me-*knacker*, while we have a touch of the *broads* with some other heaps of *coke* at my *drum*?'

Again, we have the 'Coster-slang', or the language used by the costermongers, and which consists merely in pronouncing each words as if it were spelt backwards:—'I say, Curly, will you do a *top of reeb* (pot of beer)?' one costermonger may say to the other. 'It's *on* doog, Whelkey, *on doog* (no good, no good),' the second may reply. 'I've had a reg'lar *troseno* (bad sort) to-day. I've been doing b—y *dab* (bad) with my *tol* (lot, or stock)—ha'n't made a *yennep* (penny), s'elp me.' 'Why, I've cleared a *flatch-enorc* (half-a-crown) a'ready.' Master Whelkey will answer, perhaps. 'But *kool the esilop* (look at the police); *kool him* (look at him) Curly! *Vom-us!* (be off). I'm going to *do the tightner* (have my dinner).'

Lastly comes the veritable slang, or English '*Argot*', *i.e.*, the secret language used by the London thieves. This is made up, in a great degree, of the mediaeval Latin, in which the Church service was formerly chanted, and which indeed gave rise to the term *cant* (from the Latin *cantare*), it having been the custom of the ancient beggars to 'intone' their prayers when asking for alms. 'Can you roker Romany (can you speak cant)?' one individual 'on the cross' will say to another who is not exactly 'on the square'; and if the reply be in the affirmative, he will probably add —'What is your monekeer (name)?—Where do you stall to in the huey (where do you lodge in the town)?' 'Oh, I drop the main toper (get out of the high-road),' would doubtless be the answer, 'and slink into the ken (lodging-house) in the back drum (street).' 'Will you have a shant to gatter (pot of beer) after all this dowry of parny (lot of rain)? I've got a teviss (shilling) left in my clye (pocket).'

Henry Mayhew and John Binny, The Criminal Prisons of
London, 1862

2nd – Foxhounds

What beautiful creatures they are, too! Next to a Greek statue ... I know few such combinations of grace and strength as in a fine foxhound ...

Theirs is the sort of form which expresses to me what I want Art to express—Nature not limited, but developed, by high civilization. The old savage ideal of beauty was the lion, type of mere massive force. That was succeeded by an over-civilized ideal, say the fawn, type of delicate grace. By cunning breeding and choosing, through long centuries, man has combined both, and has created the foxhound, lion and fawn in one; just as he might create noble human beings; did he take half as much trouble about politics (in the true old sense of the word) as he does about fowls. Look at that old hound, who stands doubtful, looking up at his master for advice. Look at the severity, delicacy, lightness of every curve. His head is finer than a deer's; his hind legs tense as steel springs; his fore-legs straight as arrows: and yet see the depth of chest, the sweep of loin, the breadth of paw, the mass of arm and thigh; and if you have an eye for form, look at the absolute majesty of his attitude at this moment. Majesty is the only word for it. ... Is it not a joy to see such a thing alive? It is to me, at least. I should like to have one in my study all day long, as I would have a statue or a picture.

Charles Kingsley, *Prose Idylls*

3rd – Nature Sings to the Artist

And where the evening mist clothes the riverside with poetry, as with a veil, and the poor buildings lose themselves in the dim sky, and the tall chimneys become campanili, and the warehouses are palaces in the night, and the whole city hangs in the heavens, and fairy-land is before us— then the wayfarer hastens home; the working man and the cultured one, the wise man and the one of pleasure, cease to understand, as they have ceased to see, and Nature, who, for once, has sung in tune, sings her exquisite song to the artist alone, her son and her master—her son in that he loves her, her master in that he knows her.

J. M. Whistler, *The Gentle Art of Making Enemies*

4th – The Poor Man and the Rich

The poor man's sins are glaring;
In the face of ghostly warning
   He is caught in the fact
   Of an overt act—
Buying greens on a Sunday morning.

The rich man's sins are hidden,
In the pomp of wealth and station;
   And escape the sight
   Of the children of light,
Who are wise in their generation.

The rich man has a kitchen,
And cooks to dress his dinner;
   The poor who would roast
   To the baker's must post,
And thus become a sinner.

The rich man has a cellar,
And a ready butler by him;
   The poor must steer
   For his pint of beer
Where the saint can't choose but spy him.

The rich man's painted windows
Hide the concerts of the quality;
   The poor can but share
   A crack'd fiddle in the air,
Which offends all sound morality.

The rich man is invisible
In the crowd of his gay society;
   But the poor man's delight
   Is a sore in the sight,
And a stench in the nose of piety.

The rich man. has a carriage
Where no rude eye can flout him;
   The poor man's bane
   Is a third-class train,
With the daylight all about him.

The rich man goes out yachting,
Where sanctity can't pursue him;
   The poor goes afloat
   In a fourpenny boat,
Where the bishop groans to view him.

Thomas Love Peacock

Published in Sir Henry Cole's *Fifty Years of Public Work*

Thomas Love Peacock (1785–1866) wrote many satirical novels, as well as poems and essays. He worked for most of his life for the East India Company, becoming Examiner in 1837. He occasionally appeared before Parliament to defend the Company's interests. In 1838 and 1840 he oversaw the construction of iron steamers for the Company's use. His poem *The Paper Money Lyrics*, which appeared in 1837, was a satire about bankers and political economy. He died as a result of injuries he received when trying to save his library from a house fire.

5th – Avoiding Cholera

The secret of our immunity was that we never drank any water that had not been filtered elsewhere or distilled on board. In the naval fleet the water was never brought on board from the shore but was always distilled. On land this precaution was perforce not taken. Still, something might have been done to prevent the soldiers from drinking the water of stagnant pools and streams polluted with the carcases of dead animals that had been dumped into them to save the trouble of burial. It really seemed as if the Allies were not content with being killed in their engagements with the Russians, but were determined to add to battle, and murder, the sudden death they brought upon themselves.

J. Codman, *An American Transport in the Crimean War*

John Codman (1814–1900) was an American, captain of the steamship *William Penn*. The ship was chartered by the French, and sailed from Marseilles with troops and ammunition for the Crimean War. The ship continued to ferry materials from Turkey to the Crimea until the contract ran out. Then Codman and the ship took service with the Turks until the end of the war. John Codman claimed to have commanded one of the first American steamships working in the Mediterranean.

6th – Advice to Female Migrants

Among the many books that have been written for the instruction of the Canadian emigrant, there are none exclusively devoted for the use of the wives and daughters of the future settler, who for the most part, possess but a very vague idea of the particular duties which they are destined to undertake, and are often totally unprepared to meet the emergencies of their new mode of life.

As a general thing they are told that they must prepare their minds for some hardships and privations, and that they will have to exert themselves in a variety of ways to which they have hitherto been strangers; but the exact nature of that work, and how it is to be performed, is left untold. The consequence of this is, that the females have everything to learn, with few opportunities of acquiring the requisite knowledge, which is often obtained under circumstances, and in situations the most discouraging; while their hearts are yet filled with natural yearnings after the land of their birth (dear even to the poorest emigrant), with grief for the friends of their early days, and while every object in this new country is strange to them. Disheartened by repeated failures, unused to the expedients which the older inhabitants adopt in any case of difficulty, repining and disgust take the place of cheerful activity; troubles increase, and the power to overcome them decreases; domestic happiness disappears. The woman toils on heart-sick and pining for the home she left behind her. The husband reproaches his broken-hearted partner, and both blame the Colony for the failure of the individual.

Catherine Traill, *Female Emigrant's Guide*

Catherine Traill (1802–99) had a successful career as a writer in England, before marrying in 1832 and migrating to Canada. Letters, journals and novels describe Canadian life in wide variety, and she also collected information to help new settlers. She was also a keen botanist, collecting plants and making sketches, publishing three books devoted to Canadian flora. Her collection is in the National Herbarium of Canada.

7th – Modestine the Donkey

It remained to choose a beast of burden. Now, a horse is a fine lady among animals, flighty, timid, delicate in eating, of tender health; he is too valuable and too restive to be left alone, so that you are chained to your brute as to a fellow galley-slave; a dangerous road puts him out of his wits; in short, he's an uncertain and exacting ally, and adds thirty-fold to the troubles of the voyager. What I required was something cheap and small and hardy, and of a stolid and peaceful temper; and all these requisites pointed to a donkey.

There dwelt an old man in Monastier, of rather unsound intellect according to some, much followed by street-boys, and known to fame as Father Adam. Father Adam had a cart, and to draw the cart a diminutive she-ass, not much bigger than a dog, the colour of a mouse, with a kindly eye and a determined under-jaw. There was something neat and high-bred, a quakerish elegance, about the rogue that hit my fancy on the spot. Our first interview was in Monastier market-place. To prove her good temper, one child after another was set upon her back to ride, and one after another went head over heels into the air; until a want of confidence began to reign in youthful bosoms, and the experiment was discontinued from a dearth of subjects. I was already backed by a deputation of my friends; but as if this were not enough, all the buyers and sellers came round and helped me in the bargain; and the ass and I and Father Adam were the centre of a hubbub for near half an hour. At length she passed into my service for the consideration of sixty-five francs and a glass of brandy. The sack had already cost eighty francs and two glasses of beer; so that Modestine, as I instantly baptized her, was upon all accounts the cheaper article. Indeed, that was as it should be; for she was only an appurtenance of my mattress, or self-acting bedstead on four castors.

Robert Louis Stevenson, *Travels with a Donkey*

8th – To Phoebe

"Gentle, modest little flower,
Sweet epitome of May,
Love me but for half an hour,
Love me, love me, little fay."
Sentences so fiercely flaming
In your tiny shell-like ear,
I should always be exclaiming
If I loved you, PHOEBE dear.
"Smiles that thrill from any distance
Shed upon me while I sing!
Please ecstaticize existence,
Love me, oh, thou fairy thing!"
Words like these, outpouring sadly
You'd perpetually hear,
If I loved you fondly, madly;
— But I do not, Phoebe dear.

Sir W. S Gilbert, *The Bab Ballads*

Sir William Schwenck Gilbert (1836–1911) turned to journalism when he failed to do well as a barrister. He sent humorous poems to *Punch*, later published as *The Bab Ballads*, and he wrote plays. It was his partnership with the composer Sir Arthur Sullivan that brought the greatest fame to both men: the Savoy Operas – burlesques of contemporary behaviour

– were enormously popular. He died as a result of rescuing a woman from drowning in a lake on his property.

9th – Nutting

I used to love to gather strawberries, and cut asparagus, and above all, to collect the filberts from the shrubberies: but this hedgerow nutting beats that sport all to nothing. That was a make-believe thing, compared with this; there was no surprise, no suspense, no unexpectedness—it was as inferior to this wild nutting, as the turning out of a bag-fox is to unearthing the fellow, in the eyes of a staunch foxhunter.

Oh, what enjoyment this nut-gathering is! They are in such abundance, that it seems as if there were not a boy in the parish, nor a young man, nor a young woman,—for a basket of nuts is the universal tribute of country gallantry; our pretty damsel Harriet has had at least half a dozen this season; but no one has found out these. And they are so full too, we lose half of them from over-ripeness; they drop from the socket at the slightest motion. If we lose, there is one who finds. May is as fond of nuts as a squirrel, and cracks the shell and extracts the kernel with equal dexterity. Her white glossy head is upturned now to watch them as they fall. See how her neck is thrown back like that of a swan, and how beautifully her folded ears quiver with expectation, and how her quick eye follows the rustling noise, and her light feet dance and pat the ground, and leap up with eagerness, seeming almost sustained in the air ... See, she has caught that nut just before it touched the water; but the water would have been no defence,—she fishes them from the bottom, she delves after them amongst the matted grass—even my bonnet—how beggingly she looks at that! 'Oh, what a pleasure nutting is!—Is it not, May? But the pockets are almost full, and so is the basket-bonnet, and that bright watch the sun says it is late; and after all it is wrong to rob the poor boys—is it not, May?'—May shakes her graceful head denyingly, as if she understood the question—'And we must go home now—must we not? But we will come nutting again some time or other—shall we not, my May?'

Mary Russell Mitford, *Our Village*

10th – Drawing in the Margins

For myself, my own early margins chiefly served to note, cite, and illustrate the habits of crocodiles. Along the lower or "tail" edge, the saurian, splendidly serrated as to his back, arose out of old Nile; up one side negroes, swart as sucked lead-pencil could limn them, let fall their nerveless spears; up the other, monkeys, gibbering with terror, swarmed hastily up palm-trees — a plant to the untutored hand of easier outline than (say) your British oak. Meanwhile, all over the unregarded text Balbus slew Caius on the most inadequate provocation, or Hannibal pursued his victorious career, while Roman generals delivered ornate set speeches prior to receiving the usual Drawing in the Margins satisfactory licking. Fabius, Hasdrubal — all alike were pallid shades with faint, thin voices powerless to pierce the distance. The margins of Cocytus doubtless knew them: mine were dedicated to the more attractive flesh and blood of animal life, the varied phases of the tropic forest. Or, in more practical mood, I would stoop to render certain facts recorded in the text. To these digressions I probably owe what little education I possess. For example, there was one sentence in our Roman history: "By this single battle of Magnesia, Antiochus the Great lost all his conquests in Asia Minor." Serious historians really should not thus forget themselves. 'Twas so easy, by a touch of the pen, to transform "battle" into "bottle"; for "conquests" one could substitute a word for which not even Macaulay's school-boy were at a loss; and the result, depicted with rude vigour in his margin, fixed the name of at least one ancient fight on the illustrator's memory. But this plodding and material art had small charm for me: to whom the happy margin was a "clear sky" ever through which I could sail away at will to more gracious worlds. I was duly qualified by a painfully acquired ignorance of dead languages cautiously to approach my own; and 'twas no better. Along Milton's margins the Gryphon must needs pursue the Arimaspian — what a chance, that Arimaspian, for the imaginative pencil! And so it has come about that, while Milton periods are mostly effaced from memory by the sponge of Time, I can still see that vengeful Gryphon, cousin-german to the gentle beast that danced the Lobster Quadrille by a certain shore.

Kenneth Grahame, Pagan Papers

11th – Epitaph

Not here: the white north has thy bones; and thou,
Heroic sailor-soul,
Art passing on thine happier voyage now
Toward no earthly pole.
Alfred, Lord Tennyson, the Epitaph to Sir John Franklin on the
Cenotaph in Westminster Abbey

Sir John Franklin (1786–1847) was a noted seaman and explorer. With two ships, the *Erebus* and *Terror*, he set out in 1845 to discover the North-West Passage – a route for ships from the Atlantic to the Pacific along the northern edge of Canada. He never returned. There were at least forty expeditions to find out what had happened to Franklin and his men, but it was not until 1859 that the truth about the disaster was discovered.

12th – On the Projected Kendal and Windermere Railway

October 12th, 1844
Is then no nook of English ground secure
From rash assault? Schemes of retirement sown
In youth, and mid the busy world kept pure
As when their earliest flowers of hope were blown,
Must perish; – how can they this blight endure?
And must he too the ruthless change bemoan
Who scorns a false utilitarian lure
Mid his paternal fields at random thrown?
Baffle the threat, bright Scene, from Orrest-head
Given to the pausing traveller's rapturous glance:
Plead for thy peace, thou beautiful romance
Of nature; and, if human hearts be dead,
Speak, passing winds; ye torrents, with your strong
And constant voice, protest against the wrong.
William Wordsworth

William Wordsworth (1770–1850) had travelled in France in his youth, and adopted revolutionary principles (though he was extremely unhappy about the Terror and Jacobinism). As the years went by, his politics changed, and towards the end of his life he was very conservative, supporting the Tory Lord Lonsdale in a general election. Some of his fellow-poets, heavily influenced by his poetic innovations, were distressed by this change. He became Poet Laureate in 1843 and was the only one who never wrote any official verses. In the last years of his life he was resolutely opposed to the building of the Kendal and Windermere railway, which he thought would destroy the landscape of the Lake District – one of the engineers replied (in verse) describing the democratising influence of the railway, and the social and cultural benefits it would bring. He did not mention economics!

13th – Through the Looking-Glass: the Artwork

The story, as originally written, contained thirteen chapters, but the published book consisted of twelve only. The omitted chapter introduced a wasp, in the character of a judge or barrister, I suppose, since Mr. Tenniel wrote that "a *wasp* in a *wig* is altogether beyond the appliances of art." Apart from difficulties of illustration, the "wasp" chapter was not considered to be up to the level of the rest of the book, and this was probably the principal reason of its being left out.

"It is a curious fact," wrote Mr. Tenniel some years later, when replying to a request of Lewis Carroll's that he would illustrate another of his books, "that with 'Through the Looking-Glass' the faculty of making drawings for book illustration departed from me, and, notwithstanding all sorts of tempting inducements, I have done nothing in that direction since."

S. Dodgson Collingwood, *The Life and Letters of Lewis Carroll*

14th – Drummer Hodge

They throw in Drummer Hodge, to rest
Uncoffined – just as found:
His landmark is a kopje-crest
That breaks the veldt around:
And foreign constellations west
Each night above his mound.

Young Hodge the drummer never knew –
Fresh from his Wessex home –
The meaning of the broad Karoo,
The Bush, the dusty loam,
And why uprose to nightly view
Strange stars amid the gloam.

Yet portion of that unknown plain
Will Hodge for ever be;
His homely Northern breast and brain
Grow to some Southern tree,
And strange-eyed constellations reign
His stars eternally.

Thomas Hardy

15th – Evolution and Progress

Our race's progress and perfectibility is a dream, because revelation contradicts it.

J. H. Newman, *The Idea of a University*

John Henry Newman (1801–90) was a scholar and theologian. He was a founder of the Oxford Movement, a High-Church group, which – amongst other things – reintroduced ritual, vestments and incense into Anglican services. When he wrote a pamphlet arguing that the 39 Articles of the Anglican Church were compatible with Catholicism, he was condemned by the Bishop of Oxford. Continuing his studies of the early church, John Henry Newman converted to Roman Catholicism in 1845. He eventually became a cardinal.

16th – Moving to a Country Living

Many persons rejoice in the possession of a living and in going into residence thereupon, but it was *Duty* – obedience to the orders of the Bishop of Norwich – who ordered me to go into residence – which compelled me to leave my native Town, Ipswich, and to come and live here. With a heavy broken heart I left all the ties of my youth, the house I was born in and in which all my children were born, and came to form new associations and to do the duties of a large straggling Parish. I was Curate to my Uncle at St Mary Tower Ipswich, and never shall I forget the agony I endured at my farewell duty at that Church. Such a crowded congregation and such dear old faces and friends whom I had known from my birth. One only feeling pervaded my soul, namely, that – as I had promised my bishop that when Old Mr Merest, my predecessor the curate should die, who had lived here forty years, I would go to Wortham, till which time he gave me licence for non residence – I thought it my duty to come. I knew not what it would cost me. Nor can any man tell, till experience shall teach him, what is the cost he must ever pay to do his duty. I know what it has cost me ... but God has not deserted me, though if I had received my deserts, I should have perished long ago.

Richard Cobbold, *Account of Wortham*

The Reverend Richard Cobbold (1797–1877) originally worked in a parish in Ipswich, but moved to Wortham, a village parish in Suffolk, in 1825. His first task on arrival was to build a rectory. He remained there until he died. He wrote several successful historical novels, but mostly used the money he received from them for charitable purposes. At Wortham, he recorded details of the lives of his parishioners, and the four volumes of text and illustrations are now in the Suffolk Record Office.

17th – Siege Rations

Saturday, October 17th. My busy day. We had had a slight attack during the night. Two letters came from Cawnpore, giving accounts of our reinforcements. They will not be here quite so soon as was expected. The 93rd are to be at Cawnpore on the 23rd instant, and the 23rd on the 2nd of November. Sir Colin Campbell is coming over here himself with the troops. I trust they will not delay it too long; for, famine is too horrible to contemplate. Our daily rations of meat are now 12 oz. for a man, 6 oz. for a woman, and 2 oz. for a child, and this is bone inclusive, which is sometimes nearly half; and we have had 9 lbs. (the ration for our party for one day) of which 5 lbs. was actually bone. Then seventeen of us (some choosing to have their rations separate) have 15 lbs. of unsifted flour for our chupatties, 6 lbs. of gram to be made into dal (this is private store food, generally given to horses), 1 lb. 12 oz. of rice, and a little salt. We generally make a stew of the meat and rice and a few chupatties, as it goes farther; but I think the gentlemen generally get up from table hungry. We have still a little tea, but neither sugar, milk, wine, nor beer; our beverage is toast and water, a large jug of which is always placed on the centre of the table; it is made of the old chuppatties, if any are left of the previous day. All horses under 150 rupees value were, by orders, destroyed at the river yesterday, as they were eating up the gram.

Mrs R. C. Germon, *A Diary Kept by Mrs R. C. Germon at Lucknow*

18th – A Cunning Fox

At one of our meets, a fox was found in Bracken Wood, which, after giving us a good run round the neighbourhood, eventually took refuge in a cottage near High-hall Wood. Entering by the open door, it mounted the ladder which formed the staircase to the one bedroom above; there it crept under the bed. The hounds hunted all round the premises, but the door having been shut by the occupier, an aged, retired keeper, and there being a strong wind which blew the scent from the door, his retreat was not discovered. He remained in this place of concealment until the hounds had gone to a safe distance, and then, descending by the ladder, bolted out of the door and made off.

J. Conway Walter, *Records of Woodhall Spa and Neighbourhood*

19th – Death of Lord Palmerston

He has left none like him—none who can rally round him so many followers of various opinions, none who can give us so happy a respite from the violence of party-warfare, none who can bring to the work of statesmanship so precious a store of recollections. It is impossible not to feel that Lord Palmerston's death marks an epoch in English politics. "The old order changeth, yielding place to new." Other Ministers may carry into successful effect organic reforms from which he shrunk. Others may introduce a new spirit into our foreign relations, and abandon the system of secret diplomacy which he never failed to support. Others may advise Her Majesty with equal sagacity, and sway the House of Commons with equal or greater eloquence; but his place in the hearts of the people will not be filled so easily. The name of Lord Palmerston, once the terror of the Continent, will long be connected in the minds of Englishmen with an epoch of unbroken peace and unparalleled prosperity, and cherished together with the brightest memories of the reign of Queen Victoria.

The Times, 19 October 1863

20th – Enchanting Coffee

To Abyssinia, otherwise an unknown factor in the history of good living, belongs the credit of producing the first coffee-drinkers. All honour where honour is due. The debt of the modern to Greece and Rome is smaller far than to that remote country which not one man in ten, to whom coffee is a daily necessity, could point out upon the map.

Arabs, wandering hither and thither, came to Abyssinia as they journeyed, and there drank the good drink and rejoiced. Among them were pious Moslems, who at times nodded over prayers, and, yawning pitifully as texts were murmured by lazy lips, knew that damnation must be their doom unless sleep were banished from their heavy eyes at prayer time. And to them as to the sheep and lambs, as to the goats and kids, the wonder-working berry brought wakefulness and gaiety. And into Arabia the Happy, they carried it in triumph, and coffee was drunk not for temporal pleasure but for spiritual uses. It kept worshippers awake and alert for the greater glory of Allah, and the faithful accepted it with praise and thanksgiving.

But, again, like the flocks in Abyssinian pastures, it made them too alert, it seems. After coffee, prayer grew frolicsome, and a faction arose to call it an intoxicant, to declare the drinking of it a sin against the Koran. Schisms followed, and heresies, and evils dire and manifold. But coffee fought a good fight against its enemies and its detractors; and from Arabia it passed to Constantinople, from Turkey to England, and so on from country to country, until in the end there was not one in Europe, or in the New World (which men had not then so long discovered), but had welcomed the berry that clears the clouded brain and stimulates the jaded body.

Elizabeth Robins Pennell, *The Feasts of Autolycus*

21st – Amateur Nurses Not Needed

War Office, October 21 – The duties of a hospital nurse, if they are properly performed, require great skill as well as strength and courage, especially where the cases are surgical cases and the majority of them are from gunshot wounds. Persons who have no experience or skill in such matters would be of no use whatever; and in moments of great pressure, such as must of necessity at intervals occur in a military hospital, any person who is not of use is an impediment. Many ladies, whose generous enthusiasm prompts them to offer their services as nurses, are little aware of the hardships they would have to encounter, and the horrors they would have to witness, which would try the firmest nerves. Were all accepted who offer, I fear we should have not only many inefficient nurses, but many hysterical patients themselves requiring treatment instead of assisting others ...

No additional nurses will be sent out to Miss Nightingale until she shall have written home from Scutari and reported how far her labours have been successful, and what number and description of persons, if any, she requires in addition.... No one can be sent out until we hear from Miss Nightingale that they are required.

Sidney Herbert

22nd – The Toys

My little Son, who look'd from thoughtful eyes
And moved and spoke in quiet grown-up wise,
Having my law the seventh time disobey'd,
I struck him, and dismiss'd
With hard words and unkiss'd,
His Mother, who was patient, being dead.
Then, fearing lest his grief should hinder sleep,
I visited his bed,
But found him slumbering deep,

With darken'd eyelids, and their lashes yet
From his late sobbing wet.
And I, with moan,
Kissing away his tears, left others of my own;
For, on a table drawn beside his head,
He had put, within his reach,
A box of counters and a red-vein'd stone,
A piece of glass abraded by the beach
And six or seven shells,
A bottle with bluebells
And two French copper coins, ranged there with careful art,
To comfort his sad heart.
So when that night I pray'd
To God, I wept, and said:
Ah, when at last we lie with tranced breath,
Not vexing Thee in death,
And Thou rememberest of what toys
We made our joys,
How weakly understood
Thy great commanded good,
Then, fatherly not less
Than I whom Thou hast moulded from the clay,
Thou'lt leave Thy wrath, and say,
"I will be sorry for their childishness."

Coventry Patmore

Coventry Patmore (1823–96) started work as a librarian at the British Museum, and continued there for nearly twenty years. He published several books of poems, mostly about married love (he married three times). He was connected to the Pre-Raphaelite Brotherhood – Millais used one of his poems as the basis of a painting – and knew many literary personages, such as Ruskin, Browning and Tennyson. Patmore also wrote critical and philosophical essays.

23rd – Mango wins the St Leger

October 23rd, 1837
Since August 30th, nearly two months, I have written not a line, for I have had nothing to record of public or general interest, and

have felt an invincible repugnance to write about myself or my own proceedings. Having nothing else to talk of, however, I shall write my own history of the last seven weeks, which is very interesting to me inasmuch as it has been very profitable. Having asked George Bentinck to try my horse 'Mango' before Doncaster, we went down together one night to Winchester race-course and saw him tried. He won the trial and we resolved to back him. This we accomplished more successfully than we expected, and ten days after he won the St. Leger, and I won about 9,000Ł. upon it, the first *great* piece of good fortune that ever happened to me. Since Doncaster, I have continued (up to this time) to win at Newmarket, so that my affairs are in a flourishing condition, but, notwithstanding these successes, I am dissatisfied and disquieted in my mind, and my life is spent in the alternations of excitement from the amusement and speculation of the turf and of remorse and shame at the pursuit itself.

Charles Greville, *Memoirs*

24th – A Diary

A diary. Dies. Hodie. How queer to read are some of the entries in the journal! Here are the records of dinners eaten, and gone the way of flesh. The lights burn blue somehow, and we sit before the ghosts of victuals. Hark at the dead jokes resurging! Memory greets them with the ghost of a smile. Here are the lists of the individuals who have dined at your own humble table. The agonies endured before and during those entertainments are renewed, and smart again. What a failure that special grand dinner was! How those dreadful occasional waiters did break the old china! What a dismal hash poor Mary, the cook, made of the French dish which she WOULD try out of Francatelli! How angry Mrs. Pope was at not going down to dinner before Mrs. Bishop! How Trimalchio sneered at your absurd attempt to give a feast; and Harpagon cried out at your extravagance and ostentation! How Lady Almack bullied the other ladies in the drawing-room (when no gentlemen were present): never asked you back to dinner again: left her card by her footman: and took not the slightest notice of your wife and daughters at Lady Hustleby's assembly! On the other hand, how easy, cozy, merry, comfortable, those little dinners were; got up at one or two days' notice; when everybody was contented; the soup as clear as amber; the wine as good as Trimalchio's own; and the people kept their carriages waiting, and would not go away until midnight!

William Makepeace Thackeray, *Roundabout Papers*

25th – Charge of the Light Brigade

The charge of this brigade was one of the most successful I ever witnessed, was never for a moment doubtful, and is in the highest degree creditable to Brigadier-General Scarlett and the officers and men engaged in it.

As the enemy withdrew from the ground which they had momentarily occupied I directed the cavalry, supported by the Fourth Division, under Lieutenant-General Sir George Cathcart, to move forward, and take advantage of any opportunity to regain the heights; and not having been able to accomplish this immediately, and it appearing that an attempt was making to remove the captured guns, the Earl of Lucan was desired to advance rapidly, follow the enemy in their retreat, and try to prevent them from effecting their objects.

In the meanwhile the Russians had time to re-form on their own ground, with artillery in front and upon their flanks.

From some misconception of the instruction to advance the Lieutenant-General considered that he was bound to attack at all hazards, and he accordingly ordered Major-General the Earl of Cardigan to move forward with the Light Brigade.

This order was obeyed in a most spirited and gallant manner. Lord Cardigan charged with the utmost vigour, attacked a battery which was firing on the advancing squadrons, and, having passed beyond it, engaged the Russian cavalry in its rear; but then his troops were assailed by artillery and infantry, as well as cavalry and necessarily retired, after having committed much havoc upon the enemy. They effected this movement without haste or confusion but the loss they have sustained has, I deeply lament, been very severe in officers, men and horses, only counterbalanced by the brilliancy of the attack, and the gallantry, order and discipline which distinguished it, forming a striking contrast to the enemy's cavalry, which had previously been engaged with the heavy brigade.

The Chasseurs d'Afrique advanced on our left and gallantly

charged a Russian battery, which checked its fire for a time, and thus rendered the British cavalry an essential service.

> Lord Raglan, from Dispatch, 28 October 1854, to the Duke of
> Newcastle, Secretary of State for War and the Colonies

The Charge of the Light Brigade was one of those extraordinary events in which a defeat or a disaster enters the national conscience. The folly of the orders to the Brigade, and the heroism of the charge have resulted in admiration and controversy ever since. Fitzroy Somerset, 1st Baron Raglan (1789–1855) had served with Wellington in Spain and at Waterloo, where he was badly wounded. Given command of the British forces in the Crimea, it was soon evident that he could not manage high command. He was much criticized for the orders that had led to the charge. Raglan died in the Crimea the next year, of dysentery.

26th – To the Terrestrial Globe, By a Miserable Wretch

Roll on, thou ball, roll on!
Through pathless realms of Space
Roll on!
What though I'm in a sorry case?
What though I cannot meet my bills?
What though I suffer toothache's ills?
What though I swallow countless pills?
Never *you* mind!
Roll on!
Roll on, thou ball, roll on!
Through seas of inky air
Roll on!
It's true I've got no shirts to wear;
It's true my butcher's bill is due;
It's true my prospects all look blue—
But don't let that unsettle you!
Never *you* mind!
Roll on!
It rolls on.

> Sir W. S. Gilbert, *The Bab Ballads*

27th – Some Awards for Gallantry

ELIJAH HALLAM (*Silver*), FREDERICK VICKERS (*Silver*). For saving, at imminent risk of their lives, six follow-workmen in great peril in the shaft of a coal-pit near Chesterfield, September 6th, 1875, Presented by Sir Edmund Lechmere, Bart, at a public meeting at Whittington Moor, November 18th, 1875.

ARTHUR H. STOKES (Assistant Inspector of Mines (*Silver*), CHARLES MALTBY (*Bronze*), JOHN HANCOCK (*Bronze*), THOMAS DAVIS (*Bronze*), JOHN DAVIS (*Bronze*). For remarkable constancy, courage, and daring, during the operations leading to the rescue of Dennis Bagshawe, buried for five days and nights without food in the Black Engine Mine, Eyam, July, 1879. Presented on behalf of the Order by John Furley, Esq., a Member of the Council, January 21st, 1880, at a public meeting at Sheffield.

HENRY SPAVIN (*Bronze*). For rescuing, at great personal danger, December 17th, 1879, from a small sewer at Silvertown, a fellow-workman, rendered insensible by poisonous gases. Presented by Sir Edward G. L. Perrott, Bart., March 9th, 1880 at a meeting at the Town Hall, Stratford.

Register of Medals Awarded by the Order of St John

28th – Mongolia and Beyond

One thing I sometimes think of. I left Britain with no intention of travelling; I expected to settle down quietly and confine myself to a circle I could impress. This plan has been completely changed and overruled. Two months have I been in Peking; two weeks have I been in Kalgan; a month have I been in the desert; a month have I been in Kudara, a small Russian frontier military post; a month and a half have I been in Kiachta; two months have I been in Mongolia; and now two weeks have I been travelling in Russia. A year and a month have elapsed since I left home, and during that time I have been walking to and fro on the face of the earth, and going up and down in it. In this way I have not found my life at all dull, but very stirring. Indeed, many people would have left home to travel as I have done. I sought it not; it came, and I took it. So as yet I have no hardships to complain of. To see the places and things I have seen—Liverpool, Wales, Rock of Lisbon, Gibraltar, Malta, Egypt, Port Said, Canal, Suez, Red Sea, Cape Gardafui, Indian Ocean, Penang, Straits of Malacca, Singapore, Hong Kong, Shanghai, Tientsin, Peking, Kalgan, Desert, Urga, Kiachta, Russia, Baikal, Irkutsk—only even to see these, men will make long journeys. I have seen them all without seeking them, with the exception of Baikal and Irkutsk.

Richard Lovett, *James Gilmour of Mongolia*

James Gilmour (1843–91) was a Scottish missionary who spent twenty-one years working in Mongolia. He travelled widely on foot, carrying his belongings, or sometimes with a donkey. He tried to provide simple medicines, as well as preaching and teaching, and for eleven years his wife went with him. He spoke and read the language, and his books about his travels and work were a revelation to Western readers, some of whom did not know anything about this country.

29th – The Covered Market, Covent Garden

Inside, the market all is bustle and confusion. The people walk along with their eyes fixed on the goods, and frowning with thought. Men in all costumes, from the coster in his corduroy suit to the greengrocer in his blue apron, sweep past. A countryman, in an old straw hat and dusty boots, occasionally draws down the anger of a woman for walking about with his hands in the pockets of his smock-frock, and is asked, "if that is the way to behave on a market-day?" Even the granite pillars cannot stop the crowd, for it separates and rushes past them, like the tide by a bridge pier. At every turn there is a fresh odour to sniff at; either the bitter aromatic perfume of the herbalists' shops breaks upon you, or the scent of oranges, then of apples, and then of onions is caught for an instant as you move along. The brocoli tied up in square packets, the white heads tinged slightly red, as it were, with the sunshine, – the sieves of crimson love-apples, polished like china, – the bundles of white glossy leeks, their roots dangling like fringe, – the celery, with its pinky stalks and bright green tops, – the dark purple pickling-cabbages, – the scarlet carrots, – the white knobs of turnips, – the bright yellow balls of oranges, and the rich brown coats of the chestnuts – attract the eye on every side. Then there are the apple-merchants, with their fruit of all colours, from the pale yellow green to the bright crimson, and the baskets ranged in rows on the pavement before the little shops. Round these the customers stand examining the stock, then whispering together over their bargain, and counting their money. "Give you four shillings for this here lot, master," says a coster, speaking for his three companions. "Four and six is my price," answers the salesman. "Say four, and it's a bargain," continues the man. "I said my price," returns the dealer; "go and look round, and see if you can get 'em cheaper; if not, come back. I only wants what's fair." The men, taking the salesman's advice, move on. The walnut merchant, with the group of women before his shop, peeling the fruit, their fingers stained deep brown, is busy with the Irish purchasers. The onion stores, too, are surrounded by Hibernians, feeling and pressing the gold-coloured roots, whose dry skins crackle as they are handled. Cases of lemons in their white paper jackets, and blue grapes, just seen above the sawdust are ranged about, and in some places the ground is slippery as ice from the refuse leaves and walnut husks scattered over the pavement.

Henry Mayhew, *London Labour and the London Poor*

30th – A Father's Hopes for his Son

Indeed, the Squire's last words deserved to have their effect, for they had been the result of much anxious thought. All the way up to London he had pondered what he should say to Tom by way of parting advice, something that the boy could keep in his head ready for use ... To condense the Squire's meditation, it was somewhat as follows: "I won't tell him to read his Bible and love and serve God; if he don't do that for his mother's sake and teaching, he won't for mine. Shall I go into the sort of temptations he'll meet with? No, I can't do that. Never do for an old fellow to go into such things with a boy. He won't understand me. Do him more harm than good, ten to one. Shall I tell him to mind his work, and say he's sent to school to make himself a good scholar? Well, but he isn't sent to school for that—at any rate, not for that mainly. I don't care a straw for Greek particles, or the digamma, no more does his mother. What is he sent to school for? Well, partly because he wanted so to go. If he'll only turn out a brave, helpful, truth-telling Englishman, and a gentleman, and a Christian, that's all I want," thought the Squire; and upon this view of the case framed his last words of advice to Tom, which were well enough suited to his purpose.

Thomas Hughes, *Tom Brown's School Days*

31st – Progress of the voyage

TO THE EDITOR OF THE ALBATROSS.
GREAT BRITAIN, S.S., 31*st October* 1862.
MY DEAR SIR,—I am extremely happy to say that the progress of the good old ship has been (under the circumstances of light and adverse winds) very satisfactory, and, I am proud to say, still keeps her position in advance of past voyages, being still one day in advance of her fastest passage home, surpassing any steamer or sailing-ship from Australia, in point of time and speed, from that quarter to the present latitude, as mentioned in the abstract of the log which I enclose.

The health of the ship is all that can be desired, and trusting that it may so continue, believe me to remain, yours, &c.

JOHN GRAY, *Lieut.*, R.N.R,
Commander, Great Britain

NOVEMBER

1st – November

No sun – no moon!
No morn – no noon –
No dawn – no dusk – no proper time of day.
No warmth, no cheerfulness,
No healthful ease,
No comfortable feel in any member –
No shade, no shine, no butterflies, no bees,
No fruits, no flowers, no leaves, no birds! –
November!

Thomas Hood

2nd – Why Britain Remained Calm in 1848

Yes, Gentlemen; if I am asked why we are free with servitude all around us, why our Habeas Corpus Act has not been suspended, why our press is still subject to no censor, why we still have the liberty of association, why our representative institutions still abide in all their strength, I answer, It is because in the year of revolutions we stood firmly by our Government in its peril; and, if I am asked why we stood by our Government in its peril, when men all around us were engaged in pulling Governments down, I answer, It was because we knew that though our Government was not a perfect Government, it was a good Government, that its faults admitted of peaceable and legal remedies, that it had never inflexibly opposed just demands, that we had obtained concessions of inestimable value, not by beating the drum, not by ringing the tocsin, not by tearing up the pavement, not by running to the gunsmiths' shops to search for arms, but by the mere force of reason and public opinion. And, Gentlemen, preeminent among those pacific victories of reason and public opinion, the recollection of which chiefly, I believe, carried us safely through the year of revolutions and through the year of counter-revolutions, I would place two great reforms, inseparably associated, one with the memory of an illustrious man, who is now beyond the reach of envy, the other with the name of another illustrious man, who is still, and, I hope, long will be, a living mark for distinction. I speak of the great commercial reform of 1846, the work of Sir Robert Peel, and of the great parliamentary reform of 1832, the work of many eminent statesmen, among whom none was more conspicuous than Lord John Russell. I particularly call your attention to those two great reforms, because it will, in my opinion, be the especial duty of that House of Commons in which, by your distinguished favour, I have a seat, to defend the commercial reform of Sir Robert Peel, and to perfect and extend the parliamentary reform of Lord John Russell.

Thomas Babington Macaulay
From a speech delivered in Edinburgh after being re-elected to
Parliament, 2 November 1852

3rd – The Archbishop of York

The Archbishop of York is dead. He was in no way remarkable except for the wonderful felicity of his whole life from first to last. It would perhaps be difficult to find a greater example of uninterrupted prosperity. He was not a man of great capacity nor of profound learning, but he had peculiarly the *mens sana in corpore sano*. He was nobly born and highly allied. He enjoyed robust health, had a vigorous frame with a sound understanding, and he was cheerfully obliging, good-tempered, and sociable; his profession, his tastes, pursuits, and the quality of his mind cast him into the best and choicest society, where he played his part not brilliantly but with an amiable and graceful prosperity. He had many friends and no enemies, was universally esteemed and respected, and beloved by his own family. He was the most prosperous of men, full of professional dignities and emoluments, and the inheritor of a large private fortune; he was the father of a numerous family, whom he saw flourishing around him in opulence and worldly success; he lived in the exercise of a magnificent hospitality, and surrounded with social enjoyments. No misfortunes or sorrows disturbed the placid current of his life, and his mental and bodily faculties continued unimpaired to the last; his illness, which lasted only a few hours, was without pain, and no more than the natural exhaustion of ninety-one accomplished years. Such a life and such a death so irreproachable and fortunate may well excite envy and admiration. He and Mr. Grenville so conjoined in life died at the same age, each having reached his ninety-first year, and within eleven months of each other—men in their different ways equally prosperous, virtuous, and happy.

Charles Greville, Memoirs

4th – Mauve – The First Aniline Dye

It is rich and pure, and fit for anything; be it fan, slipper, gown, ribbon, handkerchief, tie, or glove. It will lend lustre to the soft changeless twilight of ladies' eyes — it will take any shape to find an excuse to flutter round her cheek — to cling (as the wind blows it) up to her lips — to kiss her foot — to whisper at her ear. O Perkins's [sic] purple, thou art a lucky and a favoured colour!

Anon

5th – Rebellion at Marlborough College

In October our pocket money (mine was 6d. weekly) was collected for providing fireworks, as had been the annual custom, for Guy Fawkes' Day. On the 5th November, after the fireworks had been purchased, and distributed, the Head Master forbade their being displayed. It did not affect me, as boys of our Form, the Lower Fourth, were considered to be too young to let off the crackers and squibs their money had purchased. When night fell, the younger masters endeavoured to enforce the prohibition; several personal acts of violence occurred in which the boys were victorious, for the Upper Fifth and Sixth averaged from seventeen to eighteen years of age, and many were as big as their teachers. Fireworks were let off in the dormitories during the night, and acts of insubordination continued throughout November.

The Head was a learned scholar and kind-hearted man, but not strong enough to master 500 boys, of whom 100 were verging on manhood. I saw him when approaching his desk in the Upper School struck by a swan-shot thrown by a crossbow. The pellet stuck in his forehead, and he allowed it to remain there till school was up. If, as I believe, the feeling of the Lower Fourth was representative of the School, a tactful man might have utilised the shame and remorse we felt, to quell the rebellion; but neither he nor his assistants understood us, and later the masters' desks were burnt, an attempt made to fire some of the out-buildings, and a Translation of the Greek Plays was burnt with the Head's desk. In December the Master expelled three or four boys, and gave the Upper Sixth the choice of being gradually expelled, or of handing up ringleaders for punishment. The low tone of the School was shown by the fact that several selected by the older lads were like myself, under fourteen years of age.

Evelyn Wood, *From Midshipman to Field Marshal*

6th – The Largest and the Smallest Churches

The largest church in England—that is the one covering the greatest number of square yards—is York Minster, St Paul's Cathedral coming second. The largest churches other than cathedrals are the abbeys of Beverley and Tewkesbury; but the largest parish church, which was built as such and not as a monastic church, is that of Yarmouth, Coventry being the next in size.*

To decide which is the smallest church in England is not quite so simple; but there are many that are as quaintly interesting for their diminutiveness as others are impressive by their vastness. The church which George Herbert served so well, at Bemerton, near Salisbury, seats but forty people; and Lullington, Sussex, holds not many more than its twenty-five parishioners. Bradford-on-Avon Church has a nave only twenty-four feet long by thirteen feet wide, with a chancel thirteen feet long by ten feet wide: this relic of past ages (it was built by St Aldhem in 705) is not now used, but is carefully preserved. The churches of Culbone and Charlcombe, in Somersetshire, and Fenton, in Essex, each claims to be the smallest in England. The churches of Woldingham, Surrey; Stopham and Selham, Sussex; Coates, Lincolnshire; Farndish, Bedfordshire, and many others, will not contain a hundred people. Probably the smallest, as originally erected, was St Laurence's Church, in the Isle of Wight; but it has been lengthened by fifteen feet, and now seats a congregation of 107. A late parish clerk has thus celebrated its proportions:—

> Its breadth, from side to side above the bench,
> Is just eleven feet and half an inch;
> Its height, from pavement to the ceiling mortar,
> Eleven feet four inches and a quarter;
> And its whole length from the east to the west end,—
> I tell the truth, on which you may depend—
> 'Twas twenty-five feet, four inches, quarters three,
> But now 'tis forty feet as you may see.
> In eleven hundred and ninety-seven
> 'Twas built to show us the way to Heaven.

A comparison of the area of these six churches, representing three classes of foundations, may be interesting to the reader; the figures in square feet are as follows: York, 63,800; St Paul's, 59,700; Beverley, 29,600; Tewkesbury, 26,000; Yarmouth, 23,265; Coventry, 22,080.

George Smith Tyack, *Lore and Legend of the English Church*

7th – Help to Emigrate

I shall not readily forget the scenes that occurred in Kenmare when I returned, and announced that I was prepared at Lord Lansdowne's expense to send to America every one now in the poor-house who was chargeable to his lordship's estate, and who desired to go; leaving each to select what port in America he pleased — whether Boston, New York, New Orleans or Quebec.

The announcement at first was scarcely credited; it was considered by the paupers to be too good news to be true. But when it began to be believed and appreciated, a rush was made to get away at once.

Two hundred each week were selected of those apparently most suited for emigration: and having arranged their slender outfit, a steady man, on whom I could depend, Mr. Jeremiah O'Shea, was employed to take charge of them on their journey to Cork, and not to leave them nor allow them to scatter, until he saw them safely on board the emigrant ship.

William Steuart Trench, Kerry Land Agent

8th – Corporal Punishment

Probably no one of us could hear that peculiar sound which is made by a heavy oak chair when pushed back over a hollow wooden stand, without involuntarily looking around. It always betokened the rising of a master to inflict corporal punishment. The familiar sound produced an instantaneous silence, and a concentration of all eyes on the spot indicated. There stood the victim and the executioner. If the latter was notorious for the strength of his right arm, it was a matter of no small interest to us to see whether the victim's pluck would suffice to bring him victorious through the limited number of strokes which custom and decency enjoined. If he never flinched or uttered cry, we regarded him as a hero who had scored one against the redoubtable wielder of the rod of justice. There was one awful occasion on which a master lost control of himself, because his victim stood as immovable as though he had been a pillar of stone, instead of a being of flesh and warm blood. Again and again the strong cane descended till 30 strokes had been passed, and yet that boy never flinched. Exhausted at last, the master desisted, and an hour later that resolute boy was having his sliced shirt extracted from his wounds by the gentle hands of dear, tender-hearted Dr. Fergus.

J. S. Thomas, Bursar, Marlborough College

9th – Arriving at Phillip's Ferry

Phillip's Ferry occupied our thoughts almost to the exclusion of every other subject. We had already travelled nearly seven thousand miles. Our food had been principally dried provisions. For many long weeks we had been oppressed with anxious suspense; there is therefore no cause for wonder, that, jaded and worn out as we were, we felt anxious to reach our destined situation. Our enquiries of the sailors 'how much further we had to go' almost exhausted their patience. Already we had been on the vessel twenty-four hours [from St Louis], when just at nightfall the packet stopped: a little boat was lowered into the water, and we were invited to collect our luggage and descend into it, as we were at Phillip's Ferry; we were utterly confounded: there was no appearance of a landing place, no luggage yard, nor even a building of any kind within sight; we, however, attended to our directions, and in a few minutes saw ourselves standing by the brink of the river, bordered by a dark wood, with no-one near to notice us or tell us where we might procure accommodation or find harbour ... It was in the middle of November, and already very frosty. My husband and I looked at each other until we burst into tears, and our children observing our disquietude began to cry bitterly. Is this America, thought I, is this the reception I meet with after my long, painfully anxious and bereaving voyage? In vain did we look around us, hoping to see a light in some distant cabin. It was not, however, the time to weep.

My husband determined to leave us with our luggage in search of a habitation, and wished us to remain where we then stood till he returned. Such a step I saw to be necessary, but how trying! Should he lose himself in the wood, thought I, what will become of me and my helpless offspring? He departed: I was left with five young children, the youngest still at my breast. When I survey this portion of my history, it looks more like fiction than reality ... After my husband was gone I caused my four eldest children to sit together on one of our beds, covered them from the cold as well as I could, and endeavoured to pacify them ... Above me was the chill blue canopy of heaven, a wide river before me, and a dark wood behind.

Anon [now known to be Rebecca Burlend], *A True Picture of Emigration*, 1848

10th – The Steam Threshing-Machine with the Straw Carrier

Flush with the pond the lurid furnace burn'd
At eve, while smoke and vapour fill'd the yard;
The gloomy winter sky was dimly starr'd,
The fly-wheel with a mellow murmur turn'd;
While, ever rising on its mystic stair

In the dim light, from secret chambers borne,
The straw of harvest, sever'd from the corn,
Climb'd, and fell over, in the murky air.
I thought of mind and matter, will and law,
And then of him, who set his stately seal
Of Roman words on all the forms he saw
Of old-world husbandry: *I* could but feel
With what a rich precision *he* would draw
The endless ladder, and the booming wheel!

Charles Tennyson Turner

The Reverend Charles Tennyson Turner (1808–79) was an older brother of Alfred, Lord Tennyson. He too was a poet (as was another brother, Frederick). Charles Tennyson added 'Turner' to his name when he inherited an estate from a great-uncle. Many of his poems were written in sonnet form. He felt somewhat overshadowed by his famous brother.

11th – Designing Books

It was only natural that I, a decorator by profession, should attempt to ornament my books suitably: about this matter, I will only say that I have always tried to keep in mind the necessity for making my decoration a part of the page of type. I may add that in designing the magnificent and inimitable woodcuts which have adorned several of my books, and will above all adorn the Chaucer which is now drawing near completion, my friend Sir Edward Burne-Jones has never lost sight of this important point, so that his work will not only give us a series of most beautiful and imaginative pictures, but form the most harmonious decoration possible to the printed book.

William Morris, Note On His Aims In Founding The Kelmscott Press

William Morris (1834–96) began work as an architect, but, influenced by the Pre-Raphaelites, he turned to painting, then to designing such things as textiles, furniture, wallpaper and glass. He wrote novels and poetry, learning Icelandic so he could use material from the sagas in his work. Politically a socialist, he was involved in founding the Socialist League. He thought the Fabian Society was too middle class, and was introduced to Engels – who thought he lacked practical skills. The Kelmscott Press, founded in 1890, aimed to produce books that were beautiful in themselves, rather than being cheap. He raised the standards of art, design and craft, and was a major influence in the Arts and Crafts movement.

12th – Boys and Their Mothers

Think what it is to a boy, to grow up to manhood in the belief that without any merit or any exertion of his own, though he may be the most frivolous and empty or the most ignorant and stolid of mankind, by the mere fact of being born a male he is by right the superior of all and every one of an entire half of the human race: including probably some whose real superiority to himself he has daily or hourly occasion to feel; but even if in his whole conduct he habitually follows a woman's guidance, still, if he is a fool, she thinks that of course she is not, and cannot be, equal in ability and judgment to himself; and if he is not a fool, he does worse — he sees that she is superior to him, and believes that, notwithstanding her superiority, he is entitled to command and she is bound to obey. What must be the effect on his character, of this lesson? And men of the cultivated classes are often not aware how deeply it sinks into the immense majority of male minds. For, among right-feeling and wellbred people, the inequality is kept as much as possible out of sight; above all, out of sight of the children. As much obedience is required from boys to their mother as to their father: they are not permitted to domineer over their sisters, nor are they accustomed to see these postponed to them, but the contrary; the compensations of the chivalrous feeling being made prominent, while the servitude which requires them is kept in the background. Well brought-up youths in the higher classes thus often escape the bad influences of the situation in their early years, and only experience them when, arrived at manhood, they fall under the dominion of facts as they really exist. Such people are little aware, when a boy is differently brought up, how early the notion of his inherent superiority to a girl arises in his mind; how it grows with his growth and strengthens with his strength; how it is inoculated by one schoolboy upon another; how early the youth thinks himself superior to his mother, owing her perhaps forbearance, but no-real respect; and how sublime and sultan-like a sense of superiority he feels, above all, over the woman whom he honours by admitting her to a partnership of his life. Is it imagined that all this does not pervert the whole manner of existence of the man, both as an individual and as a social being?

John Stuart Mill, *The Subjection of Women*

13th – The House of Commons

CARLYLE'S QUESTION

I must tell you a story Miss Bremet got from Emerson. Carlyle was very angry with him for not believing in a devil, and to convert him took him amongst all the horrors of London—the gin shops, &c.,—and finally to the House of Commons, plying him at every turn with the question, 'Do you believe in a devil noo?'

George Eliot, *Life*

14th – The Milliner

We first find Miss Willing located at that eminent Court milliner and dressmaker's, Madame Adelaide Banboxeney, in Furbelow Street, Berkeley Square, where her elegant manners, and obliging disposition, to say nothing of her taste in torturing ribbons and wreaths, and her talent for making plain girls into pretty ones, earned for her a very distinguished reputation. She soon became first-hand, or trier-on, and unfortunately, was afterwards tempted into setting-up for herself, when she soon found, that though fine ladies like to be cheated, it must be done in style, and by some one, if not with a carriage, at all events with a name; and that a bonnet, though beautiful in Bond Street, loses all power of attraction if it is known to come out of Bloomsbury. Miss Willing was, therefore, soon sold up; and Madame Banboxeney (whose real name was Brown, Jane Brown, wife of John Brown, who was a billiard-table marker, until his wife's fingers set him up in a gig), Madame Banboxeney, we say, thinking to profit by Miss Willing's misfortunes, offered her a very reduced salary to return to her situation; but Miss Willing having tasted the sweets of bed, a thing she very seldom did at Madame Banboxeney's, at least not during the season, stood out for more money; the consequence of which was, she lost that chance.

R. S. Surtees, *Ask Mama*

15th – The Lord Mayor's Coach

The state coach for the Lord Mayor elect will be furnished by Mr. J. Offord, of Wells Street and Brook Street, who has also supplied the chariot for Mr. Sheriff Johnson. The coach for the new Lord Mayor is quite in harmony with modern ideas and taste. The side windows, instead of being rounded off in the corners as formerly, are cut nearly square, to follow the outlines of the body. This novelty renders the body of the carriage much lighter than usual, and more elegant in appearance. Another 'innovation' is the painting. It has hitherto been usual to paint the under part of the carriage white or drab, relieved by the same colour as the body, but in the present case the whole vehicle has been painted a dark green, the family colour of the Lord Mayor elect, relieved by large lines of gold upon the body, and gold and red upon the under carriage. The natural elegance of this arrangement of colouring is heightened by the beautiful heraldic paintings of the City arms and those of the Fishmongers' and Spectacle Makers' Companies, of which Mr. Alderman Lusk is a member. These have been executed by Mr. D. T. Baker, the celebrated deaf and dumb artist.

The Times, 1883

16th – Wellington's Lying in State

Nov. 16, 1852:—I went yesterday to the lying in state of the Duke of Wellington; it was fine and well done, but too gaudy and theatrical, though this is unavoidable. Afterwards to St. Paul's to see it lit up. The effect was very good, but it was like a great rout; all London was there strolling and staring about in the midst of a thousand workmen going on with their business all the same, and all the fine ladies scrambling over vast masses of timber, or ducking to avoid the great beams that were constantly sweeping along. These public funerals are very disgusting *mea sententia*. On Saturday several

people were killed and wounded at Chelsea; yesterday everything
was orderly and well conducted, and I heard of no accidents.

Charles Greville, *Diary*

17th – Birds at Winter Nightfall (Triolet)

Around the house the flakes fly faster,
And all the berries now are gone
From holly and cotoneaster
Around the house. The flakes fly!–faster
Shutting indoors that crumb-outcaster
We used to see upon the lawn
Around the house. The flakes fly faster,
And all the berries now are gone!

Thomas Hardy

18th – Poor Ginger

One day, while our cab and many others were waiting outside
one of the parks where music was playing, a shabby old cab drove
up beside ours. The horse was an old worn-out chestnut, with an
ill-kept coat, and bones that showed plainly through it, the knees
knuckled over, and the fore-legs were very unsteady. I had been
eating some hay, and the wind rolled a little lock of it that way,
and the poor creature put out her long thin neck and picked it up,
and then turned and looked about for more. There was a hopeless
look in the dull eye that I could not help noticing, and then, as I
was thinking where I had seen that horse before, she looked full at
me and said, "Black Beauty, is that you?"

It was Ginger! but how changed! The beautifully arched and glossy
neck was now straight, and lank, and fallen in; the clean straight legs
and delicate fetlocks were swelled; the joints were grown out of
shape with hard work; the face, that was once so full of spirit and
life, was now full of suffering, and I could tell by the heaving of her
sides, and her frequent cough, how bad her breath was.

Our drivers were standing together a little way off, so I sidled up
to her a step or two, that we might have a little quiet talk. It was a
sad tale that she had to tell.

After a twelvemonth's run off at Earlshall, she was considered to be fit for work again, and was sold to a gentleman. For a little while she got on very well, but after a longer gallop than usual the old strain returned, and after being rested and doctored she was again sold. In this way she changed hands several times, but always getting lower down.

"And so at last," said she, "I was bought by a man who keeps a number of cabs and horses, and lets them out. You look well off, and I am glad of it, but I could not tell you what my life has been. When they found out my weakness they said I was not worth what they gave for me, and that I must go into one of the low cabs, and just be used up; that is what they are doing, whipping and working with never one thought of what I suffer—they paid for me, and must get it out of me, they say. The man who hires me now pays a deal of money to the owner every day, and so he has to get it out of me too; and so it's all the week round and round, with never a Sunday rest."

I said, "You used to stand up for yourself if you were ill-used."

"Ah!" she said, "I did once, but it's no use; men are strongest, and if they are cruel and have no feeling, there is nothing that we can do, but just bear it—bear it on and on to the end. I wish the end was come, I wish I was dead. I have seen dead horses, and I am sure they do not suffer pain; I wish I may drop down dead at my work, and not be sent off to the knackers."

I was very much troubled, and I put my nose up to hers, but I could say nothing to comfort her. I think she was pleased to see me, for she said, "You are the only friend I ever had."

Just then her driver came up, and with a tug at her mouth backed her out of the line and drove off, leaving me very sad indeed.

A short time after this a cart with a dead horse in it passed our cab-stand. The head hung out of the cart-tail, the lifeless tongue was slowly dropping with blood; and the sunken eyes! but I can't speak of them, the sight was too dreadful. It was a chestnut horse with a long, thin neck. I saw a white streak down the forehead. I believe it was Ginger; I hoped it was, for then her troubles would be over. Oh! if men were more merciful they would shoot us before we came to such misery.

Anna Sewell, *Black Beauty*
First published 18 November 1844

Anna Sewell (1820–78) damaged both her ankles as a child, on the way home from school. As a result, she could not walk without a crutch, and often used horse-drawn carriages to get around. This started a love of horses that lasted all her life. Anna Sewell only wrote one book. She began it in 1871, when ill-health meant she was confined to bed. *Black Beauty* came out in 1877 and Anna Sewell was able to see how popular her story was before she died. It has never been out of print.

19th – A Proud Author

The author who speaks about his own books is almost as bad as a mother who talks about her own children.

Benjamin Disraeli
From a speech given at a banquet in Glasgow, 19 November 1873

20th – The Worst Weather for Poaching

The weather most unsuitable is that kind of frost which comes on in the early morning, and is accompanied with some rime on the grass—a duck's frost, just sufficient to check fox-hunting. Every footstep on grass in this condition when the sun comes out burns up as black as if the sole of the boot were of red-hot iron, and the poacher leaves an indelible trail behind him. But as three duck's frosts usually bring rain, a little patience is alone necessary. A real, downright six weeks' frost is, on the contrary, very useful—game lie close. But a deep snow is not welcome; for, although many starved animals may be picked up, yet it quite suspends the operations of the regular hand: he can neither use wire, net, nor ferret.

Windy nights are disliked, particularly by rabbit-catchers, who have to depend a great deal upon their sense of hearing to know when a rabbit is moving in the 'buries,' and where he is likely to 'bolt,' so as to lay hands on him the instant he is in the net. But with the 'oak's mysterious roar' overhead, the snapping of dead branches, and the moan of the gale as it rushes through the hawthorn, it is difficult to distinguish the low, peculiar thumping sound of a rabbit in his catacomb. The rabbit is not easily dislodged in rain; for this animal avoids getting wet as much as possible: he 'bolts' best when it is dry and still.

Richard Jefferies, *The Gamekeeper at Home*

21st – Critics

My critic Hammond flatters prettily,
And wants another volume like the last.
My critic Belfair wants another book
Entirely different, which will sell (and live?) —
A striking book, yet not a startling book.
The public blames originalities
(You must not pump spring water unawares
Upon a gracious public, full of nerves),
Good things, not subtle, new, yet orthodox,
As easy reading as the dog-eared page
That's fingered by said public fifty years,
Since first taught spelling by its grandmother,
And yet a revelation in some sort;
That's hard, my critic Belfair! So, what next?
My critic Stokes objects to abstract thoughts;
"Call a man John, a woman, Joan," says he,
"And do not prate so of humanities;"
Whereat I call my critic simply Stokes.
My critic Johnson recommends more mirth,
Because a cheerful genius suits the times,
And all true poets laugh unquenchably,
Like Shakespeare and the gods. That's very hard.
The gods may laugh, and Shakespeare; Dante smiled
With such a needy heart on two pale lips,
We cry, "Weep, rather, Dante." Poems are
Men, if true poems; and who dares exclaim
At any man's door, "Here, 'tis understood
The thunder fell last week and killed a wife,
And scared a sickly husband—what of that?
Get up, be merry, shout, and clap your hands,
Because a cheerful genius suits the times?"
None says so to the man—and why, indeed,
Should any to the poem?

                              Elizabeth Barrett Browning

Elizabeth Barrett Browning (1806–61) began to write poetry as a child. When the family moved to London, she corresponded with various literary figures and published poetry, which was well-received.

However, illness, and her father's determination not to allow any of his children any independence meant she was tied to the family house in Wimpole Street. She was able to write poetry and essays, and began a correspondence with the poet Robert Browning, who admired her work. Eventually this turned to love: because of her father's domineering behaviour they were married secretly and at once left for Italy, where they lived until she died.

22nd – The Frozen Fowls

During a very severe frost and fall of snow in Scotland, the fowls did not make their appearance at the hour when they usually retired to roost, and no one knew what had become of them; the house-dog at last entered the kitchen, having in his mouth a hen, apparently dead. Forcing his way to the fire, the sagacious animal laid his charge down upon the warm hearth, and immediately set off. He soon came again with another, which he deposited in the same place, and so continued till the whole of the poor birds were rescued. Wandering about the stack-yard, the fowls had become quite benumbed by the extreme cold, and had crowded together, when the dog observing them, effected their deliverance, for they all revived by the warmth of the fire.

Edward Jesse, *Anecdotes of Dogs*

23rd – Ladysmith

But Ladysmith has an evil reputation. Last year the troops here were prostrated with enteric. There is a little fever and a good deal of dysentery even now among the regulars. The stream by the camp is condemned, and all water is supplied in tiny rations from pumps. The main permanent camp is built of corrugated iron, practically the sole building material in South Africa, and quite universal for roofs, so that the country has few "architectural features" to boast of. The cavalry are quartered in the tin huts, but the Liverpools, Devons, Gordons, and Volunteers have pitched their own tents, and a terrible time they are having of it. Dust is the curse of the place. We remember the Long Valley as an Arcadian dell. Veterans of the Soudan recall the black sand-storms with regretful sighs. The thin, red dust comes everywhere, and never stops. It blinds your eyes, it stops your nose, it scorches your throat till the invariable shilling for a little glass of any liquid seems cheap as dirt. It turns the whitest shirt brown in half an hour, it creeps into the works of your watch and your bowels. It lies in a layer mixed with flies on the top of your rations. The white ants eat away the flaps of the tents, and the men wake up covered with dust, like children in a hayfield. Even mules die of it in convulsions. It was in this land that the ostrich developed its world-renowned digestive powers; and no wonder.

H. W. Nevinson, *Ladysmith, the Diary of a Siege*

Henry Woodd Nevinson (1856–1941) was a war correspondent and campaigning journalist. He reported on the Graeco-Turkish War in 1897 for the *Daily Chronicle*, and in 1899 went to South Africa for the same paper to report on the Second Boer War. Later, he exposed slavery in Angola, and reported on the First World War, being wounded at Gallipoli. During his life he campaigned for many causes, writing essays, newspaper articles and sometimes stories and poems. When he was seventy-seven, he married his long-time mistress at Hampstead Registry Office. She scandalised guests by wearing a black dress for the ceremony.

24th – A Superscription

Look in my face; my name is Might-have-been;
I am also call'd No-more, Too-late, Farewell;
Unto thine ear I hold the dead-sea shell
Cast up thy Life's foam-fretted feet between;
Unto thine eyes the glass where that is seen
Which had Life's form and Love's, but by my spell
Is now a shaken shadow intolerable,
Of ultimate things unutter'd the frail screen.

Mark me, how still I am! But should there dart
One moment through thy soul the soft surprise
Of that wing'd Peace which lulls the breath of sighs,—
Then shalt thou see me smile, and turn apart
Thy visage to mine ambush at thy heart.
Sleepless with cold commemorative eyes.

Dante Gabriel Rossetti, *The House of Life*

Dante Gabriel Rossetti (1828–82) was born in London to Italian parents resident there. He trained as an artist: meeting Holman Hunt and John Everett Millais, the three formed the Pre-Raphaelite Brotherhood, which sought to revolutionise art by proclaiming the virtues of those artists who had worked before Raphael. As well as painting and drawing, he also wrote poetry, criticism and translations. Later, he created designs for William Morris's firm.

25th – The Man Who Wanted to Be Transported

At Queen Street Office on Tuesday, November 25th, 1845, John Bedsted, a poor, miserable, attenuated being, was charged with felony.

He had been observed on the previous evening, by the waiter at the Pineapple Inn, William Street, Pimlico, carrying a quart pot partially concealed in a bag and, on being stopped, the pot was found to belong to the proprietor of the Phoenix Inn in the same neighbourhood. It was further proved that he had been seen in possession of another pot a night or two previously.

The prisoner, when asked by the Magistrate, "How do you answer to the charge?" replied, "I'm afraid I haven't done enough. I wish to be transported. I'm starving, I've scarcely a rag to cover me and I've no food to eat. It isn't true that I stole the pot – I found it in the street and took it to get a little milk in. I'm tired of my existence and beg you to transport me, if you can."

The Magistrate committed him to prison for a month and the prisoner said: "I am very much obliged to you, even for that, but I was in hopes that you would have done more and transported me."

Clipping from an unknown newspaper 1845

26th – Three Women Prepare to Explore the Holy Land

The Holy Land seems to be considered quite the tour for a gentleman. 'And a strong lady may accompany her husband,' says Dr Macleod. So when two friends and myself resolved, in the summer of 1868, to absent ourselves for a year from home, for the purpose of visiting scenes endeared to us by so many hallowed associations, great was the consternation expressed by our friends, at the idea of three ladies venturing on so lengthened a pilgrimage alone. 'Do you think they will ever come back? They are going amongst Mohammedans and barbarians,' said some, who knew of our intention. But for what reason? The means of communication are now so much improved, the art of providing for a traveller's comfort is carried to such perfection, that any woman of ordinary prudence (without belonging to the class called strong-minded) can find little difficulty in arranging matters for her own convenience. And if our education does not enable us to protect ourselves from the influence of such dangerous opinions as, it is said, we shall hear in the varied society with which it may be our lot to mingle, what is that education worth?

But before going further, let me introduce the reader to our party. Three is a very manageable number. We are all sisters in affection, though only two are so by birth. We are provided with the best of all auxiliaries—viz: a knowledge of the French, German, and Italian languages. A courier we do not want, as without his services we are in a much more advantageous position for gathering information. We agree to a division of labour. Violet makes herself responsible for the management at hotels, and for the direction of the party in general; Edith examines the accounts; Agnes studies the guide-book, and sketches routes for the approval of her companions. Violet is gifted with prudence and liveliness; Edith is quick at arithmetic; whilst Agnes is very happy to benefit by the practical activity of her friends. But some preparations must be made beforehand. The most useful kind of trunk is that made by Edward Cave, Wigmore Street. It is a basket, covered with strong tarpaulin, needs no extra cover, and is at once light and impervious to rain. For short journeys, a small leather portmanteau called 'The Gladstone' is most suitable, as it holds more than would appear at first sight, and will strap easily on the back of a mule. Each traveller buys a pair of mackintosh sheets; they cost a guinea, and will be invaluable in the tents. A portable bath is only unnecessary lumber, the cost of carrying it being more than the price of a substitute in any good hotel. Side saddles are to be sent for us straight to the Peninsular and Oriental Company's agent at Alexandria: riding costumes of white serge are purchased at Nicoll's, and with Murray's excellent guide-book to Syria in our hands, we feel that we are tolerably well provided for.

Agnes Smith, *Eastern Pilgrims*, 1870

Agnes Smith (1843–1926) and her twin sister Margaret (1843–1920) were linguists (together they knew twelve languages). They travelled to Greece in 1883, then in 1892 to the Sinai. Here, in St Catherine's Monastery, they found the earliest Syriac version of the Gospels thus far known. Further journeys produced more discoveries. In 1923, they catalogued the monastery's Syriac and Arab manuscripts – 'the contribution the twins made in cataloguing the Arabic and Syriac manuscripts at Saint Catherine's Monastery was literally incalculable'. Living and working in Cambridge, Agnes was known as an internationally renowned Syriac scholar – but neither sister could take a Cambridge degree, which were not available to women. Agnes Smith wrote a number of books about her journeys, as well as translations of some of the manuscripts she found.

27th – Rugby Chapel

Coldly, sadly descends
The autumn-evening. The field
Strewn with its dank yellow drifts
Of wither'd leaves, and the elms,
Fade into dimness apace,
Silent;—hardly a shout
From a few boys late at their play!
The lights come out in the street,
In the school-room windows —but cold,
Solemn, unlighted, austere,
Through the gathering darkness, arise
The chapel-walls, in whose bound
Thou, my father! art laid.

There thou dost lie, in the gloom
Of the autumn evening. But *ah!*
That word, gloom, to my mind
Brings thee back, in the light
Of thy radiant vigour, again;
In the gloom of November we pass'd
Days not dark at thy side;
Seasons impair'd not the ray
Of thy buoyant cheerfulness clear.

Such thou wast! and I stand
In the autumn evening, and think
Of bygone autumns with thee.

Matthew Arnold

Matthew Arnold (1822–88) was the son of Thomas Arnold, the famous headmaster of Rugby School. He worked as private secretary to Lord Lansdowne before becoming a school inspector. Education at every level was a concern throughout his life. He wrote poetry for the first part of his life: when he was appointed professor of poetry at Oxford in 1858 he produced only one more volume of verse – otherwise he wrote prose for the rest of his life.

28th – Toast Sandwiches

INGREDIENTS.—Thin cold toast, thin slices of bread-and-butter, pepper and salt to taste.
Mode.—Place a very thin piece of cold toast between 2 slices of thin bread-and-butter in the form of a sandwich, adding a seasoning of pepper and salt. This sandwich may be varied by adding a little pulled meat, or very fine slices of cold meat, to the toast, and in any of these forms will be found very tempting to the appetite of an invalid.

Mrs Isabella Beeton, *Mrs Beeton's Book of Household Management*

29th – Working Conditions Before the Industrial Revolution

Before the introduction of machinery, the spinning and weaving of raw materials was carried on in the working-man's home. Wife and daughter spun the yarn that the father wove or that they sold, if he did not work it up himself. These weaver families lived in the country in the neighbourhood of the towns, and could get on fairly well with their wages, because the home market was almost the only one, and the crushing power of competition that came later, with the conquest of foreign markets and the extension of trade, did not yet press upon wages. There was, further, a constant increase in the demand for the home market, keeping pace with the slow increase in population and employing all the workers; and there was also the impossibility of vigorous competition of the workers among themselves, consequent upon the rural dispersion of their homes. So it was that the weaver was usually in a position to lay by something, and rent a little piece of land, that he cultivated in his leisure hours, of which he had as many as he chose to take, since he could weave whenever and as long as he pleased. True, he was a bad farmer and managed his land inefficiently, often obtaining but poor crops; nevertheless, he was no proletarian, he had a stake in the country, he was permanently settled, and stood one step higher in society than the English workman of to-day.

So the workers vegetated throughout a passably comfortable existence, leading a righteous and peaceful life in all piety and probity; and their material position was far better than that of their successors. They did not need to overwork; they did no more than they chose to do, and yet earned what they needed. They had leisure for healthful work in garden or field, work which, in itself, was recreation for them, and they could take part besides in the recreations and games of their neighbours, and all these games— bowling, cricket, football, etc., contributed to their physical health and vigour. They were, for the most part, strong, well-built people, in whose physique little or no difference from that of their peasant neighbours was discoverable. Their children grew up in the fresh country air, and, if they could help their parents at work, it was only occasionally; while of eight or twelve hours work for them there was no question.

Fredrick Engels, *Condition of the Working Class in England in 1844*

30th – With the Army in India

Camp near Allahabad, Nov. 30, 1837.
I sent off one journal to you two days ago from a place that, it since appears, was called Bheekee. Yesterday we started at half-past five, as it was a twelve miles' march, and the troops complain if they do not get in before the sun grows hot, so we had half an hour's drive in the dark. I came on in the carriage, as I did not feel well, and one is sick and chilly naturally before breakfast. Not but that

I like these morning marches; the weather is so English, and feels so wholesome when one is well. The worst part of a march is the necessity of everybody, sick or well, dead or dying, pushing on with the others. Luckily there is every possible arrangement made for it. There are beds on poles for sick servants and palanquins for us, which are nothing but beds in boxes. G. and I went on an elephant through rather a pretty little village in the evening, and he was less bored than usual, but I never saw him hate anything so much as he does this camp life. I have long named my tent 'Misery Hall.'

'Mine,' G. said 'I call Foully Palace, it is so very squalid-looking.' He was sitting in my tent in the evening,, and when the purdahs are all down, all the outlets to the tents are so alike that he could not find which crevice led to his abode; and he said at last, 'Well! it is a hard case; they talk of the luxury in which the Governor-General travels, but I cannot even find a covered passage from Misery Hall to Foully Palace.'

This morning we are on the opposite bank of the river to Allahabad, almost a mile from it. It will take three days to pass the whole camp.

Most of the horses and the body-guard are gone to-day.

E. Eden, from *Up the Country: Letters from India*

Emily Eden (1797–1869) was the sister of George Eden, 1st Earl of Auckland, who was Governor-General of India from 1835 to 1842. Emily Eden and her sister Fanny visited their brother in India, and Emily travelled about with him. Her letters to her sister were later collected and published in book form. As well as books on India, Emily Eden also wrote novels.

DECEMBER

1st – The Gravedigger

Willy Dog-whipper's successor, as I have said, both as to the office and its badge, was his brother John. Him I induced, by the addition of sixpence from the parson's magnificent burial-fee of eighteenpence, to his own pittance of one shilling and threepence for digging the grave, attendance at the funeral, and filling up the grave at the close, to dig the graves an extra foot in depth. But it was an innovation to which, despite the—by comparison—easily earned sixpence extra, he never completely grew reconciled. He thought a coffin with twenty or twenty-two inches of soil upon it was "weel eneugh happed oop for owght." John wore a ring, made out of the old coffin-tyre he met with in digging the graves in the well-worked churchyard the Danby "kirk-garth" was, until I got an additional half acre laid to it. This ring was good against "falling fits." His predecessor's particular wear had been earrings of the same material.

These two worthies held other offices, either by favour or by inheritance or descent. Willy was the "bidder to the burials," while John was in extensive request on occasions of pig-killing; and, having a considerable number of patrons and friends among the farmers, and others who had pigs to kill in the course of the winter, he had very many engagements of that kind. It was said that, in addition to his food and a small money fee on these occasions, he had the pigs' ears as his perquisite; and that he always kept count of how many pig executions he had attended in the course of the season, by aid of small reserved and preserved pieces of the said ears.

J. C. Atkinson, *Forty Years in a Moorland Parish*

2nd – Repealing the Corn Laws

With respect to the past, gentlemen, I have perhaps a little to explain, but certainly nothing to repent or to retract. My opinions, from the day on which I entered public life, have never varied. I have always considered the principle of protection of agriculture as a vicious principle. I have always thought that this vicious principle took, in the Act of 1815, in the Act of 1828, and in the Act of 1842, a singularly vicious form. This I declared twelve years ago, when I stood for Leeds: this I declared in May 1839, when I first presented myself before you; and when, a few months later, Lord Melbourne invited me to become a member of his Government, I distinctly told him that, in office or out of office, I must vote for the total repeal of the corn laws.

But in the year 1841 a very peculiar crisis arrived. There was reason to hope that it might be possible to effect a compromise, which would not indeed wholly remove the evils inseparable from a system of protection, but which would greatly mitigate them. There were some circumstances in the financial situation of the country which led those who were then the advisers of the Crown to hope that they might be able to get rid of the sliding scale, and to substitute for it a moderate fixed duty. We proposed a duty of eight shillings a quarter on wheat. The Parliament refused even to consider our plan. Her Majesty appealed to the people. I presented myself before you; and you will bear me witness that I disguised nothing. I said, "I am for a perfectly free trade in corn: but I think that, situated as we are, we should do well to consent to a compromise. If you return me to Parliament, I shall vote for the eight shilling duty. It is for you to determine whether, on those terms, you will return me or not." You agreed with me. You sent me back to the House of Commons on the distinct understanding that I was to vote for the plan proposed by the Government of which I was a member. As soon as the new Parliament met, a change of administration took place. But it seemed to me that it was my duty to support, when out of place, that proposition to which I had been a party when I was in place. I therefore did not think myself justified in voting for a perfectly free trade, till Parliament had decided against our fixed duty, and in favour of Sir Robert Peel's new sliding scale. As soon as that decision had been pronounced, I conceived that I was no longer bound by the terms of the compromise which I had, with many misgivings, consented to offer to the agriculturists, and which the agriculturists had refused to accept. I have ever since voted in favour of every motion which has been made for the total abolition of the duties on corn.

Thomas Babington Macaulay
From a speech in Edinburgh, 2 December 1845

3rd – Two Limericks

There was a young man of Oporta,
Who daily got shorter and shorter,
The reason he said
Was the hod on his head,
Which was filled with the *heaviest* mortar.

His sister, named Lucy O'Finner,
Grew constantly thinner and thinner;
The reason was plain,
She slept out in the rain,
And was never allowed any dinner.

Lewis Carroll, *The Rectory Umbrella*

4th – Gladstone Crosses the Road

Dec. 4, 1880:—By the bye apropos of o.c's I saw Mr. Gladstone last week. He came out of Lord Selborne's house in Portland Place. He was looking fearfully cross and very yellow. He seemed very undecided as to where he should cross the street, and he stared at me in a helpless sort of way, as if he expected me to offer him some advice on the matter, but as there was no possibility of putting him in the way of being run over, I refrained from giving an opinion. The crossings about Portland Place are so stupidly safe.

Eliza Savage, *Letters between Samuel Butler and Miss E. M A Savage, 1871–1885*

5th – Timely First Aid

"Amongst many others the following cases have occurred in which those who have passed through the classes have applied successfully the instruction imparted in rendering '*first aid to the injured*'":–

Mr. Ernest Turnbull prevented a compound fracture by splinting with umbrellas and handkerchiefs the broken leg of a patient who had fallen on the asphalt in the Eltham Road.

Mr. Sancto, lodge-keeper at the Paragon, Blackheath, saved the life of a road-mender by arresting the bleeding of an artery in the foot, wounded by the point of a pickaxe.

One of the men hereto attended Dr. Owen's (Blackheath) Course was unable to attend the examination, as he had the superintendence of a Sunday School treat. One of the children fell and broke his arm, and was successfully bandaged and splinted by our student (Jay). The doctor who examined them on the ground shortly afterwards, said that he had neither seen nor heard of newspaper splints before, and that the fracture could not have been better put up.

Extract from Register, Order of St John

6th – South African Grievances

We sailed from Southampton in December, 1895, in the *Tantallon Castle*, then one of the most modern and up-to-date of the Castle liners. The ship was crowded to its utmost capacity, and among the passengers, as I afterwards learned, were many deeply concerned in the plotting which was known to be going on at Johannesburg, either to extort concessions from President Kruger, or, failing this, to remove him altogether. I knew very little about all this then, but before I had been many days on board it was not difficult to discover that much mystery filled the air, and I was greatly excited at arriving in South Africa in such stirring times. There is no such place for getting to know people well as on a sea-voyage of eighteen days. Somehow the sea inspires confidence, and one knows that information imparted cannot, anyway, be posted off by the same day's mail. So those who were helping to pull the strings of this ill-fated rebellion talked pretty freely of their hopes and fears during the long, dark tropical evenings.

I became familiar with their grievances—their unfair taxation; no education for their children except in Dutch; no representation in Parliament—and this in a population in which, at that time, the

English and Afrikanders at Johannesburg and in the surrounding districts outnumbered the Dutch in the proportion of about 6 to 1. They laid stress on the fact that neither the Boers nor their children were, or desired to become, miners, and, further, that for the enormous sums spent on developing and working the mines no proper security existed. I must admit it was the fiery-headed followers who talked the loudest—those who had nothing to lose and much to gain. The financiers, while directing and encouraging their zeal, seemed almost with the same hand to wish to put on the brake and damp their martial ardour. In any case, all were so eloquent that by the time our voyage was ended I felt as great a rebel against "Oom Paul" and his Government as any one of them.

Lady Sarah Wilson, *Book of South African Memories*

7th – Whole Duty of Children

A child should always say what's true
And speak when he is spoken to,
And behave mannerly at table;
At least as far as he is able.
Robert Louis Stevenson, *A Child's Garden of Verses*

8th – The Death of Oscar Wilde

The announcement of Mr. Oscar Wilde's death, which took place in a small hotel in the Latin Quarter of Paris, is accompanied by tidings that tend to soften the regrets that such an event must awaken. Mr. Oscar Wilde, whose meteoric appearance in the world of *belles lettres* was succeeded by moral oblivion, belonged to a group of young men, rebels born, whose conventional Protestantism could not hold back from a relapse into paganism. According to report, Mr. Wilde attributed his catastrophe to the fact that his father would not allow him, when he was a youth, to submit himself to the discipline of the Catholic Church. Be that as it may, Mr. Wilde's reception into the Church, during his last illness, by one of the Passionist Fathers in Paris, constitutes his one act of public and voluntary repentance.

A correspondent adds : The last time I saw the name of Oscar Wilde was in a letter, written about a quarter of a century ago by Father Matthew Russell, S. J., who was asking prayers for him as a brilliant young Irishman, then an undergraduate at Magdalen College, Oxford.

The Tablet, 8 December 1900

9th – After the Siege

Tuesday, December 8th. It was such luxury to be in bed, and have my chota hazree brought to me, after having had to make it for so many months—almost the whole of the siege—and it was such delicious bread and butter! Mr. S——, the chaplain, and some gentlemen, came round to all the tents, early, bringing cakes of soap for us; and the night before all our tents were supplied with oil lamps. We went over to breakfast in the Mess tent—it was the Governor-General's Durbar tent—a most splendid one, and pitched in the centre of our camp; we had a delicious breakfast—coffee, with rich cream. I enjoyed it much, after our siege fare, and was as pleased as a child to get it. We telegraphed to Capt. P—, in Calcutta, to write home, and say we were all safe. Drs. B—and H—, and Major T— called. After this, our days passed quietly at Allahabad. Christmas Day, we dined with Capt. J—, of the Fusiliers; and Monday, January 11th, left Allahabad in country boats, to join the steamers at Sirsa, as none of them could come up higher, on account of the shallow water on the Dum-dumma Flats. We had a narrow escape! As our boat was alongside the *Charles Allen*, another steamer passed, having several Native boats attached to its flat; one came with great force against ours, and every one expected we were done for, as these Native boats generally crush up and go down instantaneously. There was a cry, "Save the women and children!" and we were dragged up on the top of the paddle-box by our arms; however, our boat did not go down, or we must have gone with it. Captain F—, of the *Charles Allen*, afterwards told me he had expected to see us go down, and thought the poor creatures had escaped Lucknow only to meet with another horrible death. We had a pleasant trip down the river, and reached Calcutta on Thursday, January 28th. We slept that night on board, and the next morning took up our abode at 3,

Harrington Street—one of the houses prepared by the Relief Fund Committee for the Lucknow refugees, where we found everything provided for us in the most luxurious style.

Mrs R. C. Germon, *A Diary Kept by Mrs R. C. Germon at Lucknow*

10th – Dickens and Dogs

Tavistock House
Thursday, December 9th, 1852.
My dear Wills,
I am driven mad by dogs, who have taken it into their accursed heads to assemble every morning in the piece of ground opposite, and who have barked this morning *for five hours without intermission*; positively rendering it impossible for me to work, and so making what is really ridiculous quite serious to me. I wish, between this and dinner, you would send John to see if he can hire a gun, with a few caps, some powder, and a few charges of small shot. If you duly commission him with a card, he can easily do it. And if I get those implements up here to-night, I'll be the death of some of them to-morrow morning.

Ever faithfully.
Charles Dickens
Letters

11th – Trouble with the Neighbours

Dec. 1865:—One morning, when I looked out of my dressing-room window to see what sort of day it was, imagine the spectacle that met my eyes: a rubbishy hen-hutch, erected over night, in the garden next to ours —next! think of that!—and nine large hens and one very large cock sauntering under our windows!!! I should have fainted where I stood had I been in the habit of fainting; but that I never was. As Mr. C. said nothing, I could not guess whether he had made the discovery or not. The crowing which occurred several times during the night, as well as abundantly during the morning, certainly did not awake him, his mind being, at present, intent on 'railway whistles'. But when he should have once opened his eyes to the thing, and as the days should lengthen, the crowing would increase. Ah! my heaven, what then?—no wonder that I lay awake thinking 'What then ?'

Jane Welsh Carlyle, Letters

12th – Buckingham Palace Invaded

On Wednesday evening, shortly after 12 o'clock, the inmates of Buckingham Palace were aroused by a report that a stranger had been discovered under a sofa in her Majesty's dressing-room. The domestics and officers of the household were immediately astir, and it was soon ascertained that the alarm was not without foundation. The fellow, whose boots were left in a corridor, was at once secured and handed over to the custody of the police. The name of this daring intruder into the abode of royalty is Edward Jones. He has a most repulsive appearance, but affects an air of extreme consequence.

Charles Hindley (compiler), Curiosities of Street Literature

13th – Memories of St James's Hall

1884:—Something vanished from the artistic life of London when St. James's Hall was pulled down. Not only do I associate Wagner and Brahms with its cheap, uncomfortable gallery, but also the hearing of Richter, Joachim, and Grieg accompanying his wife. I remember the face of the young Paderewski when he played. He was then the beautiful young man of whom Burne-Jones has left so vivid a portrait. I remember Pachmann in his prime when he neither scolded the piano nor spoke to the audience. But more than all these, I have kept till now one of my most cherished and sentimental recollections of the place. The reader must imagine an audience, unlike any of to-day, with a large percentage of quite elderly people, women of a grave and refined type, who might have been relatives of Florence Nightingale. Now one sees them no more; they died with the ceasing of the Joachim quartets. They wore lace caps, artificial Parma violets, and lilac; they had worn this kind of thing since they were forty, when to-day a woman of that age is at her sexual prime and is usually half-naked after sun-down. Sir Frederick Leighton was in the stalls, and there was a perceptible hush, then a ruffle of applause, when a little elderly woman appeared on the platform. She was trimly dressed in modest nut-brown silk, her grey hair crowned with lace and a velvet bow; her deportment was at once dignified and restrained, her bow that of a princess. Her deliberate movements before the piano suggested a very superior and respected governess or ladies' companion— do I exaggerate?—the face was kindly and serene, yet somehow determined under its tranquil expression. She played the Waldstein Sonata with delicate precision and an air of detachment, and acknowledged the applause. Her rendering had been flawless in its avoidance of all exaggeration; too refined, perhaps, too lacking in impulse, and too inward in emotion. She then played Schumann's 'Arabesque' rapidly, fluently, with a tender and ardent sense of beauty; on the pause, before the last few chords, which are like a prayer and end on a question, she raised her head as if she looked to see. After the ovation she bowed like a queen. The player was Clara Schumann.

Charles Ricketts, *Self-Portrait*

14th – Biography

It has always appeared to me a strong argument for the non-existence of spirits that these friendly microscopic biographers are not haunted by the ghosts of the unfortunate men whom they persist in holding up to public contempt.

Sir A. Helps, *Thoughts in the Cloister*

Sir Arthur Helps (1813–75) did well at Cambridge, and afterwards was appointed as private secretary to the Chancellor of the Exchequer. There followed other civil service appointments until there was a change of government in 1841, and Arthur Helps retired to the country, where he dictated books and plays to an assistant. However, his abilities were needed, and in 1860 he became Clerk to the Privy Council. For the queen, he prepared a collection of Prince Albert's speeches and addresses, and he wrote a preface when she published some of her diary, *Leaves from a Journal of our Life in the Highlands*. Eventually Queen Victoria gave him a grace and favour house near the main gates of Kew Gardens.

15th – Gama's Patter Song

Gama: I am possessed
By the pale devil of a shaking heart!
My stubborn will is bent. I dare not face
That devilish monarch's black malignity!
He tortures me with torments worse than death,
I haven't anything to grumble at!
He finds out what particular meats I love,
And gives me them. The very choicest wines,
The costliest robes the richest rooms are mine:
He suffers none to thwart my simplest plan,
And gives strict orders none should contradict me!
He's made my life a curse! [*Weeps.*]

Princess: My tortured father!

Gama: Whene'er I spoke
Sarcastic joke
Replete with malice spiteful
This people mild
Politely smiled,
And voted me delightful!
Now when a wight
Sits up all night
Ill-natured jokes devising,
And all his wiles
Are met with smiles,
It's hard, there's no disguising!
Oh, don't the days seem lank and long
When all goes right and nothing goes wrong.

Chorus:
And isn't your life extremely flat
With nothing whatever to grumble at!

Gama: When German bands
From music stands
Played Wagner imperfectly
I bade them go

They didn't say no,
But off they went directly!
The organ boys
They stopped their noise
With readiness surprising,
And grinning herds
Of hurdy-gurds
Retired apologizing!
Oh, don't the days seem lank and long, etc.
I offered gold
In sums untold
To all who'd contradict me
I said I'd pay
A pound a day
To anyone who kicked me
I bribed with toys
Great vulgar boys
To utter something spiteful,
But, bless you, no!
They would be so
Confoundedly politeful!
In short, these aggravating lads
They tickle my tastes, they feed my fads,
They give me this and they give me that,
And I've nothing whatever to grumble at!

Sir W. S. Gilbert, *Princess Ida*

16th – The Thief

Monday, 16 December

Dame Matthews used to live at the Home Farm at Langley Burrell. She was a member of the family, but she must have lived a long time ago, as Mrs. Banks remarked, because she called cows 'kine'. The Dame used to sit in the chimney corner and near her chair there was a little window through which she could see all down the dairy. One evening she saw one of the farm men steal a pound of butter out of the dairy and put it into his hat, at the same moment clapping his hat upon his head.

'John,' called the Dame. 'John, come here. I want to speak to you.' John came, carefully keeping his hat on his head. The Dame ordered some ale to be heated for him and bade him sit down in front of the roaring fire. John thanked his mistress and said he would have the ale another time, as he wanted to go home at once.

'No, John. Sit you down by the fire and drink some hot ale. 'Tis a cold night and I want to speak to you about the kine.'

The miserable John, daring neither to take off his hat nor go without his mistress's leave, sat before the scorching fire drinking his hot ale till the melting butter in his hat began to run down all over his face. The Dame eyed him with malicious fun. 'Now, John,' she said, 'you may go. I won't charge you anything for the butter.'

Francis Kilvert, *Diary*

17th – Christmas Cards

This branch of industry continues to develop rapidly. The various manufacturers vie with each other to procure the most artistic designs; and the holding of exhibitions and the awarding of prizes has given a great incentive to persons of artistic tastes to enter the lists.

Observer, 17 December 1882

18th – Children's Rooms

The principle of Privacy, which was laid down at an early stage of our investigation, whereby in every Gentleman's House a distinct separation should be made between the Family and Servants, has a similar application here: that is to say, the main part of the house must be relieved from the more immediate occupation of the Children.

Robert Kerr, *The Gentleman's House: or, How to Plan English Residences, from the Parsonage to the Palace*

19th – The Last of the Light Brigade

There were thirty million English who talked of England's might,
There were twenty broken troopers who lacked a bed for the night.

They had neither food nor money, they had neither service nor
    trade;
They were only shiftless soldiers, the last of the Light Brigade.

They felt that life was fleeting; they knew not that art was long,
That though they were dying of famine, they lived in deathless
    song.
They asked for a little money to keep the wolf from the door;
And the thirty million English sent twenty pounds and four!

They laid their heads together that were scarred and lined and
    grey;
Keen were the Russian sabres, but want was keener than they;
And an old Troop-Sergeant muttered, "Let us go to the man who
    writes
The things on Balaclava the kiddies at school recites."

They went without bands or colours, a regiment ten-file strong,
To look for the Master-singer who had crowned them all in his
    song;
And, waiting his servant's order, by the garden gate they stayed,
A desolate little cluster, the last of the Light Brigade.

They strove to stand to attention, to straighten the toil-bowed
    back;
They drilled on an empty stomach, the loose-knit files fell slack;
With stooping of weary shoulders, in garments tattered and
    frayed,
They shambled into his presence, the last of the Light Brigade.

The old Troop-Sergeant was spokesman, and "Beggin' your
    pardon," he said,
"You wrote o' the Light Brigade, sir. Here's all that isn't dead.
An' it's all come true what you wrote, sir, regardin' the mouth of
    hell;
For we're all of us nigh to the workhouse, an, we thought we'd
    call an' tell.

"No, thank you, we don't want food, sir; but couldn't you take
    an' write

A sort of 'to be continued' and 'see next page' o' the fight?
We think that someone has blundered, an' couldn't you tell 'em
  how?
You wrote we were heroes once, sir. Please, write we are starving
  now."

The poor little army departed, limping and lean and forlorn.
And the heart of the Master-singer grew hot with "the scorn of
  scorn."
And he wrote for them wonderful verses that swept the land like
  flame,
Till the fatted souls of the English were scourged with the thing
  called Shame.

O thirty million English that babble of England's might,
Behold there are twenty heroes who lack their food to-night;
Our children's children are lisping to "honour the charge they
  made-"
And we leave to the streets and the workhouse the charge of the
  Light Brigade!

Rudyard Kipling

20th – Losing Prince Albert

OSBORNE, 20th December 1861
MY OWN DEAREST, KINDEST FATHER,—For as such have I
ever loved you! The poor fatherless baby of eight months is now
the utterly broken-hearted and crushed widow of forty-two! My
life as a happy one is ended! the world is gone for me! If I must
live on (and I will do nothing to make me worse than I am), it
is henceforth for our poor fatherless children—for my unhappy
country, which has lost all in losing him—and in only doing what
I know and feel he would wish, for he is near me—his spirit will
guide and inspire me ! But oh! to be cut off in the prime of life—to
see our pure, happy, quiet, domestic life, which alone enabled me
to bear my much disliked position, CUT OFF at forty-two—when
I had hoped with such instinctive certainty that God never *would*
part us, and would let us grow old together (though *he* always
talked of the shortness of life)—is too *awful*, too cruel! And yet

it *must* be for *his* good, his happiness! His purity was too great, his aspiration too *high* for this poor, *miserable* world! His great soul is *now only* enjoying *that* for which it *was* worthy! And I will *not* envy him—only pray that *mine* may be perfected by it and fit to be with him eternally, for which blessed moment I earnestly long. Dearest, dearest Uncle, *how* kind of you to come! It will be an unspeakable *comfort*, and you *can do* much to tell people to do what they ought to do. As for my *own good, personal* servants—poor Phipps in particular—nothing can be more devoted, heartbroken as they are, and anxious only to live as *he* wished !

Good Alice has been and is wonderful.

The 26th will suit me perfectly. Ever your devoted, wretched Child,

VICTORIA R.

Queen Victoria, letter to her uncle, Leopold, King of Belgium

21st – Repealing the Contagious Diseases Act

London Dec 20 1869

Dear Madam,

I return you my signature to your Circular and Petition, in the objects of which I most heartily and deeply concur.

The only correction I offer, as you have decided it, is to omit the word 'permanent' in the petition – altho' I think, had I had the wording of the petition I should have indicated that no statistics exist, which justify the Acts protested against, (or upon which to have the Acts protested against).

I am afraid that I cannot refer you to the statistics which you desire. They exist in all the Returns & scattered thro' all the Reports on Health which reach the War Office from home, the Colonies, and India. Comparative statistics of Health from foreign armies and foreign [civilian] life being often included in them.

All these have come to me in the way of business for many years – a very melancholy business it is, I assure you. But it would take me several hours even to collect these Blue Books, to look out the passages in them referring to the subjects and to make a list of them.

The Government however is perfectly aware of their existence – since they are all Government Blue Books. Indeed the opinion of the

Medical Officer of the Privy Council was asked by the government on this very subject – and was given in conformity with the facts I have mentioned to you. You will find the last official statement in a pamphlet which you probably have – but if not, I enclose a copy. It is the best reply to your request which I am able to give. The chief points are marked in the margin; but the whole pamphlet is a refutation of the 'Society' mentioned by you in your protest. There are however, things in the pamphlet not based on experience, which are unfortunate.

I am sorry that I am really unable, from the press of business, to enter more fully into the subject in correspondence.

Pray believe me, dear Madam, ever your faithful servant,
Florence Nightingale

Letter to Josephine Butler supporting her work to repeal the
Contagious Diseases Act

22nd – Weathers

This is the weather the cuckoo likes,
And so do I;
When showers betumble the chestnut spikes,
And nestlings fly;
And the little brown nightingale bills his best,
And they sit outside at 'The Traveller's Rest,'
And maids come forth sprig-muslin drest,
And citizens dream of the south and west,
And so do I.

This is the weather the shepherd shuns,
And so do I;
When beeches drip in browns and duns,
And thresh and ply;
And hill-hid tides throb, throe on throe,
And meadow rivulets overflow,
And drops on gate bars hang in a row,
And rooks in families homeward go,
And so do I.

Thomas Hardy

23rd – Left on a Train

The most astonishing kind of property to leave behind at a railway station is mentioned in an advertisement which appeared in the newspapers dated Swindon, April 27th, 1844. It gave notice "That a pair of bright bay horses, about sixteen hands high, with black switch tails and manes," had been left in the name of Hibbert; and notice was given that unless the horses were claimed on or before the 12th day of May, they would be sold to pay expenses. Accordingly on that day they were sold.

Anon, *Household Words*, reprinted in *Railway Adventures and Anecdotes*

24th – Snowed up for Christmas

I might greatly move the reader by some account of the innumerable places I have not been to. But I will leave the reader unmoved, and proceed with the object before me: to give a plain account of the Holly-Tree Inn; in which place of good entertainment for man and beast I was once snowed up.

I forget now where … we ought to have been; but I know that we were scores of miles behindhand. It snowed and snowed, and still it snowed, and never left off snowing.

At nine o'clock at night, on a Yorkshire moor, a cheerful burst from our horn, and a welcome sound of talking, with a glimmering and moving about of lanterns, roused me from my drowsy state. I found that we were going to change.

They helped me out, and I said to a waiter, whose bare head became as white as King Lear's in a single minute, "What Inn is this?"

"The Holly-Tree, sir," said he.

"Upon my word, I believe," said I, "that I must stop here."

I thought I had never seen such a large room as that into which they showed me. It had five windows, with dark red curtains that would have absorbed the light of a general illumination; and there were complications of drapery at the top of the curtains, that went wandering about the wall in a most extraordinary manner. I asked for a smaller room, and they told me there was no smaller room.

My bedroom was some quarter of a mile off, up a great staircase at the end of a long gallery. It was the grimmest room I have ever had the nightmare in; and all the furniture, from the four posts of the bed to the two old silver candle-sticks, was tall, high-shouldered, and spindle-waisted. Below, in my sitting-room, if I looked round my screen, the wind rushed at me like a mad bull; if I stuck to my arm-chair, the fire scorched me to the colour of a new brick. The chimney-piece was very high, and there was a bad glass—what I may call a wavy glass—above it. If I stood with my back to the fire, a gloomy vault of darkness above and beyond the screen insisted on being looked at; and, in its dim remoteness, the drapery of the ten curtains of the five windows went twisting and creeping about, like a nest of gigantic worms.

Before I had finished my supper of broiled fowl and mulled port, I had impressed upon the waiter in detail my arrangements for departure in the morning. Breakfast and bill at eight. Fly at nine. Two horses, or, if needful, even four.

Tired though I was, the night appeared about a week long.

In the morning I found that it was snowing still, that it had snowed all night, and that I was snowed up. Nothing could get out of that spot on the moor, or could come at it, until the road had been cut out by labourers from the market-town. When they might cut their way to the Holly-Tree nobody could tell me.

It was now Christmas-eve. I should have had a dismal Christmas-time of it anywhere, and consequently that did not so much matter; still, being snowed up was like dying of frost, a thing I had not bargained for. I felt very lonely.

Charles Dickens, from The Holly Tree

25th – Merry Christmas

Christmas comes! He comes, he comes,
Ushered with a rain of plums;
Hollies in the windows greet him;
Schools come driving post to meet him;
Gifts precede him, bells proclaim him,
Every mouth delights to name him;
Wet, and cold, and wind, and dark
Make him but the warmer mark;

And yet he comes not one-embodied,
Universal's the blithe godhead
And in every festal house
Presence hath ubiquitous.
Curtains, those snug room-enfolders,
Hang upon his million shoulders,
And he has a million eyes
Of fire, and eats a million pies,
And is very merry and wise;
Very wise and very merry,
And loves a kiss beneath the berry.

Leigh Hunt, from *Christmas Omnipresent*

Leigh Hunt (1784–1859) got into trouble in his early days as a journalist: he and his brother founded a radical weekly journal, but a critical piece about the Prince Regent resulted in a fine and two years' imprisonment. Throughout his life he worked for various magazines, as well as writing poems and some plays. His great contribution to literature was his thoughtful criticism and he promoted many poets, including Keats, Shelley, Browning and Tennyson, recognising their worth.

26th – Maria Kilvert's Funeral

The coffin had been brought downstairs and was waiting in the hall covered with the black velvet sweeping soft pall, white bordered. Boom went the great bell of the Cathedral. Church was over, and someone said they ought to have used the tenor bell, but they were using the great bell and no mistake. Boom went the bell again. The coffin went out immediately and the pall bearers filed out in pairs after it, taking their places and holding each his pall tassel on either side. My Father and I followed as Chief mourners in crape scarves and hatbands. All the rest in silk. The bearers had been selected not at all with reference to their fitness for the task, but with reference to the friendship entertained for them by the servants of the house. One of the bearers on the right side was very short, so short that he could not properly support the coffin level. The coffin seemed very heavy. As the procession moved across College Green to the Cloister arch, the men staggered under the weight and the coffin lurched and tilted to one side over the short bearer. One very fat man had constituted himself chiefest mourner of all and walked next the coffin before my Father and myself. The bearers, blinded by the sweeping pall, could not see where they were going and nearly missed the Cloister arch, but at length we got safe into the narrow dark passage and into the Cloisters. The great bell boomed high overhead and the deep thrilling vibration hung trembling in the air long after the stroke of the bell.

So the clergy and choir came to meet us at the door, then turned and moved up the Cathedral nave chanting in solemn procession, 'I am the Resurrection and the Life saith the Lord'. But meanwhile there was a dreadful struggle at the steps leading up from the Cloisters to the door. The bearers were quite unequal to the task and the coffin seemed crushingly heavy. There was a stamping and a scuffling, a mass of struggling men swaying to and fro, pushing and writhing and wrestling while the coffin sank and rose and sank again. Once or twice I thought the whole mass of men must have been down together with the coffin atop of them and some one killed or maimed at least. But now came the time of the fat chief mourner. Seizing his opportunity he rushed into the strife by an opening large and the rescued coffin rose. At last by a wild effort and tremendous heave the ponderous coffin was borne up the steps and through the door into the Cathedral where the choristers, quite unconscious of the scene and the fearful struggle going on behind, were singing up the nave like a company of angels. In the Choir there was another dreadful struggle to let the coffin down. The bearers were completely overweighted, they bowed and bent and nearly fell and threw the coffin down on the floor. When it was safely deposited we all retired to seats right and left and a verger or beadle, in a black gown and holding a mace, took up his position at the head of the coffin, standing. The Psalm was sung nicely to a very beautiful chant. The Dean had the gout and could not appear, so Canon Wood read the lesson well and impressively in a sonorous voice. The Grave Service was intoned by the Sacristan Mr. Raisin and sung by the choir, standing on the planking round the vault whilst a crowd of people looked in through the cloister windows.

Francis Kilvert, *Diary*, 26 December

27th – Lewis Carroll Dancing

December 27, 1873

My dear Gaynor,—My name is spelt with a "G," that is to say "*Dodgson.*" Any one who spells it the same as that wretch (I mean of course the Chairman of Committees in the House of Commons) offends me *deeply*, and *for ever!* It is a thing I *can* forget, but *never can forgive!* If you do it again, I shall call you "aynor." Could you live happy with such a name?

As to dancing, my dear, I *never* dance, unless I am allowed to do it *in my own peculiar way.* There is no use trying to describe it: it has to be seen to be believed. The last house I tried it in, the floor broke through. But then it was a poor sort of floor—the beams were only six inches thick, hardly worth calling beams at all: stone arches are much more sensible, when any dancing, *of my peculiar kind*, is to be done. Did you ever see the Rhinoceros, and the Hippopotamus, at the Zoölogical Gardens, trying to dance a minuet together? It is a touching sight.

Give any message from me to Amy that you think will be most likely to surprise her, and, believe me,

Your affectionate friend,
Lewis Carroll.

Letter to Gaynor Simpson, *Life and Letters of Lewis Carroll (Rev. C. L. Dodgson)* by S. Dodgson Collingwood

28th – Disaster at the Pantomime

Friday, Dec. 28th, 1860.

My dear Mary,

I cannot tell you how much I thank you for the beautiful cigar-case, and how seasonable, and friendly, and good, and warm-hearted it looked when I opened it at Gad's Hill.

I pass my time here (I am staying here alone) in working, taking physic, and taking a stall at a theatre every night. On Boxing Night I was at Covent Garden. A dull pantomime was "worked" (as we say) better than I ever saw a heavy piece worked on a first night, until suddenly and without a moment's warning, every scene on that immense stage fell over on its face, and disclosed chaos by gaslight behind! There never was such a business; about sixty people who were on the stage being extinguished in the most remarkable manner. Not a soul was hurt. In the uproar, some moon-calf rescued a porter pot, six feet high (out of which the clown had been drinking when the accident happened), and stood it on the cushion of the lowest proscenium box, P. S., beside a lady and gentleman, who were dreadfully ashamed of it. The moment the house knew that nobody was injured, they directed their whole attention to this gigantic porter pot in its genteel position (the lady and gentleman trying to hide behind it), and roared with laughter. When a modest footman came from behind the curtain to clear it, and took it up in his arms like a Brobdingnagian baby, we all laughed more than ever we had laughed in our lives. I don't know why.

We have had a fire here, but our people put it out before the parish-engine arrived, like a drivelling perambulator, with the beadle in it, like an imbecile baby. Popular opinion, disappointed in the fire having been put out, snowballed the beadle. God bless it!

Your ever affectionate

Joe

Charles Dickens, *Letters*

29th – Charles Dickens Expands His Views on Hanging

You have no idea what that hanging of the Mannings really was. The conduct of the people was so indescribably frightful, that I felt for some time afterwards almost as if I were living in a city of devils. I feel, at this hour, as if I never could go near the place again. My letters have made a great to-do, and led to a great agitation of the subject; but I have not a confident belief in any change being made, mainly because the total abolitionists are utterly reckless and dishonest (generally speaking), and would play the deuce with any such proposition in Parliament, unless it were strongly supported by the Government, which it would certainly not be, the Whig motto (in office) being "*laissez aller.*" I think Peel might do it if he came in. Two points have occurred to me as being a good commentary to the objections to my idea. The first is that a most terrific uproar was made when the hanging processions were abolished, and the ceremony shrunk from Tyburn to the prison door. The second is that, at this very time, under the British Government in New South Wales, executions take place *within the prison walls*, with decidedly improved results. (I am waiting to explode this fact on the first man of mark who gives me the opportunity.)

Charles Dickens, 29 December 1849, *Letters*

30th – The Knell of the Year

Passing away, saith the World, passing away:
Changes, beauty, and youth, sapped day by day:
Thy life never continueth in one stay.
Is the eye waxen dim, is the dark hair changing to grey
That hath won neither laurel nor bay?
I shall clothe myself in Spring and bud in May:
Thou, root-stricken, shalt not rebuild thy decay
On my bosom for aye.
Then I answered: Yea.
Passing away, saith my Soul, passing away:
With its burden of fear and hope, of labour and play,
Hearken what the past doth witness and say:
Rust in thy gold, a moth is in thine array,
A canker is in thy bud, thy leaf must decay.
At midnight, at cockcrow, at morning, one certain day
Lo the Bridegroom shall come and shall not delay;
Watch thou and pray.
Then I answered: Yea.
Passing away, saith my God, passing away:
Winter passeth after the long delay:
New grapes on the vine, new figs on the tender spray,
Turtle calleth turtle in Heaven's May.
Though I tarry, wait for Me, trust Me, watch and pray:
Arise, come away, night is past and lo it is day,
My love, My sister, My spouse, thou shalt hear Me say.
Then I answered: Yea.

Christina Rossetti

Christina Rossetti (1830–94) was the sister of Dante Gabriel Rossetti Her first poetry was published privately when she was twelve, followed by another collection when she was fifteen and she was nationally published at seventeen when *The Athenaeum* took two poems. She was a devoted High Church Anglican, and much of her work is religious in nature. Whether religious or secular, her work indicates a keen interest in nature. Her brother sent the poem 'Goblin Market' to Ruskin, who was very rude about it, but when it was published the next year, it was well-received, with many good reviews.

31st – Burglars at Carlyle's House

Dec. 31, 1852:— ... I have been meaning to write to you without waiting for New Year's Day; but in all my life I never have been so driven off letter-writing as since the repairs began in this house. There were four months of that confusion, which ended quite romantically, in my having to sleep with loaded pistols at my bedside! the smell of paint making it as much as my life was worth to sleep with closed windows, and the thieves having become aware of the state of the premises. Once they got in and stole some six pounds' worth of things, before they were frightened away by a candlestick falling and making what my Irish maid called 'a devil of a row'. It was rather to be called 'an angel of a row', as it saved further depredation. Another time they climbed up to the drawing-room windows, and found them fastened, for a wonder! Another night I was alarmed by a sound as of a pane of glass cut, and leapt out of bed, and struck a light, and listened, and heard the same sound repeated, and then a great bang, like breaking in some panel. I took one of my loaded pistols, and went downstairs, and then another bang which I perceived was at the front door. 'What do you want?' I asked; 'who are you?' 'It's the policeman, if you please; do you know that your parlour windows are both open?' It was true! I had forgotten to close them, and the policeman had first tried the bell, which made the shivering sound, the wire being detached from the bell, and when he found he could not ring it he had beaten on the door with his stick, the knocker being off while it was getting painted. I could not help laughing at what the man's feelings would have been had he known of the cocked pistol within a few inches of him.

Jane Welsh Carlyle, *Letters*

ACKNOWLEDGEMENTS

I should like to thank Mrs Rachel Roberts, archivist at Cheltenham Ladies' College, and Ms Clare Russell, archivist at Marlborough College, who both allowed me to visit, and helped me to find good things. I'd also like to thank the London Library, not just for books, but for their patience and kindness.